the Socceroos

VOODOO TO DESTINY

the Socceroos

VOODOO TO DESTINY

ANDY HARPER

limelightpress

This book is based on the author's interviews with the players and the players' recollections of their own personal stories and experiences. The recollections of others may be different. A reference to any person in these stories is not intended to suggest an association, approval or endorsement of any kind.

Limelight Press Pty Ltd
Unit 15, 6 Thames Street
Balmain NSW 2041
ABN 80 095 617 897

Published by Limelight Press Pty Ltd 2006

National Library of Australia
Cataloguing-in-Publication data:

Harper, Andy.
The Socceroos : voodoo to destiny.
ISBN 0 9757080 9 0.
1. Socceroos (Team) - Biography. 2. Soccer players - Australia - Biography. 3. Soccer - Australia. I. Title.

796.33466092

Designed by Jacqueline Richards

Author photo supplied by Andy Harper
All other images supplied by Getty Images Pty Ltd
Printed and bound by Griffin Press, South Australia

Limelight Press would like to thank Elise Brown and John O'Sullivan of Football Federation Australia and John Didulica of Australian Professional Footballers' Association for their help and support.

This book is dedicated to the two most important of football's constituents, the players and the fans. They provide the colour, noise and theatre that makes the football world go around. Without them, this would be a drearier place. With them, worlds and lives across the planet are able to connect and celebrate in each other's humanity.

You have both made my life more.

Contents

Foreword

I met Andy Harper for the first time in May of 2005. The occasion was, quite literally, the birth of the Hyundai A-League and more specifically, Sydney FC. Andy was one of the people instrumental in setting up Sydney FC as not only a viable football franchise, but as a club that would set the standard for the new league.

I was immediately struck by Andy's quiet, thoughtful intelligence and his vast knowledge of the game. He was a highly successful footballer who also had an acute understanding of the broader issues involved off the pitch in creating an exciting and functional football franchise.

I was impressed by his ability to articulate complex ideas and strategies in a way that most ex-players could not. I was, and still am, also impressed with his ability to listen to a wide range of ideas and concepts; and his ability to process them without judgement, but always with well-thought-out consideration.

However, behind that quiet, measured demeanour that for me defines Andy's outward persona, is his unbridled love and devotion to the game, not only in Australia, but all around the globe.

To have a conversation with him about anything football-related, from the history of the game in Brazil to the current state of the game at home, is an opportunity to see his face light up and his genuine love of the game bubble to the surface with all the passion and enthusiasm of a teenager discovering his one great love.

Therefore it was with great excitement that I first read *The Socceroos: voodoo to destiny*. Of all the people I could think of, no-one was more qualified and learned in the roots of Australian football to tell these often amazing stories of the incredible migration of Australian footballers to all corners of the globe, playing at the highest levels.

These stories are inspirational and enlightening, particularly in light of how lowly regarded Australian football is in the world forum.

They are also a testament to the courage and resilience of those individuals who have left the island continent to seek not only fame and fortune at the game's highest levels with little or no guarantee of success, but to simply pit their skills against the best in the world.

Each player's story is unique. Each road travelled different. What remains constant is the kind of hardship and determination it took to make the grade, and more impressively, stay there.

In this book we get a unique glimpse of the men who will represent us this year on the greatest of international stages—the 2006 World Cup in West Germany.

This inside look gives us an insight to not only the current squad, but to those great Australian players of the past whose experience and wisdom was passed on to many of the current squad in their formative years, providing them with the foundation to push on and persevere.

Right now, we are in the middle of the great resurrection of Australian football. With the resounding success of the new A-League in its first year, and our well-overdue return to the World Cup, football's popularity in Australia has never been higher.

For me, it's a strange kind of closure. Having been part of the first National Soccer League in 1978 as a player, I remember still riding high on having seen my country play (ironically) in West Germany in 1974. As a football-mad teenager, I watched every Australian game on my parents black and white TV with intense pride and enthusiasm. I argued endlessly with friends and family over how well or badly we had done in each game, but ultimately I was captivated and inspired to make football a permanent fixture in my life.

When the first National League came into existence four years later, the possibilities seemed endless. As a teenager in 1978 I too had dreams of playing in Europe, and it felt then as it does now, that it was not just a dream but it was actually possible.

The subsequent demise of the old National Soccer League and our often heartbreaking inability to return to the world stage have held the game in Australia in what seemed an endless state of limbo.

Andy's beautifully painted portraits of our current crop of heroes could not be more timely. They let us get a little closer to the players who will bear the flag in Germany and, that, in turn, I am sure will inspire us to support them in the way they deserve—with total unabashed Aussie pride and enthusiasm—no matter what the outcome of the games.

Through Andy's book we can see one thing clearly. They deserve to be there. They belong.

My one great hope is that through the work of people like Andy Harper we can learn from our past mistakes. This book, if nothing else, demonstrates the need for a healthy and fertile domestic league—if for no other reason than to ensure that young players now and in the future have a creative and vital place to learn their trade before embarking on the quest for the ultimate. A place on the world stage of football. The players in this book did it the hard way (not that it's ever easy).

Their stories and their ultimate legacy provide us with the insight and opportunity to create the foundation of a new Australian football dynasty.

I applaud Andy's dedication to the game and for giving us this insightful and always interesting "peek" behind the lives of our Socceroos.

I, for one, will watch every game this year with great interest but through this book, with a greater appreciation and understanding of the individuals who got us there.

Anthony LaPaglia

Voodoo to Destiny

In 2005 Australia set its stall against Uruguay in qualifying for the 2006 FIFA World Cup finals. Australia had not qualified for this, the world's biggest sporting event since 1974, when the tournament was hosted by West Germany. At regular quadrennial intervals thereafter, Australia's national football team, the Socceroos, would enter the respective qualifying campaigns full of hope and desire, but exit with hearts broken and reputations dented. There has been a curious combination of variables that has made failure a bitter pill, a repeated series of disasters that has increased the pressure each time to exorcise the demons of campaigns past. Over the years, the crescendo had reached deafening decibels. Surely, this couldn't go on. Surely, something would have to give. Surely, Australia had a destiny to fulfil, to win through and compete at the world's most popular game, in the world's biggest event. Surely, Australia, this sport-obsessed nation tucked away in the South Pacific, would again, one day, make its re-entry into the world's most important sporting fraternity.

To many people, from a variety of backgrounds, destiny is a powerful life force. There is a measure of presumptuousness, however, perhaps arrogance even, for Australians to believe it to be our destiny to be at the World Cup. The world of football is a massive global movement of people. FIFA, the sport's governing body internationally, has more members than the United Nations, and probably wields more influence. The World Cup only opens itself for thirty-two nations, which means the qualification process is cutthroat and prolonged. Qualification is a highly sought after prize in its own right—to win the tournament and be crowned Champions of the World is inordinately difficult. For many countries, their single biggest focus is the fortune of their national football team. Its success or failure can have vast repercussions. This means the world, to most of the world.

At this point in Australia's development, the same couldn't be said of it. Our players and the sport's fans have deserved qualification, but has the country earned that right? The World Cup is, or should be, our dream. But our destiny? At this point? That is arguable.

Johnny Warren worked for his entire adult life to make this game more important to more of Australia. He drove the football agenda to build the case for destiny. He wanted nothing more than for Australia to be able to place its hand on its heart, knowing that it had embraced this game, and by extension the world, to the point where it could reasonably expect football World Cups to be part of Australia's destiny.

But his life experience hinted to him that there was perhaps another force at work. In his 2002 biography *Sheilas, Wogs and Poofters*, Johnny Warren tells the story of the Mozambican witchdoctor who placed a curse on Australia's football. The litany of qualification failures strewn through our football history since "the curse" led Warren to say, "Every time some new disaster befalls our national teams, I think back to Mozambique. I can't help wondering if there's something extraordinary to blame."

Warren was himself no spiritual intermediary, nor did he proselytise on anything other than football, but he was an astute observer of the goings-on around him.

The story of the witchdoctor involved Australia's attempt to qualify for the 1970 World Cup finals held in Mexico. It is a convoluted tale, told by Warren in his biography, that took the Socceroos through three continents in an attempt to earn the right to play Israel for the last spot at Mexico 1970.

The penultimate stage of this quest for Israel was a series of matches against Rhodesia (now Zimbabwe), to be played in "neutral" Mozambique. Australia was heavily fancied to win through untroubled and earn the home-and-away series against Israel. But the two-match series against Rhodesia ended even, at one game each. Warren tells of the amazing performances of Rhodesia's goalkeeper that kept that country in the hunt. A third and deciding game was required.

To paraphrase Warren's story, Australian team delegates found themselves in a discussion with a local journalist about the Aussies' difficulties in scoring and the superlative form of Rhodesia's goalkeeper. The journalist suggested that a visit to a witchdoctor might be worth considering. A meeting was convened, the issues discussed and, as the legend has it, the burying of bones by the witchdoctor, set to "curse" Rhodesia's goalkeeper, worked a treat. Australia won the game 3-1, with the goalkeeper reportedly displaying a 180-degree form reversal, and qualified for the last round of qualifying against Israel.

But there is nothing for nothing, apparently, even in the metaphysical world of black magic, and the witchdoctor approached Australian officials demanding a £1000 fee for his part in Australia's victory. When the money wasn't forthcoming, the witchdoctor carried through with his threat to put a curse on Australian football.

Australia failed against Israel and missed Mexico in 1970. The team did then, famously, qualify for the 1974 finals. But from then on, the story of the Socceroos' quest for the World Cup finals has been a torturous tale of disappointment and disaster.

From the political chicanery within international football that has severely prejudiced Australia's qualifying chances (such as having to qualify through South America—one of the world's most difficult pathways), to uncharacteristic errors from highly reputable and seasoned internationals in key matches at key times (including, to name a few, Georgie Keith in 1969 against Israel, Charlie Yankos in 1989 against Israel, Milan Ivanovic in 1993 against Argentina), Australia stumbled from one World Cup exit sign to the next.

In 1993, Australia lost the away leg against the Maradona-led Argentina 0-1, with an Alex Tobin-deflected own goal—a cruel outcome after a brave team performance from a position as clear underdogs, care of one of the Socceroos' greatest servants.

Then, in 1997, when Australia was cruising at 2-0 against Iran at the MCG, with qualification for France 1998 well within sight, a pitch invader ran into one of the goal areas and tore down the goal's netting. There was a fifteen-minute interlude whilst the goal was repaired. Iran regrouped, Australia lost control, Iran scored two goals and qualified, Australia wallowed.

Through all this, the sport's administration lurched from disaster to incompetent disaster. The politics of pettiness and self-interest overruled any proper policy formation. The game was a basket case. Australia sat by and watched, while vested interests took pot shots. The football faithful were at their wit's end. Cursed is an understatement.

Until 16 November 2005, when, at Sydney's Olympic Stadium, it was almost as though voodoo met destiny head on in a winner-take-all battle for existential supremacy. There was more than football at stake—there was the future of the country.

Australia's history in this competition demanded that a penalty shoot-out be the decisive factor. The match could only go in this direction. Uruguay's failure to score from very good chances were pointers to the bigger picture struggle that was underway. As it was, though, Australia was the only team to score, and by the end of "normal time", the aggregate score over the two games was 1-1. It was to be a penalty shoot-out that would decide the issues. This was never going to be easy for Australia. Exorcisms are rarely trouble-free experiences.

Australia had taken an early lead in the penalty shoot-out. Mark Schwarzer had saved Uruguay's first penalty by Dario Rodriguez. Australia held the advantage, but it remained slender. Gustavo Varela and Fabian Estoyanoff scored their penalties for Uruguay to keep Australia under pressure.

The tension in the stadium was thickening. Mark Viduka, one of Australia's grandest ever talents and team captain, addressed the stationary ball and prepared to take his penalty. He moved in and stroked the ball to his left, aiming for the inside of the post. Uruguay's keeper had guessed the right direction to dive. It didn't matter—Viduka's penalty rolled harmlessly past the post and outside the goal. Australia's advantage teetered on the precipice.

The 83,000 in attendance were silenced. So many people have never made less noise. The voodoo "curse" had played its trump card. Another of Australia's greats could be added to the casualty catalogue. He'd be in good company, but that would be little consolation.

Uruguay's Marcelo Zalayeta now has the chance to expunge Australia's advantage and restore parity. In the duel of who blinks first, Schwarzer stands firm on his goal line. The South Americans are foxy. They will wait to see which direction the keeper will guess before hitting the ball the other way. But Schwarzer doesn't move. With nerves of steel he holds his ground. Zalayeta is forced to make the first decision. He hits the ball across his body. He hits it to Schwarzer's left, and it is goal bound. Schwarzer has dragged Zalayeta into his game. He has forced the Uruguayan to make the first, crucial move. He now knows which way to throw himself. He dives and saves magnificently. There's a renewed sense in the stadium. Australia is ascendant again. Viduka exhales violent relief. Destiny has the upper hand. John Aloisi strides forward to play his part in the unfolding drama. Probably he is unaware of the third-dimension struggle that is being played out. He only has his job to do. He only has this to send Australia to the World Cup. His left foot propels the ball past the goalkeeper, Fabian Carini, and into the back of the net. Celebrations abound, people are hysterical, strangers are hugging each other, cynical and battle-hardened former internationals break into tears, the curse is finally broken, the stadium becomes a shrine to destiny and Australia has arrived.

Voodoo's clash with destiny provides the sub-text to the enormity of what football in Australia is experiencing. These are heady days for a sport that was once the focal point of ridicule. Since the restructure of the game led by Frank Lowy and John O'Neill, Australia has secured the hat-trick of achievements—an attractive and vibrant domestic league, the A-League; formal integration with Asia by being admitted into the Asian Football Confederation, effective 1 January 2006; and, finally, qualification for the World Cup.

It is time for football in Australia. If destiny really won the day on 16 November 2005, then the game will now only go from strength to strength. The engine room for that growth will need to be driven by the A-League, the most important part of the puzzle. It is the league that provides the activity to run the business of the sport. It is the A-League that breeds culture—the culture of technical excellence and the culture of football appreciation. It provides the talking points, the economy, the educational forums and the career paths for players and coaches. Without a viable domestic competition, the organisational objectives for football will be unattainable. The start-up success of the A-League, culminating in the sell-out 2006 Grand Final and unprecedented media coverage, shows that people want it. All football needed was to be packaged and presented properly, and the A-League provided this. It isn't football that needed to be sold, it was the competition that needed to be sold. 2005–06 has shown that with the right vehicle, albeit one with more improvements to be made, people will support an Australian competition.

It is the time for Australia to hitch its wagon to football. No other sport can do for Australia what football can. This isn't about preferences or traditions, sports we like or sports we don't, it is about importance. Australia hasn't ever placed enough importance on football and that has been to its own detriment. Australia's national football team is the country's most important sporting team. This is too important not to be done properly.

We are fortunate to be so well represented. This current Socceroos team will be the most effective part of Australia's entire diplomatic corps in 2006. More people will engage with Australia this year through this team and because of the World Cup than any other initiative Australia could concoct. Of their own volition, people from around the world will watch the Socceroos play and immediately, by association, form a link with Australia. It is a quirky part of the fan's psychology. Trade deals don't permeate it. Official visits by heads of government don't penetrate it. Not like football does, not like footballers can. It may be an unusual concept for Australia to digest, but it is true.

The personalities included in this book are all outstanding young Australians. They are outstanding sportsmen, great players and tremendous ambassadors for our country. We ought to be immensely proud of them. They are, each of them, inspirational people. Theirs are stories of achievement, of defying the odds, of not giving in, of continually believing in themselves and persevering. They are everything that is often upheld as "Australian virtue". They should be secrets in their own country no more. Australia should know what they do and what they did to get here, because Australia is better for it. Australia basks in the glow of their achievements.

That is the point of this book. To introduce you to this wonderful, and inspirational, group of Australians. Every day they are pushing themselves to the limit, and in doing so, pushing the case for Australia on the international stage. There is no better embodiment of what it is to be Australian in the twenty-first century than the Socceroos. The game on 16 November showed that nothing can unite Australia better than this team, this sport.

Australia is now faced with a question of confidence. Does it have the national self-confidence to ride this football "thing"? There can be no doubt that if, and when, Australia does football properly, it will be a serious player internationally. Does Australia have the maturity and the confidence to embark on such a mission? Or will it develop separation anxiety at leaving its comfort zone? It is not a question of Australia's capacity, it is a question of Australia's will.

While all this is being played out, the pit of one's stomach is knotted. The question as to why Johnny Warren was taken before he had a chance to watch all this and to contribute to this debate and growth remains unanswered. In November 2004, he lost his battle with cancer. He passed in the same week that the A-League was launched. In 2005, Australia brokered its deal with the Asian Football Confederation for it to become a member of Asia in 2006. This had been a lifetime ambition of Warren's. And in 2006, his beloved Socceroos will re-enter football's atmosphere after being in such a meaningless orbit for such a long time.

Football was Warren's crown of thorns. It is almost as though he was the price the game had to pay. It is almost as though his passing was to atone for the sins of the past. By his death, apparently, football now has life.

Australians remember Johnny Warren like he was their very own flesh and blood. On the night of Australia's qualification for Germany 2006, fans right around the stadium unfurled banners of thanks and recognition for the work he'd undertaken, for the life he'd lived and the fight he'd fought. Some banners recalled his favourite sayings and one, even, referred to the witchdoctor curse.

It was a brilliant night for football, crystallising an unbelievable renaissance for the sport and providing Australia with fresh opportunities.

At centre stage were the players. Magnificent and stout-hearted, they held their ground and realised their personal birthright and that of their country. It is Australia's destiny. Football is Australia's destiny.

They will carry our hopes and our dreams and our image to the world in Germany 2006 and beyond.

Andy Harper

March 2006

1

shirt number

"My career is full of goals. You know what you want to achieve and sometimes the journey that you take is not always the one that you want; it might be the one you are pushed onto."

Mark Schwarzer

Date of birth 6 October 1972

Position played Goalkeeper

Current club Middlesbrough, England

Australia has always seemed to have an embarrassment of goalkeeping riches—from Ronnie Lord of the '56 Olympic team, through to the first Socceroo squads of the late '60s and early '70s. This era included the likes of Nick Sokoloff, Jim Fraser and Ronny Corry, custodians who not only had potent careers that defied their relatively diminutive statures, but whose contribution to the art of goalkeeping extends right into the heart of this current Socceroo squad.

Often ostracised because of the uniqueness of their position, goalkeepers are simultaneously, and arguably, the most important position on the field. Theirs is a view that takes in the whole of the game and the whole of the field. Theirs is a job that sets a foundation for a defence and a platform for a team. Theirs is a job that goes unnoticed until the moment arrives that will determine the course of a game, the futures of teams, of coaches, of careers, of countries.

Perhaps unremarkably, Mark Schwarzer didn't start out life as a goalkeeper. What is true, however, is that he will end his career as one of Australia's most celebrated examples of the species. Probably, care of his second penalty save in the shoot-out against Uruguay, a mould will be cast of his right hand and a bronze replica installed in some museum. And if not, it should be. Because on the night of 16 November 2005, at the Sydney Olympic Stadium, in the white heat of a death or glory penalty shoot-out, the diving Schwarzer had the presence of mind to thrust this right hand skyward to block the penalty attempt of Uruguay's Marcelo Zalayeta and deliver Australia an opportunity to take an unassailable lead in the shoot-out that would decide Australia's World Cup status.

Of course, this wasn't the first time that Schwarzer had performed penalty shoot-out heroics. In 1993, as Australia sought to negotiate safe passage past Canada and into a play-off against Argentina for a place in the 1994 World Cup, it was Schwarzer again to the fore for his country, saving twice and allowing Australia to slip through to face one of the world's mightiest football countries.

So much about these two chapters of Schwarzer's life sums up the lot of a professional footballer. In the second instance, Schwarzer was fresh from winning the Australian National Soccer League Championship with his club, Marconi. Due to his club heroics, he was voted by his peers to be the best goalkeeper in the competition.

During that off-season, Schwarzer had taken holidays in Germany, a bit of relaxation and a bit of football, nothing too serious. Schwarzer's return to Sydney became anything but frivolous as it coincided with the upcoming play-offs against Canada. Australia's incumbent goalkeeper, Mark Bosnich, had "retired" from international football because of a clash of demands between his club and his country. Schwarzer was called up to join the squad as backup for Robert Zabica for the away game in Edmonton, Canada. That game had barely got into stride when Zabica fell foul of a refereeing decision and was sent from the field. Australia was a man down and without a goalkeeper. So, Schwarzer, still in shock from his selection and, by his own admission, a metaphoric mile away, "counting the Aussie flags in the stadium" (as he told Matthew Hall in the book *The Away Game*), was to be thrust into the heart of Australia's World Cup pretensions. Australia lost that game 1-2 and returned to Sydney with Bosnich still unavailable and Zabica facing a one match, automatic suspension. The Sydney match was to be Schwarzer's own.

After much huffing and puffing, it was only due to the late goal off the bandaged cranium of Mehmet Durakovic that Australia won the return leg 2-1, thereby levelling the aggregate score at 2-2. The mandatory period of extra time that followed failed to separate the two teams and a penalty shoot-out ensued. At twenty years of age, it was Schwarzer who, with two saves in the shoot-out, emerged as Australia's hero. This was to be the start of a grand journey into the world of professional football. It was the break that any aspiring player would kill for. However, for the final qualifiers against Argentina, Bosnich "unretired" himself and Zabica was reinstated as the number two. For Schwarzer, the glory and reward of a full-time European professional career would take some time yet to germinate.

Schwarzer was born in Sydney's Auburn in 1972 and grew up in North Richmond, at the base of the Blue Mountains. His first club was the Colo Cougars Soccer Club, which he joined as a seven-year-old. He was about "nine or ten" when his father, who doubled as the coach, put him in goal because he claimed Mark was "tripping over his own feet". The love affair with his new position wasn't instant, and Schwarzer recalls that his dad/coach would pacify him by "occasionally letting me out on the field to run around a bit".

For some reason though, Schwarzer stuck with keeping and by the time he was twelve he was in the Nepean Association representative squad. It was this Nepean team that brought together one of Australian sport's most peculiar, and long-serving, unions. Emerging from another junior club in the same district was Zeljko Kalac, Schwarzer's current Socceroo team-mate and number two for the national team. Back then, though, Schwarzer had to settle for the number two position because the top spot was occupied by Kalac. Theirs has been a bizarre competition that commenced with the onset of adolescence—parallel careers that have striven to forge some sort of dominance over the other. The rivalry is real and the respect very healthy; it is a great story in its own right. For so long have both known and worked with each other, it is perhaps safe to say that both wish nothing but the best for the other, except that too often that has come at the perceived expense of the other.

Kalac was so immovable that Schwarzer was forced to look for another goal to keep, so he moved to the Blacktown Association, where he stayed until the Under 16s. In search of more competition and better coaching, a mooted move to the Blacktown State League team ended after it had barely started, and Schwarzer found himself at Marconi, then one of the mainstays of Australia's football. It was at Marconi that Schwarzer came under the tutelage of Nick Sokoloff, about whose coaching and guidance Schwarzer still raves.

With a Marconi contract in hand, Schwarzer could now work to build towards some sort of launching pad for the career that he so deeply yearned. Being the son of German migrants, football probably always had some prominence in the Schwarzer household and was the obvious starting point. However, it wasn't until the Under 16 World Cup where Australia played USA, East Germany and Brazil that Schwarzer knew "100 per cent" that he wanted to be a footballer. Like many players, the

---

"The NSL was a great taste and a great foundation, but I needed to get overseas and see what the top level was."

bite of athlete commitment came early, when the commitment to football training and games bled dry the ability to socialise with mates, who were embarking on the teenage party rite of passage. "Meeting Pelé there [in Scotland] got me going too," he adds.

Kalac was Schwarzer's team-mate for that Scotland tournament, with Schwarzer in pole position. Their positional jousting would extend into the next instalment of FIFA's youth development pathway, the Under 19 World Cup. Schwarzer fell to injury, opening the way for Kalac to go to Portugal with the Young Socceroos, where he'd play understudy, this time to Mark Bosnich. Australia was to record one of its best international results at this tournament, where it lost to host, and eventual winners, Portugal, in the semifinals. This was a young Australian team of supreme quality, the golden era of Australia's youth development.

Schwarzer, although injured, had the opportunity to stay with the team but opted to get his injury treated. His career couldn't withstand any errors of judgment brought about by sentiment at this point.

It was in a training game in the Netherlands that Schwarzer's Youth World Cup hopes came unstuck. The game against FC Twente Enschede was regular and otherwise without incident or tension. But as Schwarzer recalls, "I hit a guy's head when I went to clear the ball. I knocked him out; he scored and I broke my hand. My World Cup was over before it started. It would have been a great experience and the team went on to do really well. But I was number two and the likelihood of me playing was low anyway, so I opted, under advice from Dr Corrigan, to get home and sort my hand out."

Schwarzer was twenty-one when the urge to go overseas became a constant guttural rumble. Even twenty-one is sometimes regarded as "late", but Schwarzer spent his time wisely at Marconi, playing regular football and working his options. Mark Bosnich was already in England and doing very well, and apart from serving his own career goals, Bosnich the keeper and Bosnich the personality were providing an effective warning shot across the bow of Europe that Aussie keepers were ready, and good. Schwarzer, for his part and at this time, exuded all the confidence of youth. With a long and loping stride, fashionably long hair and permanently fixed smile, he also had the important tools in his kitbag—cat-like reflexes and hands that could deliver a granite rock into a bed of eiderdown without any trace of intervention.

In consultation with the then Marconi coach Andrea Icardi, Schwarzer and team-mates Steve Corica, Luke Casserly and Glen Johnson would spend time with the former AC Milan player discussing practicalities, requirements and opportunities as they related to European football. For Schwarzer, "the NSL was a great taste and a great foundation, but I needed to get overseas and see what the top level was". Icardi pointed Schwarzer to an agent contact of his in Germany. The meat and potatoes of Schwarzer's professional sojourn was about to commence in earnest.

"Because of my parents, I had a German passport and Germany was my only real option. It was prior to the European Union and most football leagues had a three-foreigner rule. If I went anywhere other than Germany, I'd be classed as a foreigner and clubs were more likely to keep those places for on-field players. I was young too, so that would have really tested their commitment.

"The deal didn't quite materialise as expected. I remember being suspicious at the time, but at least it was a step that got me into Europe. I had a trial organised with Borussia Dortmund, or a contract at Dynamo Dresden, guaranteed deal, as number two keeper. Dortmund was a top European club at the time and Aussie Ned Zelic was there, but I was comfortable with my decision to go to Dresden. I backed the sure thing."

Or so he thought.

"Dresden didn't turn out well but it was certainly a learning experience. It was very difficult for me there and I would repeatedly ask myself, 'Is this is what I really want to do?' My German background helped with the language and I was living a reasonable life, in a nice apartment, but the culture was very strange. The Berlin Wall was only down five years or so and Dresden hadn't really embraced westernisation yet, which developed a lot later. The team was divided: East Germans were set against foreigners, the subset of which included West Germans. It gave me a taste of what the football world was about. All this was a long way from my Australian experience." We can also perhaps safely assume that line of demarcation included Aussies of Teutonic parentage.

"I never had any bad moments with individuals; it was the atmosphere. And I was there alone. I didn't like the manager [coach] and anyway, it was the president who brought me to the club. The first day I turned up, the coach didn't even know I was coming. When I mentioned who I was, he mumbled something about 'hearing something about me'."

Schwarzer's story here is one made more familiar by the stories of many players who went before, and came after him, to many destinations around Europe. The internal politics of European football clubs, the tensions and dynamics between presidents and coaches, and within dressing-rooms, are enough to test the mettle of the most determined.

Schwarzer was dealing with some personal issues, as well as the isolation of his surroundings, and a president who, having brought him to the club, was now moving to oust him. A lot of soul-searching was required, and constant re-focusing too. Schwarzer looks back on the whole thing with balance. Never would he recommend such a thing for anyone. Neither, though, would he change it for anything, "it was an unbelievable learning experience", and quite a paradox too!

Presumably, things that are learned at such times are used later down the track. Schwarzer would not have long to wait to dust off the textbook and revisit the "learning experience" chapter.

There was a change of coach at Dresden, and the new arrival was met with some good form from Schwarzer, which immediately endeared him to the new boss. Whilst the president was still antagonistic, he also realised that there was money to be made in moving Schwarzer, so he indulged the coach and keeper for the time being.

With some good form, and some good connections at Bundesliga club Kaiserslauten through Schwarzer's agent, a move was made and Schwarzer was off to be number two at this, a bigger, club.

The political merry-go-round kicked straight back into gear for the increasingly frustrated Australian. Schwarzer's arrival as number two meant, by definition, that the incumbent second choice would become Kaiserslauten's third option. He was listed as the club's goalkeeper coach, but he also had a playing contract.

It was realised very early on that whatever preconceptions Schwarzer may have had of the much acclaimed "German efficiency" there was no evidence to be found at Kaiserslauten, at least as it managed its goalkeeper stocks. Schwarzer found his

"Bradford saw me and wanted me. I had the backing of the manager and they were decisive and efficient."

---

keeper coach to be more agitator and political strongman than either keeper or coach.

"He was very powerful at the club. And he never coached us. The first team keeper and I would do extra training, keeper specific, on our own. Shooting at each other, whatever we could do. For eighteen months at Kaiserslauten, the keeper coach never once coached us. But as his player contract was geared to appearances, he would become available to be on the bench for the big games. I missed the German Cup final and watched it from the stands because he installed himself on the bench so as to be eligible for his bonus. For me, it wasn't about money at the time, just the chance to play and build my career."

Otto Raehagel (successful coach of Greece for Euro 2004) became the next to put the bamboo under Schwarzer's fingernails. He made it very clear, very early, that he wasn't keen to play young players, including Schwarzer. However, the godsend for Schwarzer, the formation of the European Union, was imminent, and his German passport would now provide an opportunity to get out of his father's land and, hopefully, go somewhere more welcoming.

The national team was to provide a timely fillip for Schwarzer. "It was Eddie Thomson's last match in charge of the national team; they were preparing for a match against Saudi Arabia", recalls Schwarzer, "and Bozza [Mark Bosnich] pulled out of the squad. It had been some time since I was called up because I hadn't been playing much at club level. But it was during this squad that

I chatted with some of the boys who were playing in England, asking them what it was like and getting contacts from them. Lucas Neill gave me Barry Silkman's number, which I used. Still, to this day, he manages my affairs.

"When I got back to Germany, the coach left me out altogether. Neither a word of reason nor barely a glance was offered my way. I called the trainer, Hans Peter Briegel, who could see what was going on. He knew that I couldn't stay where I was; it was ruining my career."

Silkman organised a trial for Manchester City in England. The trial went well and Schwarzer was invited back for a repeat dose, this time for a game against Bradford City. The intervening period when he returned to Kaiserslauten was frostier than the worst of German winters. When an injury to the number one keeper still didn't result in any game time, Schwarzer finally became convinced that he had to break away.

Manchester City was sufficiently impressed by Schwarzer's trial form that they presented him, by fax, a contract. However, what City later claimed to be a "typo" sent alarm bells through Schwarzer's considerations. "There was a zero missing from the figures that we'd agreed on. The fax also carried a comment asking me to sign and return quickly so that the paperwork could be sorted in time for the next game." Schwarzer, understandably, hesitated. As Manchester City bumbled their way through typographic inexactitudes, Bradford City, the team against which Schwarzer played on trial, looked to swoop.

"Manchester City is a big club and the money was better. But the contract thing concerned me. Bradford, for its part, was a smaller club and carried with it comparatively less pressure. I felt I could settle in there and just get playing. I had come from two clubs in

Germany, which together had gone through six managers in the two and a half years I was there, so I liked the stability that was on offer. Bradford saw me and wanted me. I had the backing of the manager and they were decisive and efficient. I only cost them £155,000 and the agreement was I could leave if they received any offer for me that exceeded £1 million."

To be out of Germany was a huge relief for Schwarzer, who tells of the acute mental anguish that went with the treatment of him by a series of coaches. "They were working me the whole time. I'd come home devastated, wondering what this was all about and whether it was all worth it. There was a lot of self-doubt, too. My wife was very supportive and remained very objective. We could always go home, if that was what I wanted, but she knew, as I did, that I didn't really want that and I'd realise I'd be making a huge mistake. But there were a lot of nights when tears were shed. This was not how the dream was supposed to go."

England was a new lease of life for Schwarzer. "I liked the football for a start. I have always thought that because of the pace and the end-to-end action, it is a great place for strikers and keepers to show their stuff. The environment was much lighter, too. Germany was dire and stifling, there was no laughter at training, no variety, everything the same."

After a brief spell at Bradford City, Middlesbrough came in for Schwarzer in 1997 and since then, he has established himself as one of the English Premier League's most consistent performers. After lengthy service at the Riverside Stadium, Schwarzer placed a

---

"The appointment of Guus [Hiddink] was pivotal, although I admire Frank Farina a lot and I have much to thank him for."

transfer request with the Middlesbrough manager Steve McLaren in January 2006. After much talk and speculation, Schwarzer has remained where he is, though for how much longer one can't be sure.

All this, of course, is the club platform that has prepared him for the dramatic role he played most recently in assisting Australia to qualify for the finals of the FIFA World Cup. Amidst the interviews and public adulation that have followed the amazing scenes in Sydney after the game, and the centre-stage cameo so wonderfully adorned by Schwarzer on that night, the tumult undergone to arrive in the spotlight, to take the bow and accept the applause, can be significant.

Up to this point, the international road has also been bumpy. Remembering the performance against Canada, it wasn't for another couple of years that Schwarzer was reunited with the national team. And this, too, wasn't much of a re-entry, because Schwarzer's international career took another hiatus when Englishman Terry Venables, who followed the departure of Thomson, took charge of the Socceroos. The circuit-breaker for Schwarzer this time was a clash of commitments between his club, Middlesbrough, and his country, which was about to take on Macedonia in a friendly match. Middlesbrough had a League Cup semifinal second leg to play at the same time. Schwarzer believed that a conversation between his club and national team bosses had sorted the issue out, but it appeared not. So, for the time of Venables's tenure, Schwarzer was left to cool his international heels. It wasn't until Frank Farina became coach and famously made Schwarzer his "first phone call" that Schwarzer's international career reignited in 1999.

Through until 2005, Mark Schwarzer has held on to the mantle of Australia's number one goalkeeper, though under increasing

"In the afternoon of the game, whilst resting, I dreamt that it was going to be a penalty shoot-out and I was going to make two saves in it."

---

pressure from perennial aspirant, Zeljko Kalac. This qualifying campaign for the 2006 World Cup was Schwarzer's third. He was still licking his wounds from the previous failure to Uruguay in 2001, where, as the last line of a blistered defence, Schwarzer had to stoop three times, depressingly, to retrieve the ball from his own net before bidding Uruguay farewell and bon voyage to Korea–Japan 2002.

For the majority of this next quadrennial cycle, the national team plodded on, with an improved program of games but, with the exception of the Confederations Cup, still without seriously contested international matches. Players returned to their clubs to continue their individual careers. Australia didn't utilise the entire four-year interval to refine their product. Instead, change came very late, very definitely and very successfully.

The ultimate achievement, according to Schwarzer, was rooted in a thorough top to bottom going-over of the national team's affairs. There are still more things to do, but there was much better preparation this time around, the likes of which haven't been seen before. "The whole organisation got us across the line, from the top of FFA [Football Federation Australia] down. The appointment of Guus [Hiddink] was pivotal, although I admire Frank Farina a lot and I have much to thank him for. The respect of the whole football world has been won by the people at FFA."

It is possible that the planning that seems to have so impressed Schwarzer may have led to a psychology that expected success.

“In the afternoon of the game, whilst resting, I dreamt that it was going to be a penalty shoot-out and I was going to make two saves in it. But I didn’t think about it again. It wasn’t until after the game, when everything slowed down, that it dawned on me that I’d had that dream that afternoon.

“Before the game I didn’t want to think about it [penalties]; we didn’t want to go that far. I enjoy them when they come up. I have been fortunate never to have lost one in a major game and also to make saves in them. But 2-0 wouldn’t have been as nice. And I didn’t have a lot to do anyway. So the penalties ended up being good for me. The penalties suited the drama. Rather than failure and heartache, it was joy. Everything was perfect.

“It was the most unbelievable night of my whole career. Uruguay was a better team themselves this time round. I really believe that we can go on, we have to believe that. There’s a lot of hard work from now until then. But we can make it. Put the recognition even higher. Put football even more on the map. It’s ironic, Germany in 1974 and it fits that we are there again. But it doesn’t just happen; you have to make it happen.”

For Schwarzer it has been a case of many roads leading to Rome. “My career is full of goals. You know what you want to achieve and sometimes the journey that you take is not always the one that you want; it might be the one you are pushed onto.”

His is also testament to the fact that a football career, like Rome, wasn’t built in a day.

Mark Schwarzer

shirt number 2

"It [self-belief] means, to me, perhaps never being brilliant, but that when things aren't going well, you still believe that sooner or later you'll turn the corner and things will be in place again. It is about the confidence to believe in your ability and to have that faith. If you lose this week, you know that you will bounce back and tackle it again next week."

Lucas Neill

Date of birth 9 March 1978

Position played Defender

Current club Blackburn Rovers, England

To sit with Lucas Neill is to be impressed by the purity and totality of his self-belief. It is simultaneously his greatest asset and self-professed Achilles heel. It is a confidence forged out of strength of purpose and laser-like, career-focused vision. It is embellished by athletic prowess and chiselled features. It is represented by a swagger that moves to the laconic beat of a man on a mission. It is preserved with a defiant aggression and exerted by its will to impose, to make a mark. It is evident in that he cuts his teeth in one of the most intense sporting competitions in the world, the English Premier League. And in a contemporary era that searches for meanings of "Australianness", it is Australian to the very core.

Unfortunately for the Australian spectator, Lucas Neill flew the football coop without participating in the old National Soccer League, that trusty old warhorse that delivered so many, so successfully, into professional European careers. He was off and away before most of us had the chance to see what he had to offer. It hasn't been until relatively recently that we have been able to watch him again, and then you have to be prepared to catch the glimpse of a television highlight or sacrifice hours of precious early morning sleep to watch his games live via satellite on the occasions that television programmers deem this appropriate.

Or, you could have attended the Sydney Olympic Stadium on 16 November 2005 and watched one of the most masterfully composed, defensive performances of the modern era as it relates to the Australian national team.

For Neill, it all began on Sydney's northern beaches, where he grew up in Frenchs Forest. His first team was the Wakehurst Tigers, the orange and blacks, where he played in the Under 7s. His time with Wakehurst was interrupted very early on, however, when his father's work took the family to England. Unlike Australia, there was no readily available club structure, so young Lucas had to join the Cubs in the local village as "that was the only way I could play football".

The Neill family was in England for the next two seasons, whereupon the family returned to Australia and Lucas's career resumed with the Wakehurst Tigers.

"But it was probably that time in England when I really got the taste for football. That first season back in Australia, we won both the local and champion-of-champions competitions. It was a great team and I have forged some very strong friendships which have endured right up until now." This, despite the fact that Neill moved to the St Augustine's club, where he also went to school. This new school was traditionally a Rugby League school, but his commitment to the football cause was evident early as he recalls, "putting soccer on the map there for at least a couple of years".

Neill's card was marked early on. From the local club sides he began playing with the Manly Warringah representative teams. He provides constant testimony to the importance of his family to the grander picture, and this, coupled with whatever "luck" was either necessary or on offer, worked to reinforce his self-belief.

"I also think my attitude is mentally strong. I have always believed in myself and always wanted to do this. I have never let anything distract me. I could have gone out on Friday nights, when I was fourteen or fifteen, when everyone was starting to learn about going out, but I stayed home because I'd have a game the next day ... it's these tiny little things ... or surfing on Saturday mornings except that there were games in the afternoon, and I'd get tired and couldn't do what I needed to do. Then there was the driving—Mum and Dad getting out of bed early on the weekends to take me across Sydney for games or extra training."

Such focus at such a raw age should be contextualised. Sydney is one of the world's wealthiest cities and its northern beaches one of its most privileged subsets. This is not to necessarily say that the Neill upbringing was in any way lavish, but it is true that there is the opportunity to explore any of life's opportunities from there. The potential downside of that is that there is too much on offer and the ability to become seriously proficient at any one thing can be compromised. The norm of the existence in this part of the world is for kids to play as many sports as possible. This is so in much of Australia. There are also the distractions of the beach culture, which has a magnetic effect on many who live within the bosom of the peninsula.

"I remember my dad saying I should choose between cricket and soccer. I liked cricket very much, but went with soccer. Being good at it when I was young helped, because your attitude doesn't deflate. Everyone wants to win and the more you do, the more you want to succeed. I had success at football, and it was supported by a close and committed group of families who made an occasion out of each weekend when the games were on, picnics and everything. It was a good crop of people, no bad apples."

Woven throughout most of the things Neill says are references to mental toughness or self-belief. It is as though the two are one and the same and he cannot sustain himself without either.

"I know who I am and what I am good at, and I know I have the right people behind me. And as long as I know I can do it, that is all that counts."

"It means, to me, perhaps never being brilliant, but that when things aren't going well, you still believe that sooner or later you'll turn the corner and things will be in place again. It is about the confidence to believe in your ability and to have that faith. If you lose this week, you know that you will bounce back and tackle it again next week. But I know players who, if they lose, for the next six days or until the next game, they're in a bad mood, their training is affected; but if they win, they are the best trainers in the world. But for me, because every day is going to be different, I am going to remain the same. I have been kicked from pillar to post by the media, people saying who I am and what I am, but I know who I am and what I am good at, and I know I have the right people behind me. And as long as I know I can do it, that is all that counts."

This could easily be fobbed off as rhetoric, except that it appears so fundamental to the core of Neill's persona that it is strewn through everything he says, and apparently, does.

But he isn't invincible, acknowledging that his weakness is too much confidence and too much optimism. "Sometimes I get caught—too much belief and not enough caution." Neill is clear in his own mind that he isn't cocky, or at least not overly so, but that is how it can sometimes be construed. But equally, he can barely contain himself when the thought of a new or bigger challenge confronts him. "When we play Brazil in the World Cup, if selected, the prospect of playing the five best strikers in the world—I don't fear it at all, I can't wait for that. Going up against those guys makes me think, 'Come on, I want some of that.'" And it's the same when he plays Thierry Henry, the famed Arsenal and France striker. "I don't fear that. I want to challenge myself, to see how good I am, playing my own game to defuse him, not worrying about his game—that's mental toughness."

From the Australian Institute of Sport, when in his mid-teens, Neill trialled in England with Queens Park Rangers. The trial went well, but he happily obliged the request of his parents to return to Australia and complete his schooling.

Soon after, however, he returned to London to be greeted by Queens Park Rangers' invitation to trial again, for them to check that all was still okay. Neill refused, and his agent secured a deal with Millwall without any trial needed. Neill accepted. "It was a guarantee, a foot in the door, for three years."

Millwall is in South London. When football's public image has suffered at times because of crowd trouble, Millwall's fans have often been right in the thick of much of the action. They have a fearsome reputation, earned throughout the years by the brutally confrontationalist style of a core of their fans. For Neill, Millwall was "a great education. Playing for them, you realise how much it means to them to be Millwall and as a result you can't take your foot off the pedal. They don't accept 99 per cent and respect the fact that you mightn't play well every week, but if you are trying your best, not giving in, they will look after you. "

"When we play Brazil in the World Cup, if selected, the prospect of playing the five best strikers in the world—I don't fear it at all, I can't wait for that. Going up against those guys makes me think, 'Come on, I want some of that.'"

On balance though, Neill recalls much "frustration there". Whilst he played that first season, the team dropped from a mid-table position to relegation. "I found that really hard to take and I didn't really know what it meant until I saw grown men crying, realising the next two or three years of their contract was going to be in a lower division. It really didn't hit me until the next season when I realised the drop in everything—crowds, quality, stadiums—everything. At the same time, you know you can be playing Premier League and you are stuck two divisions lower, thinking, 'Is anyone watching, does anyone care?'"

Neill's first brush with injury came in the lead-in to the second season when, playing for the Australian Youth Team, he broke his foot. Prior to his departure for that Youth World Cup in Malaysia, a list of potential suitors were queuing up interestedly, including the likes of Rangers, Everton and Tottenham. "Rangers bid for me, but it was rejected by Millwall, which angers me because Millwall were in administration at the time and I didn't feel they had the right to be fussy." It was during the time of the second group match in Malaysia, against Hungary, that Neill cracked his foot. He took an injection for the next game against Argentina. Australia famously won that game 4-3, but in the final stages of the match Neill snapped his foot.

The interest from the other clubs waned and Neill found himself aground in England's third-tier competition with his foot in plaster. Three months later he broke his other foot during his first week back in training and was faced with a further three months on the sidelines. Mentally, Neill's toughness was tested. Physically, he went from "a brilliant standard to skinny legs, no muscle and no 'touch'".

It can take a while to come back from a lengthy injury lay-off. Past the time when the mechanics are back in motion, a repatriated player may still take longer to get back into the rhythm of their profession, and confidence can be a major factor. For Neill, he was "still not quite right" for his return season three. The crowd was murmuring that they'd lost the kid they'd "known", the one who at seventeen had broken in at Millwall and was touted as something special. But he worked hard to regain himself and came back to contribute to a promotion-winning campaign.

Being "buried" in the nether world of English League football was not something to which Neill took kindly. He looks back now on the naivety of the young player who might have heard a whisper that a big club was coming to watch him, and then getting primed for a big game to suit, waiting afterwards by the phone for an offer to be called through. Many young players submit themselves to similarly anxious scenarios. It was later that he realised, in fact, that the offers were coming in, but Millwall was not accepting them.

But what tarnished Neill's time at Millwall more than anything was the saga surrounding his involvement in the Sydney 2000 Olympic Games. After receiving notification of his selection for the Games, Neill was informed by Millwall that he was not to go to Australia to compete. An obstinate verbal tug of war began, with Neill insisting that he was going to represent his country. "They gave me the ultimatum—play for your country or us. They threatened to 'let me rot' there. So I called their bluff. How could they seriously not want me to play for my country, in the Olympics of my home town?"

Neill found himself dropped from the squad entirely. He asked to be released early, therefore, to get to Australia with a bit more time to prepare, but that was rejected. Whilst he was in Australia, the Millwall management (coaches) was sacked. Upon his return, Mark McGhee and Ray Hartford were appointed. Hartford turned out to be one of Neill's biggest career influences.

Immediately upon his return from the Olympics, Neill was greeted by the new manager, who was sensitive to the bad blood that existed in the previous regime. McGhee knew of Neill's performances until now and had no hesitation in throwing him straight back into the team. In that first game back, Millwall won 4-1, with Neill scoring two goals and setting up another. "It was the perfect comeback. I was back in the groove, happy with proceedings, but also with my eye on the conclusion of my contract, which was approaching."

Neill made it very clear that he wasn't going to re-sign with Millwall. Having felt that he had contributed sufficiently to the Millwall cause, it was now definitely time to move. The club didn't respond well to Neill's position, and the politics started again. "Mark McGhee came to me and apologised for what was going on and said that he was 'going to have to play political games with me'", which is a strange position for a club to take, given that Neill had been playing so well.

Neill held his ground and forced the issue with Millwall. It was during this stand-off that Ray Hartford looked to broker some peace for the player. He offered to talk with his old club, Blackburn Rovers. Meanwhile, because of injuries, Millwall were forced to play Neill and, what's worse for them, he was performing with distinction. Hartford arranged for Neill to trial with Blackburn.

"Graeme Souness [Blackburn coach] picked me up from the airport. Straightaway he said he liked my swagger. He likes arrogance. I told him about what was going on at Millwall. He warned me that I would struggle day one, because of the pace, and that it would take a couple of weeks, or months even, to get used to it properly. He knew I came highly recommended. Hartford's word counted for something."

The first day was too quick for Neill. "I knew what to do, I just couldn't do it quickly enough. Passes that I can make were being cut out. But," he continued, "day two it clicked, I must have gone up another gear. My month or week of adaptation came in a day".

Then, right on cue, the regular Blackburn right back got injured. Even though Neill had arrived to trial as a right midfielder, he accepted the chance to play right back. "I gave Damien Duff [Ireland international] such a hard time that he yelled out to Souness for respite and posed the question to his boss, 'where did you get this kid from?'"

With another injury to the other right back, Souness approached Neill after training and said that he was going to sign him and that he should return to Millwall. He said that he should encourage both the club and his own manager to be sensible and that a contract would be ready for signing at midday the next day, with the view to Neill starting against Sunderland on the upcoming Saturday. Neill was asked by Souness if he could handle it. "No doubts" was the reply. Perfunctorily to the point.

Suspensions aside, Lucas Neill "hasn't missed a game from that day to this".

"From that day to this", then, has meant a life in the hyper-stratospheric world of the English Premier League, arguably the world's most popular football league and certainly one of its richest.

"A lot of people only see the glamour and the profile. Fast cars, girls, lots of money. Everybody's always onto you with something new for a test drive. It's a bit of a catwalk at training in the morning, the boys all try to outdo each other with their gear—it's very competitive.

"There is a lot of scrutiny too, everything is such a magnifying glass that little mistakes become massive ones, and so on. There are 40,000 people at the games and another couple of million every night on television judging what you do, and also thinking they know your life.

"But I live a quiet life, I don't go to nightclubs or even the local pub because people hassle you, wanting to know why you are out when you have a game to play.

"I have a house that has no neighbours around and there are no distractions. I can be my normal self. I have my two dogs and I live with my girlfriend. We don't go into the city a lot and whilst the glamour is there, I don't indulge much. Nightclubs are uncomfortable because all sorts of people come up to you and they are a bit of a jungle. You try to put up a few barriers."

For Neill, the games are so high tempo and intense, he actively seeks out opportunities to wind down and relax, to find ways to "take the high and channel it back to real life and chill". But his preoccupation with his football is such that he is always in some state of preparation for the upcoming game and not wanting to concede any advantage to a future opponent.

"I love this, though. I love the crowds and the buzz. I always dreamed about it as a kid, playing on television, in England, against the best in the world."

He is a player driven by the challenge and the totem pole. "I want fifty caps for Australia, which is difficult in this day and age. Playing for Australia is the best thing you can do, I think it is the pinnacle. Getting paid well to play in front of big crowds is great, but so too is playing for your country."

Neill has eyes on a move to one of England's big clubs and/or a move to Spain. "I am learning Spanish and would like the challenge of the Primera Liga. Johnny Aloisi tells me what it is like over there and the lifestyle sounds good. England is hustle and bustle, the football is 100 per cent, but sometimes there is a tendency to look away from tactics and technique."

It is then with the chill of the executioner, that Neill talks about the qualifying series against Uruguay. His character comes through as he recalls the "tingle" of walking out onto Uruguay's Estadio Centenario and the way his team-mates, as one, "stuck their chests out—everyone accepting the challenge. That was good to see."

The Sydney game had a huge impact on Neill. "Hiddink had mapped out the entire 120 minutes of that game. He said to me, 'You are at the back and you can see everything, tweak this, tweak that. Don't panic.' He went through every permutation. I'm going out there, into this cauldron, everyone's on edge, the emotion's high and I'm relaxed because I have the whole game mapped out and that's something I have learned from him.

"A lot of people only see the glamour and the profile. Fast cars, girls, lots of money. Everybody's always onto you with something new for a test drive."

"I never forget where I've come from. I'm a Manly boy through and through. I want to reward the kids and create a path for them, if I can."

"I never had that approach to the game before! I looked over at him, the first part of the game was a bit scrappy, but he was unfazed. His ability to man-manage, to cuddle and to kick up the arse is very good. He can hammer me all day, he can punish me, he knows that I am just going to bounce straight back up and do the same thing again. But he was so cool, so unflappable, that really helps a team perform."

Then to the decisive moments of qualification. For his part, Neill and his penalty were never in doubt. "I was actually smiling on the walk up to the spot, I was so sure, because I'd practised the day before. I was on autopilot, shut everything down around me, took my two steps and in it went ... never in doubt."

And typical of Neill, when the winning penalty was converted and pandemonium broke out, he made his way to his family, where "to see them more emotional than me was great. Their sacrifice has been immense. They have put me in a position to do all this." Paradoxically, this is also the only mention of regret for Neill, when the absence of his girlfriend from Sydney that night left him ruing that "the chance will never come again".

In the dressing rooms, Neill describes things as a "blur". The atmosphere could only have become more surreal when John Travolta entered the rooms, singing and dancing. Neill recalls the events quite vividly. "John Travolta said that was the best sporting experience of his life, that he was so thankful and humbled for the opportunity to share it with us, to which I said, 'What? You humbled to be with us? What about us?' Travolta responded, 'Yes, but I act; what you did out there was real', and he then volunteered to fly us to Germany."

Once Travolta touches the team down in Germany, Neill expects to win the first game against Japan "simply because we have to. We have to put that pressure on ourselves. I am willing to put it on myself and on the boys that we expect to do this. Our group is perfect for us and every game is a tough game. Knowing that we have to be at our best to beat teams is perfect for me. To play Brazil is fantastic. Sure it's a great shirt to go on the wall, but there's a chance to beat them. The last game has a whole heap of emotion attached to it because of the background of some of our boys. They'll be so determined to do well, but by then I reckon we'll be playing for first and second spot!"

Apart from the immediacy of the challenge, there also appears to be broader interest from Neill for this World Cup. His desire is that football grows. He has already invested in grassroots football with a capital development at the home of the Manly Association, Cromer Park. And he intends to put more back into that community. "I never forget where I've come from. I'm a Manly boy through and through. I want to reward the kids and create a path for them, if I can."

He extracts great delight from elevating the status of his sport in his country. "We've been responsible for putting football in the race to be number one in Australia, which is a great source of pride. It is what our job is, definitely, to make it number one."

shirt number 3

"I still love the game of football. The unexpectedness of it. I've been fortunate to be with Rangers. It's a successful, family-oriented club. The years have flown by very quickly. I have loved what I have been doing every day and that is why I have made it through."

Craig Moore

Date of birth 12 December 1975

Position played Defender

Current club Newcastle United, England

The roll call of great Australian players stricken by the fickleness of injury is perhaps headed by Ray Baartz. His career was ended in a friendly match against Uruguay, of all teams, in April of 1974, only months before he was to participate in Australia's first ever, and only other, World Cup finals appearance. Baartz was one of Australia's leading players at the time. His consolation was that he still made the trip to West Germany, as it was then, as a "team manager".

There is no such thing as a well-timed injury. Injury is the big foe of professional athletes. When its fearsome head looms, shudders run down the spine of the unlucky or the unwitting, years of work are jeopardised, dreams endangered. Injuries leading up to the Uruguay game threatened Australia's dream and were putting various players through some demanding times.

While Australia watched the second game unfold, everyone with their own story to tell about where they watched the game and how they coped with the tension, Craig Moore, who was captain-in-absentia, was "stuck" in the north-east of England, hamstrung by a hamstring injury, wondering from a distance about the fortunes of his team for this, his third World Cup qualifying campaign. Spare a thought for him.

He was "wondering" because he couldn't even watch. "The games weren't live on TV over here. We only got a highlight package of game one. For the second game, the Sydney game, I was on the phone to Musky [Melbourne Victory captain and former Socceroo team-mate Kevin Muscat] every five minutes. I was also calling my mum and dad to get different bits of information about the game and what was going on, to try and get a picture of what was happening."

Kevin Muscat has been many things throughout his long career, but this was surely the first time he had been a seeing-eye dog.

"I was on the phone to Musky for the whole penalty shoot-out. I had no pictures. I was just getting commentary down the phone. He did a great job, but it was a nightmare. You can't see anything, you are just hoping. You can't see the run-up, the anticipation. You can't read the body language. You can't see the ball being placed. You can't see the keeper's eyes. How close he is getting to make a save. You can't see how nervous or comfortable the players are. You are just hanging there. You only get to release when you are told to. The tension was incredible. Absolutely no way to relieve it except listen to Musky's descriptions. And you could hear it in his voice as well, when Johnny [Aloisi] got that last one, the rush of adrenaline was incredible. The buzz was amazing. Even though I wasn't involved in the game, it seemed to take so much out of me."

Taking all this in via nothing more than a phone conversation must have been as close to unbearable as anything imaginable. Even more so if you are Craig Moore and you had invested so many years in this team and this campaign and this dream, been installed as captain and now, at the final hour, excluded because of injury. Excruciating.

"It was a very strange experience, but fantastic. I watched the replay later. It was actually better on the phone because when I saw the replay, I saw that Uruguay had a couple of chances, and I would have been tearing the walls down if I was watching it live."

"I was doing some work at a leisure centre, hydro work and gym stuff, when the game was on. I had to get excused from the medical staff. 'Listen boys, we've just qualified for the World Cup. I'll have to leave you for today. I need to go and relax with my missus and share a bottle of wine.'

"I spoke to the team directly in the dressing room right after. I phoned and left a message, and as soon as the boys have come in they've all been on the phone, which was really nice. They were singing songs in the background that they were missing me and the rest of it. Although I wasn't there, I felt a big part of it, felt involved. It was a nice touch."

An even better touch was that the team had qualified and Moore now can set his sights on selection for the finals squad, a voyage that started in Sydney's western suburbs and has taken him through Brisbane, Canberra, Glasgow, London, Monchengladbach in Germany and now Newcastle in England.

"I was a westie", spurts Moore. "I was born in Canterbury but grew up in Doonside. My first junior club was Rooty Hill RSL."

He played for the local association's representative teams until he was twelve when he moved to the higher division with Blacktown City. When he was thirteen, his family moved up to Redcliffe, a northern suburb of Brisbane, on Moreton Bay.

"It was a very strange experience, but fantastic. I watched the replay later. It was actually better on the phone because when I saw the replay, I saw that Uruguay had a couple of chances, and I would have been tearing the walls down if I was watching it live."

"Moving to Brisbane was a big turning point for me when I look back. Because of the age group that the Joeys were selected from, I was ineligible because I was too young, too young in Sydney anyway. I wasn't going to be looked at for that age group, but when we moved to Brisbane I was selected for the Queensland team, playing a year above myself, which was the age group that the Joeys were picked from [for that intake]."

This is an important distinction, because the Joeys gave Moore the opportunity to press for a scholarship with the AIS, where he would later join John Aloisi, Mark Viduka and Josip Skoko.

Meanwhile, in club-land, Moore "had a year with Redcliffe City, one with Brisbane City and a year with Northstar before making the move to the AIS.

"From about the age of ten, when I was doing athletics and football, training for them both started to clash. It was getting a bit messy. It was then that I said to myself I was going to focus on football, and I chopped athletics. I was going to give it the best crack I could. My idea at the age of ten was to be a professional footballer; I would need to head to England."

"Mum and Dad worked extremely hard for me and my brother and sister, to do the best for us that they possibly could. I knew there was potential for me to make money and for me to make things a lot easier for my family. But I also knew that I was good at the game and I loved it, and that was evident from a very early age.

"As a young boy, I used to remember Craig Johnston at Liverpool, watching him, getting up early to watch Cup finals. From an early age it had a real grip on me and it was something that I wanted to achieve and experience for myself. So every opportunity I got,

"From about the age of ten, when I was doing athletics and football, training for them both started to clash. It was getting a bit messy. It was then that I said to myself I was going to focus on football, and I chopped athletics. I was going to give it the best crack I could."

---

matches on Saturdays and Sundays, training three or four nights a week, I just got right into it. Mucking around in the street or the backyard. I always seemed to have a ball around and I was a really hard worker. My brother was probably a lot more talented and naturally gifted, but I was the one who worked a lot harder.

Moore's parents moved to Brisbane for work reasons and the "opportunity to get something closer to the water, not being as expensive as Sydney up there". He found with the move, however, that whilst he was an established part of youth football down south, it was difficult finding a club because not many in the Brisbane fraternity knew of him, and "not many people were looking at me, to be honest." He started at Redcliffe and did well there in his first year, "I think two years above my own age", and then "people started talking and I ended up going to the representative stuff with Brisbane North and Queensland. The toughest was the first year. I was at a lesser known club, but when I started playing well, the word spread and other people became interested."

Moore is not from a football family. His father's sport was Rugby League. Moore followed his brother into football and he also watched as his father took it up a bit later with an Over 35s team. "My brother and dad were doing it and I found myself getting involved. There was cricket earlier on too, but I wasn't interested if I wasn't batting or bowling."

Moore never played in the NSL, which is something that "eats away" at him a little bit. "It is always something that I have wanted to go back to. I still believe that maybe, not too far down the track, I will be back there in the national league [A-League]."

He bypassed Australia's domestic competition on the back of his performances in the 1993 FIFA Youth World Cup, which was played in Australia. It was a high-quality tournament. Australia made the semifinals, where they lost to the eventual winners, Brazil. In fact, so good was that competition that the final, played in Sydney between Brazil and Ghana, is widely recognised as the most purely beautiful game of football played on Australian territory. This for an Under 20 tournament! Australia's standing as semifinalists was a good reflection, therefore, on the quality of its team. Moore was one of the stand-out players and so it was no surprise that there were "people sniffing about, saying I could go on trial here there and everywhere". This was a young player, tough in the tackle, with exceptional speed across the ground, cool in the mind, and decisive as well. This tournament was no flash in the pan for Moore; this was just a window to great things to come.

He accepted the offer to trial with two clubs, Rangers of Glasgow and Arsenal, in England. His passage was eased care of his mother's British nationality, which although at the time didn't entitle him to a passport, did provide him with the necessary permits to work and earn money, "that helped get me going over here".

Both Arsenal and Rangers offered contracts, virtually identical money and a three-year term. "I was more comfortable in Glasgow, the Scottish people were far more friendly to me, it was a big factor in signing there."

Rangers, as Moore pointed out, was also a place where he was going to get first team football more quickly. He admits that in hindsight, this was opportune because "when I look back at Arsenal, their defence rarely changed. They were very stable with England internationals and club stalwarts, and that was in place for a good seven or eight years. The first year at Rangers, I made my debut as an eighteen-year-old and have played first team football every year since."

Moore's first stint with Rangers, then, extended from August 1993 through until 1999, when he left for a five-month spell with London club Crystal Palace. "At that particular time I wasn't an established regular at Rangers. There were a lot of changes at the club. [Manager] Walter Smith was leaving, and influential players like Ally McCoist and Ian Ferguson were also on the move. I thought it would be a good time to move as well and get myself established somewhere else."

Crystal Palace was under the control of Socceroos coach Terry Venables. Venables moved to Palace after his ill-fated period at Portsmouth. His links with Australian players saw him provide opportunities at the London club for Craig Foster, Nick Rizzo and Craig Moore. "Obviously, working with Venables at the national team helped too. It was a connection for getting me down there and that was the reason why I left in the end. I really enjoyed it at Palace. I played twenty-five games in the short time I was there. But the club was having a lot of financial difficulty. I knew that Dick Advocaat, Walter Smith's replacement, was still interested in me. He didn't really want me to leave Rangers in the first place, but I told him of my decision to go. He'd been monitoring my progress since."

Advocaat knew of Palace's trouble. It was public knowledge that funds from chairman Mark Goldberg were, as far as Palace was

"My first few years were a bit of a roller-coaster though, because I wasn't established. I was playing out of position a lot, at right back or in the midfield, or coming on as a substitute and playing centre-forward. I didn't really have a position of my own and I was getting frustrated."

---

concerned, running aground. Advocaat inquired of Palace about Moore's availability, and of Moore too, and the deal for him to return to Ibrox was executed smoothly. "Palace were looked after financially, I went back to Rangers and everybody was happy again. It was quite strange because it was almost as if I hadn't been away from the place at all."

The return signalled a new future for Moore, in some senses. Prior to his departure for London, he wouldn't have described himself as a regular in the first team. The break from the club signalled a change in his playing status with Rangers too, which was to be significant.

"When I went back, I was definitely a regular. Performances had to come along with that of course, but instead of being a player who was playing maybe fifteen to twenty games a season, if I was fit and doing my job, I was playing forty or fifty games a season, so I was definitely a regular.

"My first few years were a bit of a roller-coaster though, because I wasn't established. I was playing out of position a lot, at right back or in the midfield, or coming on as a substitute and playing centre-forward. I didn't really have a position of my own and I was getting frustrated. I knew that I was a central defender and that was the position I wanted to play. Also, as a young player, like all young players, consistency wasn't great at the time."

There was also homesickness to deal with. "It was tough, but Rangers were good. They could see that I was struggling and they sent me home at Christmas in that first year for a couple of weeks. It was great to see my family, and when I got back to Scotland, from then on I was settled. I didn't feel the urge to go home and homesickness wasn't an issue again."

Interesting, the psychology. Moore speaks of his debt to his family and how, as a youngster, he wanted to provide for them in some measure. It could almost be as though his homesickness was more an anxiety at not knowing how his family was coping without him. This is amateur, and speculative, "analysis", it must be said. But it isn't uncommon for some separation anxiety to form out of concern for the people who have been left behind, more so than for those who have departed. Whatever the mix of reasons, Moore's return in that first season was enough for him to bed down those issues that were causing trouble. He was ready to set his stall for a full-time career in Britain.

But there was still the settling-in period to be done at Rangers. "For a good four to five months, I took quite a lot of stick from the Rangers fans. I was a bit-part player with the first team, and when you aren't playing as regularly as you would like, it is very hard to be consistent in your performances. That was difficult for a young boy, but Walter Smith, he stuck by me and continued to put me in the situation where I was playing out there and people eventually saw that I was a good player. I worked hard during a game and wanted to do well for my team-mates. Eventually, I won them over and that was a great feeling because it was tough at first." Moore knew it, and the fans knew it too, and they knew it of each other, probably, that they were making it tough for him.

Rangers is a demanding club. Glasgow is a demanding city for footballers. Whilst the Scottish League is a small one, the rivalry between Glasgow's two big clubs, Rangers and Celtic, is world famous. There is a lot at stake between the fans. Players of both clubs carry an enormous responsibility. There is enormous expectation. There must not be a player take to the field who isn't up to the task, and who could potentially expose the team, and by extension, the fans, to ridicule because of a loss. Because a loss, whatever the circumstances, in matches between Rangers and Celtic is unconscionable. For the young Craig Moore, his issues about not having a regular position, his regular position, would have to be sorted out at a later date. He'd just have to survive until then. It was other people's job to test him, to put him through the wringer. It was his job, as a Rangers player, as a pro, to earn his stripes. Twelve to thirteen years later, Moore is still showing that he passed that test.

There were lots of trophy successes under Walter Smith but the turning point for Moore at Rangers was the arrival of Advocaat. Moore became his undisputed number one central defender. He became a main member of a very good team. Advocaat brought in a collection of highly credentialled Dutch players, which brought about a more continental angle to the Rangers game. Moore had to adjust to fit in with that style and became a centrepiece of it. "He liked me because I wasn't the type of player, in defence, who would try anything ridiculous. I played to my limitations and maintained a simplicity that he liked." It seemed to work, and as a reflection of Moore's standing, he was made captain of Rangers.

But by the end of the 2004 season, things began to frost over for Moore at Rangers. Advocaat had vacated the manager's position in 2001 and was replaced by Alex McLeish. In the northern summer of 2004, Moore left Scotland to captain Australia's Olympic football team, the Olyroos, at the Athens Games. When he returned to Rangers immediately after the Games, though not before the Scottish League season had already commenced, the frost had become a freeze, with the former Rangers captain on the outer with manager McLeish.

"I had been speaking with Rangers about extending my contract, but I was a little disappointed with the direction the talks were taking. I decided that I would see out my contract, or if someone would come in for me, I'd move on. I made that decision with six months or a year to go. It was a decision to try and do something different, find a new challenge and see what else is out there.

"No disrespect to the Scottish League, but the chance of playing one team six times in a season was losing its appeal. It was just time to try something else. I had a fantastic time there, but I felt that if I didn't move when I did, I would have finished my career at Rangers, and I still had the urge to go and try elsewhere."

Moore had the opportunity to sign with Blackburn Rovers in England, the club of Socceroo team-mates Lucas Neill and Brett Emerton. Blackburn had agreed the fee with Rangers and manager Graeme Souness was very positive about Moore's pending arrival.

Moore's plans, and those of Blackburn, were scuppered, however, by the medical examination—the pre-contract protocol that all players undergo when signing new deals. Moore had previously had knee surgery from an injury in 2000 but had been playing since, with no apparent problems. "Blackburn was concerned

---

"He liked me because I wasn't the type of player, in defence, who would try anything ridiculous. I played to my limitations and maintained a simplicity that he liked."

because there were already three or four players there with knee problems. It went from a done deal to falling through quite quickly. Word travels quickly in the football world and rumours were flying that I had failed the medical. After that, it was hard to get something in Britain at the time."

Dick Advocaat had meanwhile moved to Borussia Monchengladbach in Germany's Bundesliga (top division). He approached Moore to see if he was interested in a reunion. "The time was right, it was another country and it was a good standard", so Moore accepted.

He went on to play "fifteen or sixteen games, but it was very hard work. I wasn't there for long enough to be fluent in the language and that barrier was big. The amount of time I'd been away from Australia had all been in English-speaking countries, British countries. I was in my comfort zone, and now to go travelling was extremely hard and the style was different, too. I was away from family a lot for the six months I was with Monchengladbach. It was just very difficult."

Moore had an opportunity, "whilst Advocaat was at Monchengladbach, and afterwards too", to extend his deal for another three years but, "I didn't feel it was a place I was going to be happy. At my stage, I wanted to be somewhere where not only me, but my family was going to be happy also.

"The standard of football was extremely good, there were loads of goals scored. Teams would really have a go at each other, a lot of last-minute goals. Nobody was happy with draws, they really wanted to win games."

But Moore's team was struggling, which always makes the time more problematic. They never moved far away from fourth bottom on the table. "Every result was a hard-earned result, fighting against relegation. Instead of buzzing with confidence, we were really grinding results out. I have no doubt it would have been a lot more fun if we were in a better position in the league. But it was still an experience football-wise and I am very glad that it happened. But I was hoping to get back to the UK, to what I knew."

In July 2005, Moore moved to Newcastle United, to take up the position underneath Graeme Souness that was denied him at Blackburn Rovers. Moore, this time, passed his medical but was soon, cruelly, to encounter the injury that would blacken his 2005 and deprive him of his chance to participate in the national team's quest for World Cup qualification.

Newcastle United's season had caused consternation on Tyneside. The "Magpies" receive incredible support from this football-mad part of football-mad England. Its stadium, St James's Park, is full every week, for every game, with 52,000 Geordies willing their team on. But the trophy cabinet is relatively bare for such a big club. Every season the pressure is on to win some silverware. When the team is struggling, the recriminations become very pointed. Moore's injury troubles were also badly timed in this respect too. A new club, a big club and an under-performing club was not really the place to have an injury from the get-go. Sideways glances dart around places, around clubs like Newcastle, when the results are below expectation. Someone, everyone, is to be made accountable, even if those people haven't been playing. They must have something to do with it, mustn't they?

Moore, frustrated in his private injury problems, was nicely placed potentially, as a sitting duck to cop some of the flak. "The knee injury in 2000 was bad but I knew what I had to do to get it right and get back playing. With the knee, it was very much do

"I reckon I will be in great shape for June. This is a marathon, not a sprint, and I think I will be peaking at the right time. My fitness will be at a very high level."

your rehab and get back into it. It is much more defined. You get on the park, fly into your first tackle, come through it and bang, you are back and you are happy. But this hamstring has been something else again. After a bad hamstring tear has healed, there is still a period of time when you have to overcome the mental barrier. Every time you have to turn and sprint, you think about your hammie and that it could possibly go. I have never experienced anything like that with any other injury. The guessing and the doubting. There is a big barrier to break through."

Up until March 2006, he hadn't yet played a senior match for his new club. There will always be a collection of people, quick to cast aspersions and cry conspiracies. But as Moore says himself, "If they thought I was happy with this, then they are mad".

But by March and beyond, Moore was back training, which has eased his peace of mind and taken the heat out of some of that "friendly fire" that has been triggered at club level. Having participated in reserve team games and pitching, ever gradually, for a first team call-up, there is now light at the end of Moore's injury tunnel, and hopefully just in time.

"I reckon I will be in great shape for June. This is a marathon, not a sprint, and I think I will be peaking at the right time. My fitness will be at a very high level.

"I still love the game of football. The unexpectedness of it. I've been fortunate to be with Rangers. It's a successful, family-oriented club. The years have flown by very quickly. I have loved what I have been doing every day and that is why I have made it through. The injuries are no fun, but everyone goes through that. The unfortunate thing is it has become a business, and at times it takes the enjoyment out of it to an extent. When you are young and running about, it's all about fun, going on the park and doing your stuff. It's like anything, as soon as money is introduced, the rules tend to change, which is unfortunate."

It is on the business of the World Cup that Moore is now focused. Preparing himself for the chance to be included in his dream team for his dream date. His actual time with coach Guus Hiddink has been minimal. It is a bizarre scenario that is another pointer to the bizarre world of Australia's national football team. Hiddink's arrival coincided with Moore's injury, and, for all intents and purposes, because of the geographic spread of all the individuals involved, the two have had very little opportunity to work together. "I've met Guus at one of the camps we had, but otherwise, there hasn't really been the opportunity."

The World Cup, and the lead-in thereto, could be a great place for them to get to know each other better. It may well be the only chance Moore gets.

4

shirt number

"I'm not a world-beater who can do tricks, but I like to have a presence in the game, tackle and do whatever I can to help the team out and then myself. If I get a goal, I get one. I always seem to be able to nick a goal."

Tim Cahill

Date of birth 6 December 1979

Position played Midfielder

Current club Everton, England

To those gathered on the terraces, he is "Tiny". In actual fact, a more appropriate nickname for Tim Cahill and the football career he has been carving out for himself since leaving Australia in his late teens would be "Huge", but that has neither any traceable pop star history nor any alliterative allure. It's cumbersome and it doesn't endear, neither of which is appropriate to Cahill's story. "Tiny" suits just fine.

As a football commodity, Cahill's vivacity is tailor-made for the rigours of the English Premier League, where he now plies his trade with Everton, the blue half of Merseyside, "the Toffees" of Liverpool. Cahill's is a playing style that reeks of his personality and approach to life; a thousand miles an hour, ask no questions and take no prisoners, with a metallurgic capacity to score goals.

So excitable is Cahill, and so absorbed is he with his football, that his stare can cut an onlooker to the bone's marrow. Spending time with him off the field gives one a clear idea of how much of a handful he is on it. Certainly, up to this point, no opposing coach has found any meaningful way of dulling his impact. Until now, it has only been Cahill himself who has let opponents off the hook, to the extent even that can be said. But players can't be perfect all the time. What is true of Tim Cahill, however, is that he is there, amongst it, all the time, looking to push his team over the line, looking to score, looking to win and looking to hurt his opponent. "Irrepressible" is the descriptor that, like Cahill, won't go away, until both it, and he, have made the point.

Yet it doesn't take long to see, as Cahill sits back, all steely glare and furrowed brow, how gloriously incapable is he of camouflaging his two greatest motivators—his passion and his family.

He "got" football from his Dagenham-born, English father. For the Cahills, football was a generational thing. He also perhaps got "to" football care of the paperwork that could be generated by that lineage. The influence from the maternal side of his family was more Rugby: Cahill's mum is from Western Samoa and "all her side of the family was into Rugby". Unlike his brothers, Cahill's physique was smaller, and in any case, his dad "put a ball at his feet as soon as he could" and it was all away from there.

When talking, Cahill never really stops at any point of his career or deliberates for any length of time. He never forgets those who have contributed and the clubs and mechanisms that have been part of the journey, for they are firmly embedded in his deep reservoir of gratitude. His are reliable, tried and tested values that unfortunately, in some sectors, have become an anachronism. But they are alive and well in the world that has been constructed by, and for, Tim Cahill. The fact is, he is living his dream and he will never forget the role his family played in getting him there. There is so much to be done and, though still only twenty-six years of age, so much football to be played in the limited amount of time left. Trophies to win, goals to score, games to play, a country to represent and, most significantly, a family to reward, cherish, nurture and thank.

Cahill, born in Sydney in December 1979, recalls a childhood where he was constantly playing football and an introduction to the club circuit that "began with the Lakemba reps". He then moved to Sydney Olympic for "six to eight" years before a final Australian stint with Belmore Hercules in the New South Wales leagues, where he "got some first team and scored some goals".

Perhaps his indebtedness to his family is rooted in the damage he caused to the family backyard. "I was just always playing football. I was about eleven or twelve I'd say, when I really decided on this game, and the sacrifices and discipline started then. Waking up at ridiculous hours to watch football from overseas on SBS. There were to be no school discos or hanging around with your mates. After school there was training and I couldn't get enough of it. When there was no training, I'd be in the backyard taking out fence posts, breaking the occasional window or destroying Mum's garden."

But such wantonness from energetic and sport-obsessed youth is not atypical and it is certainly not the crux of the story for Cahill. That came, more apparently, in his mid-teens, when Cahill left for overseas to realise his football ambitions. He had an issue about whether to finish his schooling or to follow the sport he loved, with the discussions being overseen by his father. When Cahill decided unequivocally that it was football, his parents organised to take out a loan so that he could embark upon his journey. Cahill knew he had to make the right decision. Money was tight and he had brothers and a sister, all of whom "had their dreams and desires too, this was a big sacrifice on their part".

Possibly tinged with the benefit of hindsight, Cahill says that in the end, the decision was easy. When pressed in the discussions, and particularly given his circumstances, he knew it would be difficult to leave his family and that he was going to miss home but "this is always what I wanted to do". So Cahill left, looking

---

"I was just always playing football. I was about eleven or twelve I'd say, when I really decided on this game, and the sacrifices and discipline started then."

over his shoulder at his beloved family, driven by the need to do well for them, driven to the other side of the world.

So to England, and Cahill was hosted by some family friends for the first couple of months and had some trials with clubs that had been set up by connections through his father. The trials went so well in fact, that Cahill had Millwall, two Premier League clubs and a first division club wanting to sign him. Cahill had done well and he knew that his chance was arriving; it was up to him, as he puts it, "to take the bull by the horns". All the while, Cahill was emboldened by experiencing, first-hand, the playing standard of his new surroundings, and he realised very early, knew very early, that his chances were good based on these favourable comparisons. He recalls the onlookers, those whom he was out to impress, "liked my attitude and willingness to learn".

Cahill was also armed with a very healthy self-assessment. He knew he was young and raw, "nowhere near the finished product". There was the brief flirtation with the thought of being the "newest and next Aussie kid" in the Premier League when Nottingham Forest wanted him, the flirtation fired by a fleeting desire to send a message to people at home, the usual suspects who thought Cahill to be "too small and not good enough", that they could stick their thoughts up their analytical jacksies.

But after consideration, for Cahill, there could be only one choice, Millwall, "because they first gave me a chance, I had to pay my dues, that's the way I was brought up".

For Cahill it was about his value system, not about money. He wanted to learn to be a good footballer, and with a confirmed deal with Millwall, he knew that he'd "have three years of playing football, 365 days a year, earning enough money to live and pay my way, learning from good players along the way".

Cahill's time at Millwall was made easier by the presence of Australians Lucas Neill and Jason van Blerk. "It was all about learning for me. I was scoring loads of goals in the youth team and establishing myself at the club by making the right noises on the field."

Cahill's first team debut came towards the end of the 1997–98 season against Bournemouth, and through the next season he was a first team regular. It wasn't just England that suited Cahill. Millwall was a hand-in-glove symbiosis. Even within the umbrella English culture, there are different nuances between clubs, idiosyncrasies, histories and reputations that mark clubs as different from each other. Millwall is a high-octane football club. It has spent the majority of its existence outside the top window of English football, but its reputation goes way beyond this. So too is Cahill a high-octane player, who operates on the most refined of fuels that drives his Formula One physiology up and down, in and around a football field. While sections of Millwall's fans have at times crossed the line into unacceptability, there does remain a club with a palpable and clearly defined spirit. It is this spirit that so embraced Cahill and it was to this that he so responded. He became a crowd favourite at "the Den", Millwall's famously named stadium. Truth is, Cahill has become the same at Goodison Park, home to his current club, Everton. The other "coincidence" is that both teams play in blue.

"I was a massive favourite at Millwall. I was there for six or seven years, played over 250 games and scored just under sixty [fifty-seven] goals. I played at Wembley for them, met George Best as a Millwall player, which was a huge honour, enjoyed getting promotion with Millwall and nearly won promotion to the English Premier League with them, scored a winner in an FA Cup semifinal and played in an FA Cup final against Manchester United—all for Millwall."

Cahill rattles off this sequence with barely a breath taken. It gushes from his mouth, the pride at being involved in things like this, the enjoyment he gave people and the manner in which he represented the fans. He uses the word "massive" a lot, and it is totally appropriate. It is no wonder that he loved his time there so much, and it is even less of a wonder that he was so popular with the fans.

FA Cup goals don't come regularly for Australian players. When Craig Johnston scored for Liverpool against Everton in the 1986 FA Cup final, it was the last of Liverpool's three goals that day, and so technically it was the winner. This game was significant to Australia because Craig Johnston, although born in South Africa, was raised in Lake Macquarie, near Newcastle, Australia. Johnston's career, and this goal, had for a long time been a defining aspect for Australia's football, a sport looking desperately for a hook on which it could hang its hat.

Liverpool, in Johnston's day, was riding the crest of a magnificent wave that made them the envy of English football and champions of Europe. To illustrate the power of Liverpool then, in 1986 they became only the third team of the twentieth century to win the English League Championship and FA Cup double. This FA Cup final was significant also because in beating Everton, Liverpool had triumphed over their great cross-city foes—their derby battles, and others like them, are the beating heart of English football.

The English FA Cup is the oldest codified soccer football competition in the world. It is a knockout format and is open to all of England's football clubs, whether professional or amateur. Because of the nature of the competition, it is difficult to win and because of the history attached to it, it is a keenly sought prize. Moreover, in Australia, the FA Cup final has been an annual check-in for Australian sports fans. It is on their list of sporting "things to do" each year. And prior to the regular television exposure of the English League football, the FA Cup final was the only televised football available to Australians in any regular sense. Probably because of our colonial association with England, and the importance of the FA Cup to them, so too, it meant something to us. Irrespective of the historicity, the FA Cup has always been news in Australia, and when an Australian scores a decisive goal at a decisive moment, the country sits up and takes notice.

Not since Johnston then, has an Australian scored a goal of "significance" in the FA Cup. Not until "Tiny" of course. For in the semifinal of 2003–04 and playing for Millwall against Sunderland, Cahill popped up to score the winner and take his team to that FA Cup final against Manchester United.

Former Everton player Mick Lyons, who was in the thick of the Everton–Liverpool battles of Johnston's day, spent some time coaching in Australia, for Canberra in the National League. It was Lyons's considered belief that the semifinal was a bigger day for the fans, because the final was party day and anything could happen. They'd have their day at Wembley and it would be fun (and great to win the Cup), but the real angst and tension and deliverance was for semifinal day.

Against this backdrop then, did Cahill bob up and smash home his goal opportunity, to send Sunderland spiralling and Millwall soaring. The young Aussie from Lakemba ripped his shirt from his torso and ran bare-chested with ripped midriff, arms aloft, shirt swirling, saluting the fans, a thousand miles an hour of course, pursued by his adoring team-mates. Millwall had never done anything like this before and, according to Cahill, "Millwall will never get to an FA Cup final again. It is just one of those things; it was our year—a good team of good players." Cahill says this with no egotism and with respect to the Millwall fans. One might suggest he wishes it weren't true and he'd be happily proved wrong, unless it meant Everton falling by the wayside. (Cahill scored to knock Milwall out of the 2006 FA Cup, and his "non-celebration" at scoring was reported as, "They gave me my big break. It would have been like kicking them in the teeth".) But it is true that these were rarefied heights for a club like Millwall. It probably isn't a coincidence that in the engine room at the time, worked Tim Cahill.

With Cahill's star rising, and time ticking, a departure from Millwall was imminent. Performances such as those dished up by Cahill don't go unnoticed. "I had loads of approaches to leave Millwall over the years, but the chairman wasn't ready to sell. I honestly thought we could get to the Premier League, which we very nearly did. My contract was up the year after, and moving football clubs, especially to the Premier League and playing regularly, is a big thing, so I had to know I was ready, I'd want to get straight into it.

"With Everton, I could see myself playing for David Moyes [the manager] and I could see myself playing for that team week in and week out. They had good footballers there. It was a good time for me to go."

Crystal Palace was another team that had come in for Cahill, too, and it is reported that a fee was agreed between Palace and Millwall, but the deal wasn't consummated because of agency fees.

Before Cahill had a chance to join Everton in person, he had to fly to Japan to meet up with the Australian Olympic Games team. Frank Farina had selected Cahill as one of his permitted three over-age players for the Athens Games. (The Olympic Football tournament is an Under 23 competition, with an allowance to nominate three players in the squad who exceed the age boundary.) Not only did it delay his arrival at Everton, but it also added fuel to a fire that would burn in the next off-season, a fire that burned around concern that Cahill was burning out.

"When I got to Everton, the League was already four games old. I hadn't really met anyone from the club because the team was away on pre-season when I moved up there and then I went to the Olympics. When everyone was back together, I had four days training with the team. The new team-mates were really good, everybody was welcoming. In a team meeting, the gaffer [manager] wrote the weekend's team on the board, and there was a vacancy due to illness." Moyes wrote Cahill's name into the vacant space and then turned to him and said, "Man United away; Old Trafford. You're starting, you right with that?" Recalling, "no nerves or anything", Cahill responded "Yes!", and in his own words, in his own mind, he knew that this was sink or swim time. "The boys were a bit surprised because I'd only had four days of training." But he was in, and he was going to give this his very best.

A player turning out for a new set of fans is a big occasion. This is particularly so when you are an off-season purchase and already, through the media, known in some way to them. The relationship, particularly in England, between the players and fans is very important. English football is renowned for the passion of the fans, and if a player can manage to synchronise his play with their passion, it can be an amazing ride. Up to this point, Cahill had done that with Millwall. Everton was another challenge. It is one of England's biggest clubs. The Toffees hadn't had a great time of it recently—it had been many years since silverware had come their way and even longer since they had won the League. They had spent many more years than they'd care to recall looking across town at Liverpool's successes. Into this stepped Cahill, in an away game to the mighty Manchester United.

"When you get to the ground, that's when you get your nerves. Walk on the pitch at Old Trafford and I knew straightaway, this was amazing. I want to do this every week. I played really well, had a chance in the first ten minutes. Could have scored a debut goal. I came off after seventy-five minutes but from then on never sat on the bench or have been rested once. It's been a dream."

Sink or swim! No flotation devices or other aids, just the willingness to seize the moment and the self-belief to realise it. And just to mention, Cahill's first year at Everton contributed to the team defying the expectation that they would be candidates for relegation from the Premier League and instead they qualified for the European Champions League care of a fourth place League finish!

"Now it's ridiculous, absolutely ridiculous. Finished leading scorer that year and already signed a second contract. I picked up every player-of-the-year award and man-of-the-match award through the season, Champions League and UEFA Cup." Ridiculous? Remarkable is perhaps a more apt description.

The off-season arrived and Cahill, on the back of this monstrously successful first season with Everton, was now scheduled to

---

"When you get to the ground, that's when you get your nerves. Walk on the pitch at Old Trafford and I knew straightaway, this was amazing. I want to do this every week."

take his place in the Australian team to compete at the FIFA Confederations Cup in Germany. It meant an off-season without rest.

Everton didn't start the 2005–06 season very convincingly. "At the start of the year when we were bottom, four points in ten games, this was the toughest period in my career so far, only because I have had it good so far. But you didn't see me hiding. I didn't get a 'sore' groin or calf. I played every game. It's great playing in the good stuff, but fans recognise when you are working through the bad stuff too. You can only change it by playing football." Interestingly, Cahill refers to this patch as his darkest, and there is no mention of the injury problem that reduced his 2002–03 season to just eleven or so games. Perhaps this is poignant, perhaps not, but there is the possibility that the problems faced by the group are of more significance to Cahill than the problems of an individual through injury.

In any event, and unfairly, much of the talk about the Everton malaise was falling at the feet of Tim Cahill. Reports in Australia focused on Moyes's irritation with Cahill's international commitments, of which Cahill says "David Moyes didn't want me to play for Australia. He said that it would be better if I settled down and concentrated on the club football. As a footballer, you never ask to be rested and you never ask not to play. I'm only twenty-six, with only so many years left. I don't regret anything. People can say what they like about me being jaded or burnt out. But when I have hit form again and started scoring goals and winning games, people have mistakenly said I am fit again. But I have been doing the same thing, the only difference has been not finishing off what I had been finishing.

"I feel there is a big onus on me to do well. When I don't, the fans and the gaffer look at me. I'm not a world-beater who can

"My family has everything to do with my football and it is the reason why I am good and also the reason why I am so down to earth. Without them, I'd have nothing."

---

do tricks, but I like to have a presence in the game, tackle and do whatever I can to help the team out and then myself. If I get a goal, I get one. I always seem to be able to nick a goal."

Although defined by the green rectangle that is his workspace, it is at home that Cahill transfuses into his heartfelt reality. "I have two lovely young boys and a beautiful missus and when I am not playing football, I am generally playing with the kids or helping her do something. My family has everything to do with my football and it is the reason why I am good and also the reason why I am so down to earth. Without them, I'd have nothing. I don't want my parents to ever have to work again. I want my dad to do his hobbies: birds, electrics—whatever he wants. I want my mum to relax. And the rest of the family too, I want the best for them. Every competition I have played in, my family has been there. Doesn't matter how much it costs, how much it puts me out. All because they are part of it."

The nice things that Cahill wants for his family, he also enjoys. "I like the nice things too, nice cars, houses and clothes, but it's no good if you are by yourself. Who you going to share it with? Every time my brothers come over, they take all my gear anyway. I get hammered at training for it by the lads. They don't rate it anyway.

"My life is crazy. Training every day, spending time with family and relaxing. In Liverpool people are either red or blue. I am a massive icon in Liverpool and people look up to me so I have to live up to it. It's constant. When I am with my family, I don't like to involve them in things. It is hard, but it is part and parcel of what we do. If they didn't buy my tops and things, I'd be a nobody. I am very complimentary about them. I have to live with it. When away from it though, I like to take time to rest. If I could, I would sleep or play pool or watch TV."

Cahill's international career has been quite a saga. As a fourteen-year-old, Cahill played for the Western Samoa Under 20s team, and FIFA regulations forbade players from representing two countries. It seemed, for a while, that Cahill's international career for Australia would never ignite. It wasn't until FIFA altered its eligibility laws that Cahill could become a Socceroo and Australia could rest easy. Mike Cockerill, of *The Sydney Morning Herald*, would write about Cahill to promote the cause, and (then coach) Frank Farina invited him to camps in anticipation that the rules would be changed. Thankfully for both Cahill and fans of the national team, the decks have been cleared.

The injection that Cahill gives the Socceroos is significant. Goal-scoring midfielders like him are highly cherished football items. He had no doubts Australia would qualify past Uruguay, a belief that stemmed from the Oceania round of matches. "We knew we had a chance from then. It's all positive because we are a brilliant unit."

Hiddink was a big play for the national set-up too. "Farina was great and whatever happened, happened, but Guus, even the Uruguay team were nervous of his presence.

"The only expectations we have of ourselves is to get through our group. There's no middle ground for Aussies. We want to win."

"The only expectations we have of ourselves is to get through our group. There's no middle ground for Aussies. We want to win. The gaffer strives to succeed and we are like that as players. Without saying we are going to win the World Cup—but we aren't going there to make up the numbers."

Qualifying was "crazy" for Cahill. "This wasn't the city I grew up with. They were magical moments, the fans and the family. You can't explain it, one of those freak incidents. It's opened Australia's eyes to the world. It is just amazing. And I never get sick of talking about this, it's the best thing that has ever happened, so just enjoy it."

Tim Cahill

5

shirt number

"Scotland was the best time of my football life.
The size of Rangers, and winning things,
not all players get the chance to do it.
I wanted to establish myself in Europe
and to win medals and trophies.
Rangers gave me that opportunity."

Tony Vidmar

Date of birth 4 July 1970

Position played Defender

Current club NAC Breda, the Netherlands

Most of Australia will have an enduring image of Tony Vidmar. It was a photo of him being assisted from Montevideo's Estadio Centenario, in November 2001, after Australia had succumbed to Uruguay at the final hurdle of 2002 World Cup qualifying. It was a photo that was strewn across every major metropolitan newspaper in the days following Australia's defeat. It was an image that was also transmitted across televisions and into the lounge rooms of Australia's households.

Perhaps it was the immediacy of the defeat, or perhaps it was a sobering consideration that his World Cup dreams may have been extinguished then, and forever. More than likely it was a combination of the two. The picture of the inconsolable Vidmar, whose beaten body was trudging its way forlornly to the players' tunnel, has been an image that has been used to sum up the total experience of Australia's repeated World Cup anguish.

For at least the first half of the 1990s, Adelaide was commonly considered the home of football in Australia. Its two national league teams were very competitive and Adelaide City, in particular, was consistently producing a type of player and brand of football that made it one of the powerhouses of the Australian game.

Like many parts of Australia, the "serious" football community moved, for many clandestine years, in isolation from the broader Australian community. Whilst Adelaide was reinforcing its obsession with indigenous football—Australian Rules—a generation of youth were growing up with a foot in both camps, indoctrinated to the accepted "Australian" ways whilst dipping the toe into this new world brought alive by post-war migration.

For Tony Vidmar, this mightn't be a surprise because as an Australian-born son of a Slovenian father and Italian mother, his sensibilities would have been alive to the world of migrant Australia, at least to a degree. And football was so central to the general story of migrant Australia that many would presume that football was a natural thing for Vidmar to adopt as his own.

But such a simplistically presumptuous approach belies the reality of Tony Vidmar's "Australian" childhood. Firstly and most definitely, the impression one gets of him is that he is a sportsman. He appears to have been born to play sport but born into a family, so says he, where his parents "weren't sporty types". His parents' apparent apathy towards things athletic perhaps created the space for Tony to explore and develop in his own way and in his own time.

In a memory slightly cobwebbed by the passing of the years, Vidmar recalls his first football club being Woodville Soccer Club, though the exact when's and how's don't exactly come flooding back. Either that or it is a point of little consequence. What seems to particularly resonate is that his older brother, Aurelio, had started playing and the younger Tony guesses that he followed him into it. Tony's eldest brother was playing Aussie Rules, so one can imagine that the youngest Vidmar boy could quite easily have gone in that direction too.

But, as with so many like-minded youth, there was too much to do to focus on one sport. Vidmar was a keen and handy cricketer, with devilish if "slow" medium pace bowling and a capacity to wield the willow with aplomb. An all-rounder at cricket and, as it would eventuate, a considerably versatile top-level footballer as well, although that course was to take a deal of time to unfold.

"I must have been seven or eight when I started playing soccer at primary school. Some of my friends were doing it, so it also must have been a function of the peer group. I first got selected with the South Australia primary schools team, which was when I first realised I was any good. It was an Under 12s competition, I was ten, the youngest in the team, and got selected the next year also, so the two years in that sort of got me going in football. As a kid, you don't really think about it much, except to think that 'okay, this isn't bad and I'm not bad, now what else can I do?' I was playing school soccer on Saturday and club on a Sunday. As a kid, I was thinking, this is great."

It was an unaffected and unstructured sporting career at this point. Vocational disinterest may have contributed, but with so many sports so available to young Australians, the challenge is almost to see if you can be good at all of them rather than set out to be really good at one.

In his early teens, Vidmar started to dabble in Aussie Rules, "I went through a stage when I was fourteen or fifteen, a friend of mine played Aussie Rules and his father was the coach. For one game I was invited to play because they were short of players. At the same time, our high school didn't have a soccer team because none of the teachers wanted to take it. In the past there had been fights between our school and other schools."

So at this time during his high school years, Vidmar was playing on the wing for his Aussie Rules team on Saturday mornings. "I had a bit of pace about me. I would get the ball and take off, running the length of the field just about. I'd keep the ball on the ground, I'd be too scared to bend over and pick it up, just in case I got smacked, so I'd 'soccer' it along the ground. I remember the guys on the sideline would yell out, 'Hey, you bloody wog, pick up the ball'. It is laughable now, but at the time there was probably a bit of acid in comments like that.

"I didn't care. It was good fun and we made the grand final of that Under 15 competition. We played the game on one of Adelaide's famous SAFL [South Australia Football League] grounds. Watching that game was the coach of the West Torrens Under 17s, which was one of the big local footy clubs—prior to the Adelaide Crows and Port Power and the AFL [Australian Football League].

"At the end of the game, the coach came up to me and asked if I was interested in playing for West Torrens. I had actually stopped soccer at this point. I was a little fed up with it and so I accepted his offer. West Torrens was just down the road from us, so it was perfect. A few of the guys from school were there, which made it a bit easier to settle in, though I remember the intensity and the aggression being something to get used to."

Vidmar was asked back for a second season. At the time he was happily considering his cricket future, too. For the Under 17 season, there was a confluence of interest for the three sports. Vidmar was ready to take up soccer again, and West Torrens were preparing for their next year. At this point Vidmar's father weighed in and said that young Tony should choose, that he really couldn't do all three.

"The West Torrens coach asked about my intentions and I was quite prepared to do both footy and soccer in winter. He asked me, 'Why would you want to go out and play that sissy wog-ball game?' and that actually made up my mind for me. His attitude pissed me off—'That's not a game; that's for sheilas'. That was the real starting point for me in football. I stopped cricket and left Aussie Rules.

"I moved to Adelaide City, who had just won the championship, and it was a real golden period for football in Adelaide. Adelaide was buzzing, with the junior set-up and the players in the first team."

Vidmar's older brother, Aurelio, had earlier made the move into the Adelaide City framework. When Tony rolled up, he recalls distinctly the opposition from people who thought he was only at the club because he was Aurelio's brother. "It's always been about Aurelio's brother, never so much about Tony", he quips.

Of course, the Aurelio to whom people referred was one of the bright young pups of Australia's football at the time. Aurelio went on to have a celebrated career for Adelaide City, in Europe and for the national team. He is now the assistant coach at Adelaide United, in the newly formed Australian A-League.

During his early time at Adelaide City, Tony was bouncing around between the youth team and the reserve team, which played in the South Australia State League. Legendary coach Zoran Matic, so central to the rise of Adelaide as a football centre, spotted Tony Vidmar and tried him at left back, recognising the qualities Vidmar had for the role. "I made my debut under Zoran, in the NSL Cup, coming on as a sub, against George Cross, and scored", remembers Vidmar.

Vidmar recollects the early Adelaide City days as a "bit of a battle, getting my own space, not as Aurelio's younger brother". At this stage he had "no ambition for Europe or even the national team, I was just trying to get going and get my own oxygen at Adelaide City.

"I learned a lot from that period, and from Zoran. He was hard and tough, but I appreciated it because as a defender, the discipline that he was strong on helped me. I had very good recollections of him. He is a very good person. He'd go crazy if someone wasn't doing their job and that was jeopardising the team, but he gave me a lot of one-on-one time and advice, particularly when the Europe thing emerged."

Vidmar was about nineteen when he began settling properly into the Adelaide City team. The quality of that team provided a cushioned blow, too. To be in a team that was so good and so established eased the transition for the young player. In these circumstances, a young one's inexperience isn't exposed and the quality of those around him allows for stable and steady development and provides protection.

It was from this base that Vidmar was selected in the Olympic team that was preparing for the 1992 Barcelona Olympics. During the six-week tour in Europe, Vidmar then "got a taste for making a career out of this. The vibe and atmosphere in Europe, the facilities and seriousness, I just wanted a piece of it".

However, as a twenty-one-year-old, Vidmar didn't really know how to get to Europe. Impressions of Australians as footballers were fairly basic at the time, too. The simplest of Vidmar's problems had no answer—to whom do I send a video? Who do I contact? "Just by chance, though, a friend of ours went to Europe

"I learned a lot from that period, and from Zoran. He was hard and tough, but I appreciated it because as a defender, the discipline that he was strong on helped me. I had very good recollections of him. He is a very good person."

on holiday. He wanted to play some soccer and he bumped into a player agent. He kept his details, and I sent this agent a video of myself. The timing of it all was just lucky."

Just after the Barcelona Olympics, Vidmar left for his European odyssey, going to Germinal Ekeren in Belgium. He was accompanied to Ekeren by Olympic team-mate Milan Blagojevic. Aurelio Vidmar was also, by this time, playing in Europe. As it happened, he was also in Belgium.

"It helped, having another Aussie, but not enough. It was a total nightmare. The club was run by the president, and the coach was just a puppet. Certain players had too much influence. Things had been building up over a period, but the gasket blew during the week when we were preparing to play, of all things, Aurelio's team, Waregem. For two days we'd been training in formation, getting ready. I was playing in the centre at the back. I was asked by the coach if I had any problems playing directly against my brother. I said no, and bluntly. Then, on the Thursday before the game he said to me he was going to change the team and that he was going for experienced players and that he was leaving me out. I am not usually given to outbursts, but when he told me this, I just lost it. After the game the coach came to shake my hand, which I ignored, before giving him another spray—I got fined for that!

"It was the build-up of everything though. I was hating it. I was playing irregularly and I didn't like the surroundings. The whole adventure degenerated in six months. I was home in Australia for the winter break before returning to Ekeren. When I got there I said to Milan, 'I don't know if I want to do this'."

For Vidmar, the Ekeren experience was "shattering". "I wouldn't want to send anyone there, it's a nothing town, only about ten kilometres away from Antwerp, which is nice, but Ekeren isn't. The people weren't nice; they were nosy and jealous and it was very cold. If you had something, they'd want something better. I was in a pizza bar once, relaxing and minding my own business, when a local started talking to me. I had never seen him before. Suddenly, he asked me how much I earned. I was shocked. I hated it and I really questioned if I wanted this."

Vidmar was also in the national team that year and there was a lot of travelling. He was away from family a lot and felt disengaged. "I feel like I lost a bit of my childhood. I didn't enjoy going out. I was finding it difficult, and when I got back to Australia, I was loving being home. That confirmed to me that I wanted to get out of Europe and to come home."

Vidmar, very successfully, re-established himself and refocused during a brief period back in the NSL with Adelaide City. "About a year or so later, Arnie [Graham Arnold] called and asked if I wanted to go back to Europe. He had moved from Charleroi in Belgium to NAC Breda in Holland. I felt ready again. I needed that year and a half back home to get back into it. Arnie had recommended me to the club and recommended to me that I 'can't hold back and that I'd have to go for it'. Belgium to Holland is totally different. Ekeren to Breda is only about fifty kilometres, but it may as well be a continent away. You know when you cross the border into Belgium because the roads are crap—'yep, we're in Belgium', as you bounce along." Vidmar had two years at Breda, which he lists as "great" and a much better experience altogether than the sourness of his time in Belgium.

Vidmar then had the opportunity to move to Glasgow Rangers, in Scotland. He had enjoyed the Netherlands, but the opportunity to experience such a huge club could not be passed up. "Indescribable", says Vidmar. "The second day of pre-season

"I feel like I lost a bit of my childhood. I didn't enjoy going out. I was finding it difficult, and when I got back to Australia, I was loving being home."

---

training at Rangers and they had an open day for supporters. We played an eleven versus eleven exhibition, intra-squad game and 50,000 supporters turned up just to watch it."

Vidmar spent longer at Rangers than he has anywhere else. But Rangers (Protestant) is such a huge club, and it shares Glasgow with sectarian rivals Celtic (Catholic), a club of equal proportions, which provides many interesting experiences.

Vidmar recalls the night of a Celtic game when a group went to a pub for dinner. Just a small group of some players and their partners. At the conclusion of the evening Vidmar went outside to find that the windows of his car had been smashed. "It was difficult to go out and socialise because people would put rubbish on you. There were so many foreigners in the Rangers and Celtic teams, and many of them came from the same countries and were friends before they got to Scotland. I used to catch up with Dukes [Mark Viduka], who was with Celtic at the time. Foreigners would go out and mix because of that, but some of the fans couldn't cope with it."

All of this reminds one of arguably the most infamous lightning rod for the sectarian tensions that exist between the two clubs. In 1989, Mo Johnstone looked to return to Britain after a playing stint with Nantes in France. Johnstone, a Catholic, had previously played for Celtic. In returning to Glasgow, he was expected to return to "the Bhoys" at Celtic Park and indeed indicated that was his intention. In an amazing act of "independent thinking",

Johnstone signed for Rangers, causing an amazing fallout and media frenzy. For Celtic fans it was the ultimate act of betrayal. It proved no easier for Rangers fans to accept, as Johnstone was to become the first Catholic to sign for the team in seventy years. The outrage was voluble. The indignation, from both sets of fans, caused many to discard season tickets and there were "scarf burning" ceremonies outside the gates of both Ibrox and Celtic Park. These were the more peaceable expressions of anger.

Given this, it is understandable that Vidmar's pre-game ritual also had the potential to arouse interest. "Very early on in my time at Rangers, just before going onto the field for a game, I bent over, touched the ground and crossed myself. This was something that I had done for ages. At the time I hadn't realised the significance of what I had done. After the game, one of the players said to me that I should be careful when and where I cross myself. I found it strange because at this time there was a mix of Catholic and Protestant players in our squad. But the fans take it very seriously, or at least some do. It is a pre-game ritual for me, but from that point on I made sure that I did it well before I got out onto the pitch."

Despite the residual tensions of deep-seated historical hatreds, Scotland provided Vidmar with many happy memories. "Scotland was the best time of my football life. The size of Rangers, and winning things, not all players get the chance to do it. I wanted to establish myself in Europe and to win medals and trophies. Rangers gave me that opportunity."

After five years at Ibrox, Vidmar felt a stirring to find another challenge, although he might also have stayed for another contract. Rangers had confirmed that's what they wanted and Vidmar had told them he'd be happy to hear from them.

At the very last, Rangers withdrew their offer totally. There was nothing else on the horizon. Money was drying up in England, care of the ITV digital crash, and clubs weren't looking to add to wage bills. Vidmar was swinging in the football breeze.

He then took his family to Eindhoven in the Netherlands, where he'd lived previously, to train by himself, hoping that a football offer would eventuate. After six weeks of self-preparation, he received contact from Middlesbrough in the English Premier League. After a week and a half on trial, Vidmar signed a contract for the season ahead. He played well and enjoyed his time in England's north-east, but a contract extension wasn't offered. "I understood their view. They had a couple of young players coming through and another older guy whom they were looking to keep. I was just surplus to their requirements."

From Middlesborough, Vidmar moved to Cardiff City, a club that had previously expressed interest in the Australian. "It was a good club and a nice city. The fans were good and positive. They hated the English and so playing English clubs every weekend really generated a good atmosphere."

Vidmar enjoyed two good years at Cardiff City, captaining the club for a spell and having healthy relations with the management and president. But as "cracks started to appear", says Vidmar, he began again to consider moving.

"Very early on in my time at Rangers, just before going onto the field for a game, I bent over, touched the ground and crossed myself. This was something that I had done for ages."

"I love Holland and at every opportunity to come back, we did. I am very settled here, part of the furniture here at NAC, and the kids have started school here."

In the January transfer window of the final season in his contract with Cardiff, NAC Breda came in for Vidmar. He approached the management and said he wanted to leave and go back to his old club. Cardiff wouldn't release him, so he had to wait until the end of the season to move back to the Netherlands.

"At the end of the Rangers experience there was a chance this whole thing could have finished. There were doubts, 'God, what am I going to do?', and you start revising the decisions made until now, 'Did I do the right thing?' I wasn't ready to go back to Australia, so I just stuck it out and hung on."

The chance to return to Breda was good for Vidmar. The Netherlands has developed into a home away from home, "I love Holland and at every opportunity to come back, we did. I am very settled here, part of the furniture here at NAC, and the kids have started school here."

Vidmar's contract with NAC ends with the conclusion of the 2005–06 season and he was scheduled to meet with the club in March to discuss the future. "If they don't want to renew, it could be hard to find a club at thirty-five, thirty-six years of age. God, it was hard enough at thirty-two! But since then I've stayed fit and been playing well at a good level. A good showing at the World Cup may help me, too."

For Vidmar, the joy of the game remains, despite the trials and tribulations of his many years on the road. "It started as a hobby and I continue to try and treat it that way. Every day, I love going to training and the competition."

Durability and determination have sustained Vidmar through a club career spanning almost two decades and six countries, and an international career that has taken in four World Cup campaigns, including the most recent series against Uruguay.

"This time there was the confidence we'd do it. In the past we'd say it but perhaps they were only words, to be positive. But this time quite a few of us were like that, Dukes [Mark Viduka] was big on it, we're gonna do it.

"The whole preparation was fantastic and the confidence among the players was great. Then in Sydney, the national anthem, the booing, got me more pumped up than anything. It was a sign that finally Aussies cared. At times in football we are too nice to visiting teams. It's time we got ruthless and street-wise."

Vidmar has not only seen the heartache of the repeated disasters and "ruthlessness", he has lived them. One can only imagine what an outpouring the success against Uruguay caused. Moreover, as the players gathered at halfway, in preparation for the shoot-out, it was Vidmar who insisted on taking one of the penalties. "I wanted to control my own fate in a way. I didn't want to rely on anyone else. I didn't think anything about it and then it

---

"Then in Sydney, the national anthem, the booing, got me more pumped up than anything. It was a sign that finally Aussies cared. At times in football we are too nice to visiting teams. It's time we got ruthless and street-wise."

hit me—a little bit of panic, but then I settled and focused and was never going to miss."

Of all the pressures of a sporting career, this is a feat to be admired. So easy, it could have been, to step back and hope. Much more difficult to step forward and stare your enemy in the face.

On such things are successful careers built.

Tony Vidmar

6

shirt number

"At no stage do I think I have made it. That's all to do with family upbringing. My father never let me believe otherwise. He'd always find negatives, not harshly, just constructively critical. He loves the game and is my number one fan. He is the reason why I made it. He made me mentally strong."

Tony Popovic

Date of birth 4 July 1973

Position played Defender

Current club Crystal Palace, England

In all his thirty-two years on mother Earth, Tony Popovic has played football for a grand total of three clubs. When you consider that some players have gone through that many in a single season, it speaks volumes about the man.

In this, his thirty-third year on mother Earth, if all goes to plan, "Popa" will complete the full house of international representation for Australia, a development pathway that for the affable central defender will have seen him make appearances at all of FIFA's men's tournaments—Under 17s, Under 20s, Olympic Games and Senior World Cup. It will be an achievement of considerable merit. It will be a bookmark to one of Australia's most loyal and bankable football servants.

Tony Popovic, like many footballers, is a man of many paradoxes. He is a fan of heavy metal music, yet his demeanour is calm, courteous and reserved. He is a footballer of noteworthy culture and refinement, yet he plays in the most physical of all positions in the centre of defence. He is a player who appreciates the finer things in football, who values passing and possession, constructive and deliberate play, yet he earns his living in the rough and tumble of England's second-tier competition, nowadays called "the Championship". He is a thinker about the game, but of whom muscle and brawn is oft required.

Tony Popovic was born in Sydney. He is a product of what has been a highly fertile player nursery, Australia's Croatian community.

Sydney United, as it is now called, first received Popovic as a junior. In those days the club was called Sydney Croatia, until pressure from football's governing body at the time, Soccer Australia, required clubs of the NSL to abandon ethnic affiliations, at least in their names. In modern parlance, they were asked to "re-brand" themselves. The process was clumsy, inflammatory and poorly managed, and ultimately had little lasting material impact.

Suffice to say, that born to Croatian migrants, Popovic made a very natural entrance to football through the centrepiece of Sydney's Croatian community, its football club. His father also coached the junior team of his son.

When Tony turned fourteen, he moved into the club's youth set-up and began building to a career in its senior team. He graduated to the first grade set-up at the age of sixteen, and by twenty he was installed as club captain. It was a smooth and untroubled rise through the ranks for one who would later emerge to be the apple of his community's eye.

He is so respected in this community because he first affords others respect. It was Manfred Schafer, coach of Sydney United, who offered the captaincy to Popovic. Rather than accept immediately, Popovic's first response was to go home and talk it over with this father. Under questioning, it emerged that the young star felt uncomfortable accepting such a position with so many senior players in the club, people for whom Popovic had deep and abiding respect. Popovic approached one senior player, Ivan Petkovic, to talk the situation over. Petkovic's encouragement was founded on a desire to promote the development and growth of Popovic into the footballer that everyone wanted him to be.

"I was fortunate, I played for the national Under 17s and 20s and in the Olympics, now, God willing, a World Cup, and it's been brilliant. At no stage do I think I have made it. That's all to do with family upbringing. My father never let me believe otherwise. He'd always find negatives, not harshly, just constructively critical. He loves the game and is my number one fan. He is the reason why I made it. He made me mentally strong. He always used to make me look in the mirror. He'd listen to me rant about a game, but then would always put the focus back onto me. I will put that onto my kids too, in whatever they do, that they always work at it and try to get better."

On the topic of his three-club career, Popovic is characteristically deflective. "I guess it says a bit about me, but it is from the clubs, too. It hasn't all been one-way traffic."

In perusing international club opportunities, it wasn't uncommon for young players with Popovic's background to consider Croatia as a destination. But there was never any interest from Croatian clubs (that Popovic knew of) and his father never suggested that Croatia should necessarily be a starting point for his son's overseas club career.

From Sydney United then, Popovic moved to Sanfreece Hiroshima in Japan's J-League. Former national team coach Eddie Thomson was in charge and he gathered a posse of Australians around him, including Graham Arnold, Steve Corica and Popovic.

It was in Japan soon after he arrived, that Popovic entered the great defining phase of his career. Only six weeks after he had started playing in Japan, he was beset with a debilitating toe injury. "For some reason", says Popovic, "within those six weeks the club fell in love with me. It was greatly appreciated. However I was to basically miss the next two years. I went through two years of hell with that right toe. For a whole year I couldn't walk or run."

Then "a year and eight or nine months on", Popovic thought he was going to be released by the club and not get a new contract, a scenario that was very reasonably anticipated given the length of his lay-off.

So Popovic, a player earmarked by the Australian system for big things, and so soon after he departed to realise his dream, was already planning on returning to Australia, having had only very meagre game time. The potential emotional damage was significant, but to Popovic, by then just playing football again was the highest of his priorities. The situation was indeed a grim one.

Incredibly, however, Sanfreece said to him that they hadn't forgotten how well he had done in those first six weeks and they believed that he could still make a contribution to them. They offered him a two-year contract extension. "I wasn't expecting it at all. It was a big turning point for me. The extra two years in Japan to get fit and strong and ready for Europe. Europe was always my plan."

The injury problem that was proving so difficult for Popovic was one that sounded so innocuous. "I had bone on bone in the big knuckle of the toe. Some experts advised that I would never play again. At twenty-three I thought my career was over. To hear that was very difficult indeed."

Popovic turned to the assistance of current Socceroo assistant coach, Graham Arnold, who was then his team-mate at Sanfreece. "That was a real character builder—the injury in Japan. Arnie was unbelievable to me. Without him, I don't know how it would have turned out. I go back a long way with Arnie, stretching right back to Sydney United days, when as a senior player, he'd drag me to the front of the group for running and physical stuff, always pushing me, even then. Now, in Japan, he kept me going again. Once I got through the injury, I knew nothing would stop me."

It was surely a case of build character or wither, and the latter would have been a perfectly understandable, although unpalatable, outcome. Popovic's foot was in a cast for four months and it was that long before he could walk. The foot then went into a boot with special orthotics, and then into specially crafted runners and trainers, before he was even allowed to try to walk barefoot. This process lasted "eight to ten months, with no guarantee of success". The rehabilitation got to the point where he could "maybe train once a week on the field with the rest of the time in the gym." This lasted for months. It was a very slow process building up to a training regimen that didn't allow him to have a day off.

"The injury probably lasted eighteen months to two years and it took another twelve months before I felt comfortable with my body. I had to teach myself to jump again, to run again and to jump with taking off from my other foot. It was like going to kindergarten again."

And as he points out, with specific reference to England, "if you can't jump to head the ball, you can't play". Not in his position at least.

Through all this, Popovic developed a deep affection for Japan. "Those people were unbelievable. The help they gave me off the field was unbelievable. When my wife came over, if she was sick, with flu or something, they'd come over at two in the morning and take her to the doctors. 'Tony, you sleep, you've got training in the morning.' If I needed anything and they thought it would help, they'd do it. The professionalism in Japan was incredible. I didn't quite realise how good, until I moved to England. The difference between the two was enormous."

Japan also taught Popovic how much work went into professional football. "When you are in Australia, you think you are going okay and you are doing well, until you go overseas, you realise you are probably 50 or 60 per cent of what you should be. You think you are close, but when I got to Japan I realised how sharp and strong they are—that really blew me away. It took a little time to come to grips with that."

From Hiroshima, Popovic moved to London and the Crystal Palace club. As Croatia is not part of the European Union, and armed only with his Australian passport, Tony Popovic needed to acquire a work permit to play football in England, a process that brings grief to many hopeful players. "When I went to England, there were other difficulties again. I was waiting for my work permit and my wife was back in Australia having our first child. I got a phone call saying that my wife was two weeks early. She's there having the baby and I was stuck in England, without having received my work permit yet. So I was thinking, 'If I don't get this work permit, I'll kill somebody'. I missed the birth. Then what if I couldn't get the permit—I'd have to pack the whole thing up."

The situation with the work permit always seems to take longer than is necessary, but thankfully, and in view of the situation with Popovic's wife and newborn, the process was smoothed out rather slickly. As soon as the permit came through, Popovic was released by the manager to return to Australia to be with his wife.

But Popovic's difficulties in England seemed only to commence with the work permit issue. The troubles had by no means ended. "In England I was in a small little hotel room. The club wasn't as helpful as they said they were going to be. As a new player much was expected of me. But my newborn had colic and I'd be up until six in the morning and then have to get to training every day.

"For the first three months I was crap. I was struggling big time. I wasn't happy—I was woeful. I couldn't train, just physically tired

"For the first three months I was crap. I was struggling big time. I wasn't happy—I was woeful. I couldn't train, just physically tired the whole time. I was at a new club, with everyone watching me, waiting for me to prove myself to be better than what is already there, or else they'd think they'd be better off with a local boy."

---

the whole time. I was at a new club, with everyone watching me, waiting for me to prove myself to be better than what is already there, or else they'd think they'd be better off with a local boy. On par is not good enough, you have to be better. Steve Bruce, the manager [coach] said, 'Listen mate, you look terrible, go and have a week off and clean yourself up.' It was the breather that I needed and the introduction to England proved just to be another obstacle to overcome. From there and ever since, it has been good."

Through these difficulties, Popovic felt the cavern that was created by the distance between him and his extended family. He and his wife were adjusting to their new lives as parents, and had just arrived in a new city, to a new team. Their family network was some 20,000 kilometres away. Popovic would be tired and struggling at training, knowing that his wife and child were struggling at home. He had a new set of fans who were proving difficult to please. Their impact was lessened slightly by the fact that Popovic is steadfastly more critical of himself than any fan or journalist could be.

Popovic also drew strength from his wife. "My wife's been great. She's a strong woman, probably a lot stronger than me, actually. All the setbacks and injuries, and you come home and your moods are variable, she doesn't know if you are going to be happy or not happy, what might or might not have happened on the training pitch. They put up with a lot. My wife has always been a fantastic support. It changes a bit when you have kids. You have a bad day and you come home, the kids don't care about any injury. You walk through the door and they want to just start playing, so you quickly forget your own issues. You rearrange your priorities. Football's not the end of the world anymore. I can get hard on myself but the kids put it into a bit of perspective.

"Parenthood changed me as a player. I have become a lot more tolerant to a lot more things, in football terms. Things that bothered me before, I now know to be non-issues. I always thought I was a calm person, but having the kids has taken that to another level. I am not less dedicated. But my approach has changed a bit. Both my wife and I would say for the better, but I wouldn't say that I am less dedicated to football, because as you get older, you realise that you can't survive if you take your foot off the pedal."

The personal issues were one thing, but unfortunately for Popovic, the team's fortunes dipped at just the wrong time for him. "I knew the fans weren't happy. When I arrived at Palace, they had played their first two or three League games, which they won. When I got in the team, we lost our next three, which was terrible. It was then that the manager gave me the week off, and when I got back we went on a seven-game winning run, and I played in each one of those games. The fans warmed to me from then on."

"My wife has always been a fantastic support. It changes a bit when you have kids. You have a bad day and you come home, the kids don't care about any injury. You walk through the door and they want to just start playing, so you quickly forget your own issues."

Not only the fans, but the club also, which showed the worth it placed on Popovic by installing him as Palace captain. But to many onlookers, England is an interesting football destination for Popovic, who appreciates the observations people make about his playing style and his choice to play in England. "True, the Championship wouldn't be a league where I'd naturally put myself, but the Premiership is. I played in that last year and it was fantastic. It was everything I expected and more. With Palace, we have every chance to go back there and if that's the chance, I'd grab it."

For a player with Popovic's penchant for delivering reliable and consistent ball out from the back and into the midfield, the helter-skelter of Championship football can prove a test for him. "I understand that. I have been fortunate enough in England to have a manager who has encouraged us to play, which suits me. The Championship, it's a tough league. It's good to play in England. The buzz of the fans is amazing. You get a Cup game against a third division side, away from home at a small stadium, the atmosphere is unbelievable and you know that you are in for a game and if you aren't up for it, you lose. Where I am now, the play is just end to end. No respite at all. It is purely results orientated. It's just a grind, you want to get through it, however you have to do it."

But Popovic respects where he is currently playing, "even if the League isn't suited to me, I am still happy to be playing there. It's a great atmosphere. That balances it out a bit. During the Christmas and January periods the Championship is not something you want to be watching. The pitches are terrible, the football is terrible, but the top sides still win, which shows there is some method and reliability to it all."

Popovic is currently eyeing his options at club level. A rise to the Premiership for Palace, a new European challenge or even a return to Japan are all feasible considerations. He has had five years in England now, which has been both testing and rewarding. London is a city in which he appears to like living for the time being, although he is buttressed by the knowledge that "if I can move to Japan and be happy, I can live anywhere". It wasn't just the injury that was the focus of the time in Japan. The culture and the language were obviously big hurdles, and never having lived away from home was another consideration. It was a quantum leap from anything he had known previously. "It was tough to settle in but, in the end, I could have stayed longer in Japan. I absolutely loved the place."

The injury demons may have compartmentalised his time in Japan, and toughened him up for his professional career, but injury also excluded Popovic from World Cup qualifying four years ago and, eerily, it was almost a repeat this time round.

Popovic has been around the national team for a while now, but because his contributions at the final stages of qualifying have been interrupted, his recollections of what was right and wrong with each campaign are unreliable, according to him. "It's different when you are not involved and you are injured, you can't really get into it. It's a different mind-set from players who are about to go out on the field. So it is hard to make a comparison, because I was ready to play this time, previously I wasn't.

"I definitely thought we'd get through the last two times also and that didn't happen, so I can't say that I had an overwhelming sense that we'd qualify this time. With the new boss coming in, I expect there was more belief in everyone that we could do it."

On a personal note, injury threatened to derail Popovic's attempts to contribute to this campaign also. "I just wanted to be fit for the game. As it got closer I was getting healthier and getting excited about the prospect of making a contribution, in some way, this time."

Popovic was granted his wish of making a contribution. His performance in the away game against Uruguay was stellar. "Guus [Hiddink] had us all believing, we all knew our jobs; we believed if we executed we'd get through."

Away to Uruguay is one of football's toughest assignments, but despite this, despite the crowd factor, Popovic tells of how relaxed everything was, and the lack of fear from everyone in the team was a decisive factor. "Even at half-time, when we were 0-1 down, it was very calm. Of course we knew we were in a difficult situation but 'so what?' At 0-1, we knew we had a good chance to do the job in Sydney.

"I hadn't played for three months before the Montevideo game. Whether it was adrenaline or what, I got through the game well. No cramps and still going strong at the end of the game. The second game was only a matter of days, and a rather long international flight, away."

Popovic started the second game and thought he was going alright, but on about the half-hour mark, Hiddink made a substitution and replaced Popovic with Harry Kewell.

"I had received a yellow card for a tackle on Alvaro Recoba, their best player. I was lacking match fitness and playing against a South American team, I could have gone in for a tackle, a bit fatigued, and mistimed it and we could have been down to ten men. Irrespective, and walking off the field, I can't say I was happy. I plonked myself down on the bench and thought, 'That's it for me, I can't do anymore'."

It was a dark couple of minutes for Popovic. Thoughts flooded his mind amidst the disappointment of vacating the field. He was very proud to have won selection for the first leg and to have not played for so long in the lead-up, to have survived without cramping and execute a game plan that contributed to the team's success was very gratifying. He had put a month of very hard work in with trainer Anthony Crea and to feel the result of that was a big reward. To be able to run and fight for the cause was a fantastic thing for Popovic. But now, he was on the bench, feeling helpless.

But for Popovic, "it became a non-issue again very quickly". The anxiety returned for the extra time and penalties. The more precarious the stage of the game, the more acute were his feelings of helplessness. The greater the tension on the sideline, the sharper the pains to get back into the battle. Perhaps this is the captain coming out in him. "It was the most nervous I have ever been. When I am out on the field, I am at my most calm and relaxed, but off the field I was a nervous wreck and it got worse the deeper the game went. I have never experienced anything like that. It was a total and thorough drain on the emotions. It is much easier to play than to watch."

Welcome to the world of the fan!

Australia's World Cup group will provide a stern challenge. Apart from the game against Brazil, for which everybody will have a natural desire to do well, Popovic has direct links to both other opponents.

"It was the most nervous I have ever been. When I am out on the field, I am at my most calm and relaxed, but off the field I was a nervous wreck and it got worse the deeper the game went."

His time in Japan will make him a talking point in that country when the two countries play the first match. "When I got to Palace five years ago from Japan and having watched the way they do things, I knew it was only a matter of time before Japan would be high quality internationally. We'll have to be very ready for them."

Then the third match against Croatia won't be just another game for Popovic.

"My worst experience in football was the 0-7 drubbing given us by Croatia just before the 1998 World Cup. They gave us a heap of stick, really letting us know how bad they thought we were. They 'expected' us to be like that, because we were Australia and they Croatia. There was a measure of arrogance and I want to change their perception of us. There is only one way to do that.

"My father is very Croatian, and proud, he loves it. I speak Croatian to my kids, I want that to be part of our family and want my kids to know where their grandparents come from. Some of my extended family, especially in Croatia, will find it strange. But for me and my immediate family it isn't an issue at all, we are proudly Australian and for the match against Croatia, we can only imagine one outcome."

Imagining is believing is doing!

shirt number

7

"I got through because in this day and age, talent isn't enough. You have to be 100 per cent committed and you have to put in hard work more than anything else. Every day, practise, every day, improving yourself."

Brett Emerton

Date of birth 22 February 1979

Position played Midfielder

Current club Blackburn Rovers, England

Brett Emerton has a fancy for cars, fast ones. As a young, newly licensed driver, he'd scoot into the car park of his club's training ground with his hotted-up, or slightly modified, buzz-box whizzing and gurgling its way through the gear box to its resting point. It's uncanny really, that Emerton should have such a taste for cars, because through the formative years of his football career, when he was skinning opponents bare with his sheer pace and beguiling them with his newly learned tricks, he was always described as a "Rolls Royce" prospect for Australia's football. Whilst a "Roller" may not have been exactly the brand association to which Emerton himself would have most related, he got the point just the same.

For all the raciness of his taste in cars, Brett Emerton is unflappable, undemonstrative and quietly spoken. He has taken methodical and measured steps up the ladder of elite achievement. His star has risen steadily and, hopefully, hasn't yet hit its zenith.

Born in the western Sydney suburb of Bankstown, Emerton was raised in Macquarie Fields. His first club was the Campbelltown Gunners. He started playing at age five, "and loved it—been playing ever since".

The Emerton family, according to Brett, is a very sporty family. Any sport was a good one to play, and he played a few. He was heavily into athletics and swimming, but it was always soccer that he enjoyed the most.

"The other sports were individual and I like team sports. There was always the variety factor, too. Swimming up and down, with that black line on the bottom of the pool your only company, didn't really grab me. But mixing with other people was good and the team environment I always enjoyed."

Quantitatively speaking, Emerton isn't an "out there" athlete. The solidarity of his family upbringing and the importance he places on those relationships, so pivotal to his athletic ascendancy, is also where he houses his most personal material. Fair enough and not at all unusual. He is sustained by the depth of those commitments.

He loves his football and the associated environments, but it is almost as though he feels no real need to expand beyond this to express and gratify himself, not yet anyway. He has a world view enhanced by a rich depth of vision, but that is for him to chew on, for the time being. He is respectful and courteous; he doesn't appear to judge and wishes not to be judged. He is, after all, just an Australian kid with a very impressive physical profile who started playing football well, and who has risen, measuredly, into a full-blown professional career. And he is loving it.

Brett Emerton was a co-scholarship holder with fellow Socceroos Harry Kewell and Archie Thompson at the NSW Academy, under the coaching directorship of David Lee. Lee made quite an impression on Emerton, who makes time when back in Australia to visit Lee's latest coaching academy incarnation, wherever that may be, to lend a hand and encourage the kids. This is another insight into the world of Brett Emerton, who is obviously intent on helping others, particularly, though probably not solely, through football. It is just that perhaps football, for now, provides him with the most readily accessible forum to help out. He may be reserved or he may just be the strong, silent type, but he is always willing to "put back" where he can, always looking at ways to repay his community, and football, for the grand opportunities that he has had, and used.

Through the NSW Academy, both Emerton and Kewell went on the "big brother" program to Leeds United in England. The idea behind the scheme was to give local talent a short taste of the big time and what, exactly, went into succeeding there. The month-long visit was, as much as anything though, a benchmarking exercise, an opportunity to see how good kids in the professional clubs in England were at the same chronological stage compared with Australian players. Based on these comparisons, both Emerton and Kewell were invited to stay. Kewell hasn't been home since (in a football sense). Emerton returned to Australia, to put a few more bricks in his development wall before he unleashed himself upon the continent.

From the NSW Academy, Emerton was invited to the Australian Institute of Sport in Canberra. "I think probably once I went to the AIS, I started thinking that possibly I can make a career out of this. But I was also always intent on combining football with school."

Academia also came naturally to Emerton, who has always had the reputation of being a good student. It is apparent that there is respect for the need and worth of such things, and for as long as he felt he could manage it, the classroom got all the attention it could be given. There would have definitely been an element of the "fall-back" too, in case the precarious world of professional sport collapsed, which it can so suddenly and unpredictably do. For every athlete, there is always the spectre of injury. You can plan, pray and hope against it, and reduce the associated risks, but in the end, injury is capricious. To encounter injury is as probable as avoiding it is unlikely, and to be torpedoed by it is unfortunately common.

> "For me, the bad times are the test. You have to believe that you are good at this game. Form fluctuates and can be regained, but commitment can't waiver."

But once the course was set, Emerton didn't stray. "I got through because in this day and age, talent isn't enough. You have to be 100 per cent committed and you have to put in hard work more than anything else. Every day, practise, every day, improving yourself."

Also, says Emerton, "You have to be quite strong mentally. Football is full of ups and downs. You can play well one week, but the next it might all come tumbling down. You have to believe in your ability and give it a go."

Mental application is an interesting concept. Emerton refers to it and so, too, do almost all his Socceroo team-mates. Almost to a player, they trot out the comments referring to mental toughness. In the joint-jarring world that is professional football, a fixation with preparing and preserving the body-temple would seem obvious, but more so it is the mental toughness required that all players, Emerton included, relate to. For each player it may mean a slightly different thing, but inescapably, the last reserve that cannot be defeated or penetrated is the psychology of self-belief. The body can break and the emotions be taunted, but the mind must never yield.

By definition, the good times are easy to identify and easy to experience. Without them, nobody would chase this dream. The ability to cope when things aren't going well is the test that will either sustain or destroy the athlete. "For me, the bad times are the test. You have to believe that you are good at this game.

Form fluctuates and can be regained, but commitment can't waiver. There are a lot of pressures, from team-mates, supporters, from self. The tough learn to deal with all these things and push through." The talented, without the toughness, will fall by the wayside. It happens a lot.

Interestingly for Emerton, although armed with this realisation and steely determination, his time so far has been "pretty undramatic, and I have been pretty lucky. The progression has been slow and steady. I haven't had too many tough times." By his own admission, he has had a good run of it. Emerton has made a pre-emptive strike on career despair, the ghost for athletes that daren't speak its name. He's ready if it comes, but has been fortunate to date that his has, for the most part, remained estranged. It is a good preparedness to have.

"From the AIS I went into the NSL with Sydney Olympic. I did well there for a few years before leaving to go to Feyenoord. It wasn't long before I was playing first team there, before moving to Blackburn."

This Sunday morning stroll through Emerton's career reflects more on Emerton's no-nonsense style than it does on what was actually happening. From the time of Emerton's "release" into the NSL, there has been mega-activity in the transfer market to acquire his signature. During his time at Sydney Olympic, NSL rival Northern Spirit, based on the North Shore in Sydney, was agitating for Emerton's signature. Unfortunately for the NSL, Emerton was of more value then as a transfer property than he was as a local identity. This has been one of the more crippling problems facing football in Australia for many years.

But at the time of Northern Spirit's reported interest in Emerton, the club was owned by Scottish giants Glasgow Rangers. Rangers had bought into an Australian club for two reasons. Firstly, it was part of the "internationalisation" of the Rangers "brand". Secondly, and more importantly, by owning a club in Australia, Rangers could establish a youth structure that could develop talent on a much more cost-effective basis than it could do in Glasgow. Plus, the quality of the athletic talent on offer excited them. It was a cheap way to channel top Australian talent to the mother ship, Rangers. Emerton would have been a major coup for this program and Northern Spirit pushed it very hard. But Emerton remained with Sydney Olympic for the remainder of his NSL contract before he moved to Dutch giants Feyenoord of Rotterdam.

The Netherlands is a country of similar population size to Australia. It is far more condensed, though, as a country, being 300 kilometres from top to bottom—Sydney to Canberra, or thereabouts, in other words. There is another key difference, in the context of this story. The Netherlands have been in the final of the World Cup twice, in 1974 and 1978, on each occasion losing to the respective host country, West Germany and Argentina. Before November 2005, Australia had qualified for one World Cup finals tournament and never yet won a game there.

The Netherlands' successes were fuelled by the revolution that they foisted upon the football world, referred to as "total football". It is a concept of play that determines that all players "attack" when the team is in possession of the ball, and when not in possession, all players "defend". The outworking is more intricate than this, but this is the general principle. It therefore requires players to be adaptable and flexible, multiskilled and appreciative. It is a famous baby of the Dutch coach Rinus Michels.

As a result of total football and the game's reinvention, the world got a renewed picture of the breadth and depth of Dutch football, and of the importance of the game to the Dutch people. If the Netherlands was the boiler room for football advancement, its three big clubs in particular were the coal that was fuelling the furnace. These clubs are big institutions, internationally recognised and locally, devoutly followed, indeed almost worshipped.

Feyenoord of Rotterdam is one of these clubs. In what is one of Emerton's signature understatements, he says of his move to the Netherlands. "It's a big step over there, a different world from Australia. It was sunny at home and freezing cold there, and a totally different lifestyle. I was enjoying the football so much it didn't seem to bother me."

But beneath the understatement is the appreciation. "I had great times at Feyenoord, but I didn't realise how big it was until I became part of it. That is one reason why I decided to stay in Australia until I was twenty-one. If I had come over any younger, I feel that mentally I might not have been strong enough to cope with the demands. I mightn't have made it.

"The NSL set me up well for the move. It was a big difference when I got there, undoubtedly, but I was well prepared otherwise and it was the right time and the right decision.

"But I still remember the shock when I came here—52,000 fans every week. It was cold. It was massive. It was a bit scary at first. But to get there and play the first game was a great feeling. I had a good relationship with the fans and they seemed to like me. Feyenoord was a great club. I loved every minute of it."

And the fans loved him too, all the way to Suriname, it seemed. Suriname is in South America and was colonised by Europeans in the seventeenth century. It was ceded by England to the Dutch in 1677. Dutch football is big in Suriname. Meanwhile, deep inside

Eindhoven, PSV territory (PSV is the third of the big clubs, Ajax of Amsterdam the other), there is a Surinamese taxi driver, "Pieter", who boldly promotes his allegiance to Feyenoord and who is gushing in his adoration for Emerton, whom he first saw "when I was in Suriname" and who, in his eyes, was "a fabulous player, that Australian. I wish he'd come back to Feyenoord. Watching him play made me want to go visit Australia". Such is the power of football, to promote a country's cause, and the power of players, to randomly penetrate the consciousness of fans worldwide.

For Emerton, Feyenoord was "something special. I have never played in front of a better set of fans. They were unbelievable. I'd love to do it again one day, perhaps. Feyenoord versus Ajax was the biggest game of the year for us. Fans used to say to us as long as we won that game we could lose all the rest. Those games were the most pressurised of all. Thankfully, we ended up on top most of the time when I was there.

"I think it's hard to imagine what this life is like until you have been involved in it yourself. It's hard to describe to people what it's like to play in front of so many people. The football fluctuates, it's up and down, and it goes with you through the week. Simple things like shopping in the street with your wife. People treat you differently. Difficult to explain to people what it is like being a pro footballer in this environment. Australia has its sports fans, but I think the fans here are more fanatical."

From the raucous heights of Feyenoord, Emerton accepted the chance to move to the English Premier League, where he joined Blackburn Rovers. "England and the Premier League was always an ambition of mine and I have achieved that now. I would dearly love to win a trophy or two. It is definitely everything that I thought it would be. Football is massive over here. It is a very tough league to play in. Every week is like a final."

Moving to the Premier League may have been an ambition, even one achieved, but it has also, for the first time in his career, put Emerton in the unfamiliar position of irregular game time. Now is the time for Emerton to recall the pre-emptive lessons on mental toughness, because for him, in this period approaching the World Cup finals, this is as tough as he has had it.

"Blackburn is not going that well at the moment. But as I say, and as I know, football is full of ups and downs. I am not playing as much as I'd like, but that can change overnight. I can be playing next weekend, and then I'll be away again."

For the majority of the 2005–06 season, Emerton has been encouraging himself with these words and with this attitude. "It makes me work harder and want it more. If anything, I am more determined. If there is something I am not doing well at, I will go out there and work on it. I have to believe, in times like this, that I am a good player. It's a little test for me and I am sure I will overcome it. I don't doubt myself at all. I train harder and it is a matter of time before I am back playing again."

Lessons well learned, pre-emptively.

And what of the World Cup lessons from failures past, were those so well learned?

"I think it's hard to imagine what this life is like until you have been involved in it yourself. It's hard to describe to people what it's like to play in front of so many people. The football fluctuates, it's up and down, and it goes with you through the week."

"With Uruguay, we had the same opponents and the same pressures", which was a good starting point for Emerton, who surely still bears the scars of failure four years ago. Probably because of aggregation, "the anxiety was a bit more this time".

"But we were much better prepared this time. I certainly was. We lost 0-1 away but that was redeemable because we knew we'd played well. Back in Sydney, we had nothing to lose.

"I went into the game feeling that we'd win for some reason. That comes from Guus. He made us believe in ourselves. The public reaction surprised me. I couldn't really believe it. Everyone was part of it and this is going to be fantastic for Australian football.

"None of us will ever forget that night. It was a night Australia will never forget. Captaining Australia at the Sydney 2000 Games was great, but 16 November, I don't think anything will compare with that again. The build-ups, the failures, the pressure release, the joy. It was incredible.

"It was always going to be fantastic when we won, it was just a matter of how good. The penalties ensured that it was pretty special."

Emerton has had a special career, one that has sprouted from a special gift. His has been a carefully family-managed and

---

"I went into the game feeling that we'd win for some reason. That comes from Guus. He made us believe in ourselves. The public reaction surprised me. I couldn't really believe it. Everyone was part of it and this is going to be fantastic for Australian football."

"I'd recommend this life. I couldn't be happier and wouldn't change a thing. I am still a fan of football, I enjoy watching it and playing it, and I get paid for doing it."

faultlessly executed plan. "I have a very tight family, but you become public property as a footballer. I don't really find it difficult. I like my own space, and being so close to the family keeps me well grounded. No matter how good a footballer I become or how famous, hopefully that will never change.

"I'd recommend this life. I couldn't be happier and wouldn't change a thing. I am still a fan of football, I enjoy watching it and playing it, and I get paid for doing it. Sometimes it has to be treated like it's a job and because of that I need to get away a bit. But when I stop enjoying it, I will stop playing it. I am a very competitive person, and I need an outlet, and football serves me well there.

"I am happy in Europe but I miss Australia. I will make my home there when I finish playing here and I would like to actually finish playing in Australia, and put something back into the game there. It was a dream to play professionally, but to what extent, well, I never knew how good I could be." Emerton is probably still on his course to find out what that ultimately means for him.

"It has been a slow progression for me, with no huge leaps. When I look back on my career, sometimes I can't believe it myself. I am still young, so hopefully I can do some more good things."

8

shirt number

"I want to show how good I am. I have always wanted to play in a World Cup. We have always spoken about it, not just getting there, but winning it. This might sound crazy but it's an attitude that has got us this far, and qualifying was the first step. That was the first dream."

Josip Skoko

Date of birth 10 December 1975

Position played Midfielder

Current club Wigan Athletic, England (on loan to Stoke City)

Every life is a series of links. The intertwining of life's strands, when managed neatly, makes for a nice crochet. The weaving of football through a life and of a life into football makes for the most interesting of stories. Football endlessly fascinates with the manner in which it creates characters for positions on a field, matchmakes characters for special roles, or reconstructs characters who then go on to live life as the reconstructed model. This is one of the great things about football. Football finds you out somehow, eventually, inexorably, finally.

Josip Skoko found football out long before it did him. For a long time he has been ahead of a game that many people spend their life chasing. This is not to say that he has had things his own way, or that he has necessarily ended up where he thought he might. That career epitaph is the sole reserve of only the very best. Modestly, Skoko would concede that he is not one of those.

But Skoko is an acute thinker about the game and life, and the marriage between the two. He has a wonderfully accurate radar that can sense static before the heavens have even started to rumble. He has a personality that unites rather than divides, and a quirky form of body language that draws attention but doesn't dominate or overpower.

Still waters run very deep with Skoko. He goes about his business efficiently, backed by his sharp mind and his capable body.

Football is the most cerebral of sports and it is the reason why Skoko has thrived therein.

He moves around the midfield of a football pitch stealthily, simultaneously assessing his team's forte and his opponent's weakness. He has a keenly trained eye for these things. One gets the feeling he conducts his general affairs in a similar manner.

To the chagrin of all football fans in Australia, Josip Skoko never played on the national stage with any club in the old NSL. Apart from a small, select group, Australians never really got to see him play until he started with the national team, which has played so irregularly over the years that his image has remained effectively banished from local view.

Football began for Skoko, as did life, in Mount Gambier, South Australia, when he began playing for Mount Gambier Croatia at five years of age. His father, who emigrated from Croatia and landed in South Australia's second city to work as a pine filler, started playing for the club, and when Josip was old enough, he followed in his dad's footsteps.

As may be obvious from the name of his first club, there was quite a strong Croatian presence in Mount Gambier at the time. When Skoko was ten, the family moved to Geelong, where there was more opportunity in a bigger city and where there was also a bigger Croatian base. It is a community that has produced many fine footballers for Australia, and Skoko remembers it to be "a very tight-knit and very enjoyable community".

The "Geelong Croatians" played for the North Geelong club in the Victorian leagues. Skoko moved straight into the club when his family relocated. After being recognised in regional teams and Victorian state teams, Skoko was offered a place at the AIS where he spent two years. "I went to the Institute with an open mind. Until I went to the AIS, I didn't really think about being a professional player."

At the conclusion of his time at the AIS, he returned to North Geelong to play in the senior team. Eighteen months later, Skoko was on his way to one of Croatia's best known clubs, Hajduk Split.

"I am disappointed I never played in the NSL. At the time, when I came out of the Institute, I did go to the Melbourne Knights a few times and was offered a contract, but it was basically to play for nothing. I thought that if I was considering the possibility of going overseas, I would be better suited to a year of State League football, senior football somewhere, which would take me up to the 1995 Youth World Cup in Qatar. If nothing would have happened then, I would revisit the NSL thing."

With his eye firmly fixed on his desire to head overseas, Skoko was hesitant about dropping anchor in Australia. "A lot of people said that it would be difficult to get out of Australia. I was only eighteen. The football I was getting was good for me at that stage, and by staying away from the NSL, I had the freedom to leave when I needed to."

This was noteworthy wisdom from one so green. Australia, as a developing football country, was by definition a "selling" country. Largely ignored by sponsors of corporate significance and disregarded by commercial media and their financial resources, many NSL clubs lived a hand-to-mouth existence by finding young talent and selling it overseas. The exchange rates and economies of scale made Australian talent good value. However short-sighted this approach may have been, it kept NSL clubs ticking over, for the most part, for the term of their natural lives. This, it should be said, is not a phenomenon unique to Australia.

There are many countries and many clubs worldwide who, cognisant of their places in football's food chain, organise their affairs to capitalise on this player market. But it isn't always as easy as it sounds, and many players have had careers stalled, or even ended, by international transfers that failed to get off the tarmac, for whatever reason.

After listening to all the commentary and advice, Skoko set about ensuring that his wings wouldn't get clipped by anything he couldn't control, and it was for this reason that he shied away from the NSL. He can't regret his action, because it was one that was reached with due consideration, but it is interesting to hear how someone with such varied professional experience since has hankered for a spell in the Australian competition. But club football in Australia and Josip Skoko were apparently not to be.

"One of my coaches at North Geelong was in with the president at Hajduk. I didn't really believe it, that they were interested, but one day a faxed contract came through from them, and I was on my way.

"I had grown up immersed in the Croatian community here, but that didn't prepare me at all for what I met over there. The only thing that helped was the language and even that ... I thought I could speak really well, but in actual fact the players were taking the piss out of me every day. There was a lot of familiarity, culturally, but also a lot of differences."

Croatia, the good and the bad, made Skoko a lot wiser. "Australia is not corrupt, relatively. What you see is what you get. I was very innocent coming out of Australia. When I got to Croatia, I could not believe what I was seeing there. It was out of this world. It was in everyday life, but football, too. The war was on too, so that would have added to it."

"I was fairly open-minded about Croatia when I went. I was surprised by what I saw, but didn't really go with any perception otherwise. But it was great because I was playing professional football. It gave me my chance."

Around the time Skoko parachuted into Hajduk to play football, the former Yugoslav conglomeration, of which Croatia was part, was in meltdown. Centuries-old enmity between Croatian and Serbian cultures, which had been relatively suppressed during the Tito domination, was cascading out of the cracks of Yugoslavia's disintegration. As Croatia fought to withdraw from Serb domination, Serbia tried to firm its grip. There is no such thing as a pleasant war. The horrors of that conflict are still being told. Nothing in Joe Skoko's life to this point could have prepared him for this.

For him, whilst Croatia was in a war economy at the time, football was thankfully a relatively safe haven. For Skoko's life passage, Croatia provided many things, including "a lot of life lessons. I became more street-wise". Seemingly daily, managers were trying to rip him off, while corrupt journalists, looking for aggrandisement and thirsty for power and influence and money, would either deify or destroy people. "After Croatia, nothing surprised me anymore, and it helped deal with any other stuff that came up after that. It was a good, but tough, learning experience."

Despite the fractious surroundings, Skoko's professional football career did get going in Croatia, which was the reason for him being there. "I was fairly open-minded about Croatia when I went. I was surprised by what I saw, but didn't really go with any perception otherwise. But it was great because I was playing professional football. It gave me my chance."

Football in Croatia is a national passion. The appreciation and technical understanding of the game runs very deep there. It is a culture that repeatedly produces very good players. At the time Skoko was there, although most of the big names were playing in western Europe, Croatia was preparing for what was to be a momentously successful World Cup finals in France in '98. Competing for the first time as an independent country, Croatia finished third in the tournament, losing the semifinal to the hosts and eventual champions, France. And Croatia is a country with a population in the vicinity of only 3 million people—smaller than Sydney!

There was certainly plenty of quality around, therefore. Rising through all this was Skoko from Mount Gambier, who was appointed captain of Hajduk Split, one of the big names of European football, at the tender age of twenty, the youngest-ever captain in the history of that proud club.

Hajduk was only ever going to be a starting, and not finishing point, though. "From about two and a half years in, I started getting false approaches from 'managers' promising 'this' much money and claiming interest from 'that' club. For a while and as a youngster, you get swept up in this, getting excited about the possibilities, but soon realise it is just part of the game. It was a difficult thing but really, pretty quickly, it didn't faze me.

"I think I stayed there a bit longer than I wanted, four and half years, probably half a year earlier out of there would have been great, but it set the stage for the rest of my career."

Skoko's move to Belgium came right on cue. He was very ready for a new challenge. "I was fed up in Croatia." The corridor of escape came rather circuitously. Hajduk played a game against 1860 Munich, which they won 3-1. "I played really well", says

Skoko. Watching that game was another German club, Wolfsburg, who expressed an interest. Skoko immediately set sail to talk, taking three days off from Hajduk to go and see what was what.

Racing Club Genk was at the same game, scouting another player. Skoko did the medical at Wolfsburg and was ready to sign with the German club. But the contract that appeared was for less than what had initially been agreed. "It was a bit shifty, so I said I needed a few days to go away and think about it."

Skoko and his lawyer started on their return journey to Croatia. "On the way back, a Croatian guy called my lawyer and invited me to go to Genk, saying that they were interested in me. So we made a bit of a turn, and headed for Belgium. That same night I signed with Genk. It just felt right. I didn't know anything about Genk, had never heard of it. I never thought I would play in Belgium, yet it has turned out to be probably the best club I have played for."

The "Racing Club" part of the Genk name is a historical reference to cycling, which is such a big sport in Europe. Football clubs were to emerge from the cycling "racing clubs" and the absurd popularity of football has largely usurped the names and traditions of the clubs, though the references have remained. One of Australia's great football exports, Robbie Slater, built the substance of his career at RC (Racing Club) Lens, in northern France—another such example. Similar things occurred in places such as Brazil, where its biggest club (and one of the world's biggest football clubs) Flamengo of Rio de Janeiro, is actually known as Clube de Regatas do Flamengo, the football club originally an offshoot to the rowing club that was first formed at the end of the nineteenth century.

For Skoko, Genk, a neat city situated on the German border, was a master move. The club had "good facilities and good fans". The stadium now holds approximately 26,000 people, although when Skoko arrived, its capacity was between 12,000 and 14,000. "The building project was underway when I got there, and by the time I left the crowds were regularly topping the 23,000 mark."

As his time at Genk would highlight, Skoko has a knack for usually leaving places better than he finds them. That isn't a bad tag line to have.

"When I arrived, we won a cup straightaway. A new coach then arrived and things really started to move. We qualified for the European Champions League and the UEFA Cup there."

There was also a championship title for Genk during Skoko's time and for the last two years of this three-and-a-half-year stay, he was made captain of the team. Two professional clubs and two captaincy appointments is an indication of Skoko's standing. "Captaincy is what somebody sees in you", and in Skoko a collection of people have obviously seen similar things. His performances at the Youth World Cup in Qatar were the first to catch the eye of Australia's football public. There was something about Skoko's gait, combined with his squared-angled shoulders as well as the quality of his play—neat and incisive passing and busy linkage between team members—that made the young man stand out. It was a reason why there was such gnashing of teeth that fans never got to see him regularly in the NSL.

Even then, however, it was more than the pure football. When pressed, Skoko finds it difficult to quantify the reasons why he has been made captain. "Off the field I am not one to enforce rules and paperwork like some captains do. But I think it is just on the field, the way that I am. I understand the game fairly well, and like talking and keeping things organised. I remember the president of Genk telling me in contract negotiations what the coach said to him about me—'You're not the best player here, but you are the most important', which was nice to hear."

His importance has also permeated the national team, when twice Skoko has been made captain of Australia. He recalls with a rueful smirk his debut in the role in the 2-2 draw with the Solomon Islands—"not the best result"—but more significantly for Australia's first game in official Asian competition, when as a fully-fledged member of the Asian Football Confederation, Australia beat (with a Skoko goal) Bahrain 3-1 in an Asia Cup qualifier.

Skoko thoroughly enjoyed his time with Genk. He won things there, presided over the club's new achievements and settled into some good playing form. But, after the third year, Skoko sensed it was time to move on. "I felt I had been there for long enough. Three or four years at a club is a good amount of time. I like change.

"I still had four years left on my Genk contract, so there was no real need to leave. I was twenty-seven or so by this time and I wanted to play in a bigger league. England was the preference. There were a few nibbles but nothing concrete. Then a Turkish manager called me. I thought he was taking the piss with the money he was offering.

"Initially I refused Turkey. The offer came through and I went back with my figure. I didn't hear from them for a couple of

---

"Off the field I am not one to enforce rules and paperwork like some captains do. But I think it is just on the field, the way that I am. I understand the game fairly well, and like talking and keeping things organised."

weeks. They came and watched a few more games. They finally agreed to my wages, and I started to do some homework on the club. I wanted to leave Genk. I was worried that my football might start to deteriorate if I stayed. I wanted to go to England but maybe Turkey would provide another route to my goal.

"It was the biggest gamble I have taken. I was only there for two years, but it was fantastic. The club, Genclerberligi, is based in Ankara and living there was good. The club itself was a strange one. It was aiming for the top, it had a good standing, but was not expected to win trophies so the pressure wasn't great. Everything seemed quite good, the level was better than Belgium and, from the club's point of view, they had it in mind to move me on to one of the big three clubs, Galatasaray, Fenerbahce or Besiktas. Besiktas actually came in for me towards the end of the contract but the club didn't want to sell me."

Turkey proved a very nice place for Skoko to live. He lived in a nice estate, with nice villas. The fans were fanatical without being crazy. Different from the cauldron that is Istanbul and the fevered rivalry between its big clubs, Ankara's football fans were "normal and good, they wouldn't cause you any trouble away from football. I enjoyed a good UEFA Cup campaign there, which helped. The living standards in Turkey can be low but where I lived, ate and shopped, it was world-class stuff."

With Skoko approaching the thirty years of age mark (a milestone reached in December of 2005), his internal career call to England became too loud to ignore. "If I am going to go to England, I need to go. The World Cup was coming up as well, and England might help me with that. I wasn't overly happy with the football style of the coach in Turkey and because of that style, which didn't suit me, he started leaving me out. It was frustrating because I was one of his better players and he really couldn't afford to leave me out, but he did. The fans were becoming annoyed with him and he started playing games with me, which assisted my exit in the end.

"The club had spent quite a bit of money to get me there and wanted something for me. But the coach was putting pressure for me to be released, which I was able to use to my advantage. In the end I got away on a free transfer. It helped me get to England."

Despite the sourness of the departure, Skoko's recollection of Turkey was fond. "I had two full seasons of football, UEFA Cup, and earned a lot of money. The lifestyle was more Mediterranean than Belgium and I still had two years to go on my contract. I could easily have lived in Turkey for another couple of years. Even when I signed in England, the coach was released quickly and they wanted me back there."

Skoko's English move took him to Lancashire and the newly promoted Wigan Athletic Football Club. The 2005–06 season is Wigan's first in the top flight of English football. It was widely expected to struggle and, in fact, return from whence it came—the Championship and perhaps even beyond. Probably Skoko expected the team to struggle, too, which might have provided extra opportunities for him to shine and do his thing, remembering that to date he had exerted somewhat of a Midas touch on the clubs of his employ.

However, it wasn't quite to work out as planned. "The biggest frustration with the Wigan experience was never getting three or four games in a row to settle and establish myself. I missed the first two games, which they lost. I was going away with the national team at that stage. Then they hit a purple patch of ten wins and a draw. Coaches don't tinker with success like that and, because of the frequency of the games, there was no training forum for me to show the boss anything. I had no games to play."

Of the many things that Josip Skoko may be, and of all the places to which he may be suited, the English Championship doesn't leap to mind as one of them. But in search of football, Skoko moved on loan to Stoke City—"the Potters" from the Midlands of England. He initially moved on a month's loan, during which time Wigan retained the right of recall within a twenty-four-hour period. Thereafter, Skoko is a Stoke player until the end of the 2005–06 season. "You have to take things as they come. This is a World Cup year. This is my only World Cup chance. I need games. I don't want to be there to make up the numbers, I want to play. The lack of games might keep me fresh, but I don't want to be too fresh," he jokes.

Stoke City is merely the latest twist in Skoko's fascinating tale. He has lived a vastly different life from that which people in Australia could really comprehend. "It is impossible for people to know what it is like. You are virtually a nomad, always travelling and never settled really. Different phases of your life occur through these constant transitions, marriage, family etc. We have lived like this for so long now, but in the end it is a great experience and you have to experience as much as you can, even the hardships along the way.

"I found it difficult in the first two years, but you just get on with it—this is your path. If you don't like it, you can just pack

---

"It is impossible for people to know what it is like. You are virtually a nomad, always travelling and never settled really."

"The Croatia game that looms is exciting. I have played for years there and have many friends there. There will be a lot of people who won't know who to go for. It will be mixed with emotion."

---

up and go home. There is always choice. In the first six months in Croatia, I was moved to a smaller club to get more games—sometimes you have to go down a little to come back up again. You have to stay positive and maintain your sense of purpose.

"I am persistent and quite disciplined. Being in Croatia as a nineteen-year-old and waking up in the morning and thinking, 'What the hell is this?' But you push through it because you have bigger things planned.

"I want to show how good I am. I have always wanted to play in a World Cup. We have always spoken about it, not just getting there, but winning it. This might sound crazy but it's an attitude that has got us this far, and qualifying was the first step. That was the first dream."

Qualification for the Germany finals is listed by Skoko as his biggest single achievement. He is not one to subscribe to the inevitability of the ultimate qualification. "I am one, throughout my career, who has learned to be very wary of history repeating itself. Teams losing Cup finals two years in a row and that sort of thing. I was very wary of Uruguay this time round.

"But we were in good shape. Guus brought the sharpness that we needed. We were more ruthless about it. Qualification was always imagined but never in my wildest dreams could I have foreseen the reaction by Australians.

“I think we will be disappointed if we don’t go through to the second round. It’ll be very difficult, but that’s what we are after. The Croatia game that looms is exciting. I have played for years there and have many friends there. There will be a lot of people who won’t know who to go for. It will be mixed with emotion.”

Skoko is confronted, predictably, with people testing his allegiance—“which national anthem will I sing?” He coyly dodges the issue by answering, “Neither, I don’t want to offend anybody”.

Skoko’s nomadic football life might have less time in front of it than it has behind, but he isn’t convinced the nomadic lifestyle to which he has become accustomed is about to change. “I would like to settle down but I am so used to moving around. Also, the way my family is, I have very close ties to Croatia and Australia, so that will be some sort of juggling act. It doesn’t really matter where, just to be more settled than now is the aim.”

Josip Skoko

9

shirt number

"I was crazy about soccer. My dad used to take me to watch Melbourne Croatia. As a junior I was good. I was just obsessed by soccer. Dad was a builder. I used to get his lime out and mark a field in the backyard."

Mark Viduka

Date of birth 9 October 1975

Position played Striker

Current club Middlesbrough, England

Too often Australians must depart these shores in order to be recognised within them. This is the case in many walks of life and professional endeavour. It is particularly so in football. And in football, no-one is a better example of this than Mark Viduka.

The international stage or marketplace or ideas factory is big and wide and offers untold opportunities for Australians, with which Australia cannot compete. It's a fact, no harm done.

This, though, isn't the point. The point, irritatingly, is that talent that explores this big and wide world is not appreciated whilst it is here.

For many years, there has been a perception that football in this country has suffered irreparably because of the overseas talent drain of its best and brightest. Football's doomsayers, of which there have been a voluminous gaggle, have trotted out the argument that football will never be viable in Australia whilst ever it can't hold onto this talent. This, because of the sport's international opportunities, means for these people, conveniently, that football will never be viable in Australia. Happy to have reached this conclusion for themselves in no time flat, and for their own interests, they have then eagerly spouted the "opinion" across the nation's newspapers and airwaves. The net cumulative effect of this "thinking" is worrisome, and, arguably, as was the case for the old NSL, potentially fatal.

There can be no argument that a domestic competition isn't better served by having better players. Actually there can be few more obvious conclusions that can be reached. Rhodes Scholar analysis this is not.

But the experience of Mark Viduka provides a clear window into this particular malaise that confronts Australian society, as it relates to the broad spectrum of activities beset by the problems of talent drain.

You see, Mark Viduka was never celebrated when he was here, other than by the football communities of Australia. Amazingly, Viduka was perceived to be part of the blanket problem of the NSL, if you were to believe the doomsayers. Poor quality and nothing worth watching. Then, miraculously, and care of a 20,000 or so kilometre flight to Europe, Viduka (and others like him) was perceived to be the solution to the NSL's woes.

The problem was not the quality on show, because Viduka was available for all to see in the years he played in the NSL—and what a glorious sight. The problem was anonymity. That Viduka had to leave Australia to gain credibility is offensive.

When Mark Viduka played for the Melbourne Knights in the NSL, his (high-quality) team won the Championship, and he was voted in consecutive years by his peers as simultaneously being the best Under 21 player and the best player in the league. He also won the Golden Boot as top goal scorer.

Young, strapping, elegant, deadly in front of goal, happy, skilful, proud, gregarious, welcoming—he won all these things and he was all these things right here in Australia. And it would have cost probably ten Aussie dollars each week to see it.

Football's doomsayers wouldn't have had a clue about any of this. They wouldn't have bothered to check. It wouldn't have suited their agenda. It wasn't in their interests. Their interest lay in death-riding football. Selfish interests which, because of their currency, deprived too many people of enjoying this magnificent footballer, for the time that he was here. Australia was lesser for it and lessened by it.

We weren't going to be able to hold onto him forever, but we could have appreciated him much more whilst we had him. Certainly, this is a book about football and this is a chapter about Mark Viduka, but this is a lesson that extends beyond both.

Viduka was born in Melbourne and raised in St Albans, in the city's west. His entry to football was with Melbourne Croatia, the proud pedestal on which this vibrant migrant community displayed its sporting offerings to Australia. It is a proud club that has produced many international players.

Viduka, destined to be one of these international players, started playing for the club in 1982, when, as a six-year-old, he joined the Under 9 team. He tried to begin a year earlier but the club said he was too young.

From his earliest days, Viduka was going to be a Knight (under the insistence of the then governing body, Melbourne Croatia changed its name to become the Melbourne Knights). He was fixated on the club and the sport. "I was crazy about soccer. My dad used to take me to watch Melbourne Croatia. As a junior I was good. I was just obsessed by soccer. Dad was a builder. I used to get his lime out and mark a field in the backyard.

"There are family photos of when I was two or three years old, kicking a ball around. I still love the game and that's the main thing. The actual game, I completely love. But once you get to the highest level there is so much crap that goes with it. Shifty people, everywhere, when there is a lot of money around. They always come out. You don't know who to trust. But you can't live your life not trusting anybody. You have to keep it tight though, you can only depend on a few people."

Sadly, in the space of one paragraph's worth of conversation, Viduka fast-forwards from his infantile infatuation with this game straight to the devil that lurks in the shallowness of football's waters. In between, there has been an incredible story of achievement and self-discovery.

Viduka, from as early as he can remember, had "nothing else in my head" apart from football. He progressed through the age groups at club level and was selected in the Victorian teams when, at sixteen, he moved to the AIS on a scholarship. For Viduka, this obsessed footballer in waiting, the AIS was the sign to do something with this sport.

Another vocational prompting arrived a year earlier when, as a fifteen-year-old, Viduka fronted up for a job interview at Highpoint City in Melbourne. The job was to move boxes in a shoe shop. "I was tall and skinny, not strong then, probably good for getting the boxes in the hard-to-reach places. The lady asked me what days after school I could work, as per the advertisement. I said, 'I can't do Monday, Tuesday, Thursday, Friday, because of training'. She said, 'Don't call us, we'll call you'." Needless to say, the phone didn't ring.

The AIS was a significant change for Viduka. "I am in a big family, I have four sisters. It was difficult to leave home. But the two years I was there made me think I could focus on doing this for a living. In the first couple of months there I developed a severe case of osteitis pubis. I was told to rest for a year. I wasn't interested in that, so I knuckled down and did everything I could to get it right. A big stretching regime and a lot of physiotherapy."

From the AIS Viduka returned to the Melbourne Knights to realise his childhood dream. The Knights were a dominant team at the time. "I wasn't frustrated with the low profile of the league. It was my goal in life to play for the Melbourne Knights. That was it. Having played through the ranks there and watching them for many years, with all the disappointments, it was special to win a championship with them—it was fantastic.

"That was all that was in my head back then. I didn't think about anything else except to play for the Knights. That was such a beautiful time—we had so much fun. It was such a nice atmosphere, with such nice people, who were happy. We'd train in the morning and go to the beach in the afternoon before another session at night. It was a nice life." Viduka doesn't quite break into song as he tells this story, but there is a gentle and melodic undulation in his voice as he speaks, and his eyes sparkle with the fondness of what it all means. Not only did Viduka touch all those with whom his football brought him into contact, but he has quite clearly been touched himself by that period in his life.

"They were spectacular days. I was just lucky, really, to be in such a good team. I was really enjoying myself—you know when you enjoy yourself?" Viduka asks the question as if the intervening time has him wondering how to recognise these things anymore. But all of us, when sliding sentimentally into personal memories, often check to see if those who are with us are still in for the ride. It's a courtesy as much as anything. But it is a wistful Viduka who recalls these cherished times spent wearing the shirt of the club he idolised. And he recites his personal honour roll—players such as Andrew Marth and Josip Biskic, unknown to the sporting rank and file of Australia or even Melbourne, but deeply etched into Viduka's life and memory.

In 1995 Viduka left the Melbourne Knights and accepted a contract with Croatia Zagreb. There was much more to this move than the simple sale and purchase of a football player. Zagreb was the team of Croatian president Franjo Tudjman and he was on a mission to position his "new" Croatia to the watching world through the football team. As football is also such an obsession in Croatia, the domestic political fortunes of Tudjman could also be massaged by the team.

There was a lot riding on this and the stakes were raised because of Viduka's performance, as captain, with the Young Socceroos at the Youth World Cup in Qatar that year. Clubs from around the world were circling for his signature. Tudjman had to swoop, which he literally, and famously did, in a snatch-and-grab negotiation with Australia's hottest young football talent.

Viduka, it has been reported, found it very difficult to say no to the Croatian president, and he packed his bags and set off for Croatia.

"The Croatian experience was very much a defining experience of my life. We live in such a lucky country in Australia. Yes it's wealthy, but more than that, I think the level of consciousness in our country is much higher than in a lot of countries. I mean, when would we ever have a war with each other? You have to be on a different level to do that stuff. I went from an environment where nine times out of ten, people are positive, to Croatia, where it was the opposite.

"I was very immersed in the Croatian community here. But going there was very much a deconstructing experience for me. I had this expectation, as a kid you hear stories about this place, and it is one of the world's most beautiful places. But if you are born and raised in a place like Australia, you can never understand some of the things that happen there. You'll not be able to understand how people think in that way. I can understand the culture but I can't understand some of the things they do. It's not me, it's not my character.

"The whole experience has definitely been a mechanism to redefine myself as a human being. First of all, it was a rough situation there. Towards the end, I was copping a lot of abuse from everywhere. It was the first time in my life that I had to deal with being attacked, and I was nineteen, twenty years old at the time. It makes you stronger when you have to deal with it. Some of the most successful people in life have been through that sort of stuff."

Whilst all this nonsense was going on, Viduka was actually playing good football. His arrival was welcomed warmly. The new star, the new kid on the block. He was also Tudjman's "signing" and as long as Tudjman was well regarded with the supporters, Viduka was okay. "An element of me being there was to be used by Tudjman. I was young and naive and thinking only about playing soccer. I wasn't thinking about any political agendas; other people put that on it." And this was the real difficulty Viduka faced. He became the receptacle for any anger from the fans, because he was Tudjman's player. There was no escaping it. Goals scored by Viduka were booed by his own fans. Journalists were machete-ing a path to him one day and then using the same implement to wound him in the back the next. Understandably, Viduka did not really know what had hit him.

Thankfully for Viduka, an escape from the torment was approaching. "I wanted to get out of Croatia at about the same time as Celtic came in for me. We played a European Champions

League qualifying match against them and I played well. Alan Stubbs, one of Celtic's central defenders, was apparently talking it up in their dressing room about how they were 'black and blue' from playing against me, and they told their manager, Joe Venglos, to buy me. He must have asked them what they thought. He knew I was Australian and it went from there. They were looking for a striker."

As all teams are. Teams can never score enough goals and when there is someone of the quality of Viduka available, a club will look to move. The other thing in Viduka's favour was Venglos himself. A footballing professor from the former Czechoslovakia, he'd spent a great deal of time in Australia already, many years earlier. He knew the culture and the character of the people. In fact, there had been moves over the years to get Venglos to return to Australia in some sort of Technical Director capacity, but it didn't happen. Viduka—an exquisite player and Australian to boot—was an easy sell for Venglos.

"Venglos was such a nice man. One of the nicest I have met in football. He was just a genuine person. In Australia when I grew up, because there was no money, the experience was more with people like that, but where there is money involved there are not nice people involved.

"The move from Zagreb really put pressure on me. There was a lot of crap in the last three or four months. I didn't know what my name was; I didn't know where I was. I was on my way to Celtic, but I was depressed. I had to play a game in two days before my new crowd in Glasgow and had just come from being battered in Croatia. I had come from scoring goals for my team and my own crowd was shouting, 'Viduka's a poofter' and I'd be thinking, 'What the hell's going on here?' I have never experienced that before. You try to do your best. I didn't need that crap anymore.

"But I would like to think of myself as an honest person, a fair person, and if anybody says that when I give my word it sticks—that is more important to me than anything. I went to Venglos and said to him, 'I can't play, mentally I am gone. I need to go home and get out of here. I can't do this.' He was very nice and told me to do what I needed to do, whatever that was. I thought that was very nice. I didn't know if I wanted to play anymore.

"I signed a contract but there was a delay in paying £3.5 million to Zagreb. I told Celtic to wait. If I don't come back, don't pay it; if I do come back, pay it. That's what happened, in essence. I went home to Australia for a month and that's when Fergus McCann [Celtic chairman] wanted to not pay the money."

Viduka's time off did the trick. Consistent with the parallel theme of this chapter, his career crisis was a major news item even in Australia. Viduka was holding press conferences to explain to the Australian public what was going on, as best he could. It had only been a couple of years since he'd been playing in Australia, anonymous. It was the same person and to all intents and purposes, it was the same player. Now, though, the Australian media was desperate to know what was happening with him. Before, they couldn't have given a toss.

But once Viduka had rested and sorted himself out, he really took off at Celtic. "It's a great club. I loved playing there. I loved the fans and I loved everything about it. The only thing, which ultimately got to me, was playing each other four times in the league. That's the problem with Scotland, the league is too small and it gets boring. In my last month that I played in Scotland, we played Dundee or Dundee United [two different clubs separated along sectarian lines] four times in that month—Cup matches, a League match and a catch-up game. There was this tall guy at the back, marking me. Every game, the same guy. I'd look at him and say, 'Not you again!' It just seemed like every week I was against this guy."

At the end of that season, Viduka moved to Leeds United in the English Premier League, where he joined fellow Aussie Harry Kewell. At his first training session there, he couldn't believe his eyes when he turned up and saw "that big bastard from Dundee again, on trial at Leeds. I had to ask him, 'Are you following me around or something?'"

Viduka's time at Celtic was highly successful. He was a massive hit with the fans. Celtic is a huge club, despite the comparative smallness of the league. In fact, the sheer size of Rangers and Celtic is one of the reasons why Scottish football struggles. They are both seriously huge football clubs that almost absorb the entire football economy of Scotland. To have done well with "the Bhoys" really set Viduka up in Glasgow. Being a crowd favourite at one of the world's biggest football clubs would be an experience most could only imagine.

And the timing of his move to Leeds was impeccable. The Yorkshire club "were flying then, it was a great atmosphere. Harry [Kewell] was there and going extremely well". It was true, Leeds were about to enter a golden run. Fuelled by a golden generation of youth trained and developed at the club's training complex, Thorpe Arch Grange, Leeds were also to embark upon a highly geared financial strategy to win competitions—aka spend extravagantly on player recruitment. Viduka was part of that gearing strategy.

The gearing strategy was highly speculative, as they often can be, and the huge investment in the team wasn't underpinned by the necessary trading capacity. Unbeknown to those outside the club, Leeds United were about to run headlong into a financial twister.

But times could scarcely have been better for Viduka. Performances such as his four-goal personal haul in one game against Liverpool remain an "unimaginable" highlight. Viduka's game has that capacity. He can be totally uncontainable, when he turns it on. The English spend a lot of time writing about Viduka the "enigma". The key is to find out how to turn it on. "I don't really know", says Viduka. "I know when I am in the zone, but it is getting there. Probably too many distractions." When Viduka is in the zone, there are few better sights in world football.

Eventually, though, Leeds' financial plan began to start unravelling. Viduka was going well and there was interest from the continent. Roma was interested and AC Milan was "really interested".

"Milan made an offer for me. Zvonimir Boban [one of Croatia's biggest football stars], who I know really well, was at Milan at the time. He and my agent played together. They talked to Milan, but that was my first year at Leeds. I was so happy—I had just moved there and we had a good team. We had bought Robbie Fowler from Liverpool, Rio Ferdinand from West Ham and there was me, Harry, Robbie Keane, Alan Smith, Jonathon Woodgate—a lot of good players. I thought I would give it another year. We had just got into the semifinals of the Champions League and I thought there was more to come. And then trouble hit at Leeds. You can't predict these things.

"The last two years at Leeds we were fighting against relegation. That was tough and not as enjoyable as playing for the Champions League. When Leeds did finally get relegated, I was sold in the fire sale and ended up at Middlesbrough. I had a lot of options but clubs apparently couldn't afford me. I haven't gone that well since Leeds. The people are nice at Middlesbrough.

> "Qualifying had to happen this time. It was like destiny, like those T-shirts. In the lead-up, we were all thinking, it's got to happen for us sometime. We were desperate this time. Well, we were desperate last time too, but things fell into place for us this time."

Honest sort of workers. There isn't really a lot there, the industrial plants and the football." The "smoggies", as the people are affectionately known in the north-east of England, on Teesside—"They love their football, it means a lot to them," acknowledges Viduka.

Like many of his team-mates, qualification for the World Cup has brought the tournament into sharp focus. Certainly for what it is, but also for what it can do. "Football is so unpredictable, anything is possible. If you have a good World Cup, then who knows what might be next.

"Qualifying had to happen this time. It was like destiny, like those T-shirts. In the lead-up, we were all thinking, it's got to happen for us sometime. We were desperate this time. Well, we were desperate last time too, but things fell into place for us this time. Guus has been a big influence, the way he prepared us and his experience. The way he makes everybody in the team function. The way he can get the maximum out of everybody, it's an art. His man-management is fundamental. He has very good training sessions—all intense. He is a big leader who brings confidence to everybody."

The first game against Uruguay, in Montevideo, was one of the best Viduka has had for his country. He was a colossus that day, in very trying circumstances. "I thought I played well in the away game. I might have had a better game somewhere along the line but not in a game so important. It was a great atmosphere: it was thick, suffocating. Now it is just a memory, but there was such an atmosphere. The South Americans are so passionate and the crowd gives them extra incentive. That is the only reason they scored that goal, the crowd. I believe a lot in that mental side of things. It's a big advantage.

"The return match in Sydney was of course a highlight, except for my penalty which was disappointing. Unbelievable, the whole thing, really. You just don't expect these things in Australia. The crowd gave us the twelfth man, and apart from the first twenty minutes, I think we dominated the game.

"The way it did happen, on penalties, the drama added to it. It made people tune in. If we'd won 3-1 it would have been great, but not the same. Australia needed us to win that game that way. I tell you what, if it was a Hollywood film, you couldn't have planned it better."

Viduka is very optimistic about the finals. "I think we can surprise a lot of people and do very well. Stranger things have happened, look at Greece in the 2004 European Championships."

For Viduka, the group matches all appeal. "If we were up against Trinidad and Tobago it wouldn't be the same. But the whole world will be watching these games. Japan is a big team in Asia, which is our home now, and bragging rights for Asia are

---

"I think we can surprise a lot of people and do very well. Stranger things have happened, look at Greece in the 2004 European Championships."

"The thing that defines you as a person is your downs. Ups, anybody can cope with. I have seen players, unbelievable players, who crashed because they couldn't cope with the downs."

---

up for grabs here. Brazil is top of the world, and Croatia, well, half our team is desperate to knock them off.

"The Croatia game is extra incentive for me. I know a lot of the players, and the coach was my coach when I first went to Croatia. And they all think we are kangaroos and we don't know anything. I tell you, I want to show them. I can't wait to be there."

Most recently, Viduka has been made captain of Australia. Craig Moore's injury problems, which coincided with the Hiddink reign, left the post vacant. Viduka was given the armband by the new coach. "It was always a goal of mine to play in a World Cup for Australia. As captain—well that's another thing and won't be finalised until later, I guess. But when I was made captain, I was surprised and honoured. It was nice. I have been part of this team for a long time, through the Olympics and the Young Socceroos, and captained those teams. That was a great experience. But this is the top end, to captain your country. People have a real respect for you if you captain a national team in Australia. Here, people are very proud of it and I was proud of it and my family was proud of it."

The World Cup will be a fabulous celebration, but it will pass. Viduka is very circumspect about his world and his career. "It takes a lot of work and mental toughness to get to the highest level in anything, not just sport. The thing that defines you as a person is your downs. Ups, anybody can cope with. I have seen players, unbelievable players, who crashed because they couldn't cope with the downs. Maybe I can't cope with the downs either, but I am still going. I have this inner thing where I like to prove people wrong.

"In the Premier League, there are a lot of players who are average, but they are there and they are playing every week. I think it is the mental toughness. The down times make you—there can be no mistake about it. Living away from home, it's much tougher for us Aussies. These Poms, if something goes wrong, they have their whole network to fall back on. When you are overseas and everybody is hammering you left, right and centre, papers, coaches, fans—you have you, and you only. Your family is 12,000 miles away. You can't hide, you can't bury yourself—it sorts you out. It's unpleasant.

"We [Aussies] didn't come here for a haircut, we came here to play soccer, and when that side of it is going bad, it affects everything. That's when you wonder why you can't be at home with your family.

"The key is not to let the crap bother you. The reason why I started this was because I loved it more than anything. It's been my life and it is such a part of me, when people think of me they think of football. I can't be a box packer because I am football and it is part of me. I have some good years left in me. Enough will be enough when I am not enjoying it. I don't want to linger,

---

"We [Aussies] didn't come here for a haircut, we came here to play soccer, and when that side of it is going bad, it affects everything. That's when you wonder why you can't be at home with your family."

just for the sake of it. I want to do as well as I can for myself, to prove a few things to myself."

Viduka's decade-long journey of self-discovery may well have taken a toll, but he has provided untold enjoyment to millions of people. He hopes that he "can continue to provide more for people", which of course he can, for as long as he chooses to grace the football stadiums of the world.

Hopefully, that will be for some time yet.

Mark Viduka

shirt number

10

"I expect only good for the World Cup. Every player has got to set out into a competition to win it. If you set out to aim lower, you might as well not participate. We have something really strong here. We all want to work hard for each other."

Harry Kewell

Date of birth 22 September 1978

Position played Striker

Current club Liverpool, England

There have been many people who have contributed enormously to the shape and texture of Australia's football. Many people have worked, selflessly and with dedication, to effect positive change for the sport. A mass movement of people, who, by their sheer will, have pushed against the tide to force a place for football in the Australian community, who have resisted the antagonism they have met, challenged the poor resourcing that has impounded the sport, and confronted the ugly bigotry that has warped Australia's view of and relationship with football.

In particular, at this point, one has to mention the late Johnny Warren, who was the masthead of football's struggle in this country, the champion of the cause and its people, the soldier who would never say die, the statesman who brought honour, the Aussie who brought the world to Australia, through football. Warren was an angel, given to football by the firmaments to nurse football through its difficult birthing pains and into the delivery ward. Words can only fail to encapsulate his contribution, to mark our respect, to express the depth of our gratitude.

But in the relative twinkling of an eye, one person has changed the face of football in this country, arguably more than any "singular" other. He has not been on a mission as such, perhaps as others before him in different areas of the game may have been. He has just played football. He has, as his mantra goes, "let his feet do the talking". But he has done it so well that the extent of his impact really is difficult to quantify. Suffice to say that nothing else, in that singular sense, has been as big for football in this country, as Harry Kewell.

Naturally, this narrow assessment is offered with broad acknowledgement of the army of people hitherto referred to. It is offered with sincere affection and respect for the conga line of high-quality players who have preceded Kewell. It is offered with the appreciation that all sorts of environmental factors have had their say at different times, affecting different groups and different talents in different ways.

It is offered with understanding of all these things.

It is offered also, though, because it is true. Harry Kewell is introverted and private—he doesn't cajole or rally or lobby, he has just played football very well, and to dramatic effect in Australia.

Kewell, as he is quick to modestly point out, wasn't the first Australian football export. There is an under-reported history of who actually left Australia to first play football in Britain, but our most famous "first" was Joe Marston, who left Australia for England at a time when Aussies were either cricketers or lifesavers. Actually, Marston was a lifesaver too, but for football he went to England, from the Leichhardt–Annandale club in Sydney to play for Preston North-End, then one of England's top teams. Marston had five years with the club, played in the 1954 FA Cup final, was selected to play in an England League XI against the Scottish equivalent, and has been included in Preston's official best-ever list.

Kewell, of his own volition, when this topic is raised, mentions Craig Johnston and Mark Bosnich. Both did wonderful things in big clubs and with real panache. And anything could have happened with John Kosmina, Australian legend, if he had continued with Arsenal in the days of his youth.

Also predating Kewell were David Mitchell, Frank Farina, Eddie Krncevic, Graham Arnold and Robbie Slater, all forging a new path and new reputation for Australians in Europe. It was difficult for them.

And closer to Kewell, Paul Okon and Ned Zelic, two of Australia's best products, were re-emphasising what Australian talent can do and be in Europe.

And the list goes on. All these fabulous players, pioneers all in their own way, determined and talented exponents of football, pursuing their dreams, and each one of them, all the time, changing the way the world viewed Australia's football.

Warren himself testified to the magnitude of the Kewell football phenomenon post-Uruguay 2001, when Australia had been so humiliated at that final stage of World Cup qualification. "Australia will have made it when we have produced a team that has more than one Harry", he famously said. And in his biography, *Sheilas, Wogs and Poofters*, Warren says of Kewell, "He is one the best dribblers of a football in Britain. He also possesses one of the best left feet I have ever seen in action." Remember, Johnny Warren had been around, seen a lot. It is high praise indeed.

It wasn't only Warren who was so struck by Kewell. Leeds United, Kewell's club for the first nine years of his career, were like the cat that got the cream. Having not outlaid much to move Kewell to England, the Yorkshire club was in possession of a player worth many millions of pounds.

But it wasn't the commercial value of Kewell, it was the way he played the game. Kewell electrifies a stadium better than any

Snowy Mountains hydro scheme ever could. The impact has been the frenzy that his football has generated. For England, Kewell was a message that Australia was a golden development pathway waiting to be exploited. Manchester United, Arsenal, West Ham, Glasgow Rangers and Leeds United are just a few of the clubs that looked to set up relationships and academies over here, to find the next Kewell.

The essence of the Kewell factor lies in this: the rest of the world has known of the quality of the Australian athlete for a long time—the Olympic Games success has had a lot to do with that. What they have been waiting for, however, is that same proficiency to be transmitted into our football. Kewell was a green light for them that this has happened, and the stampede has been on since.

For other players now wanting to go to Britain (and there are many), Kewell's football has smoothed the way for them. It is the influx of British interest here, greater than at any time in our past, and the acceptability of Australians in return, that has been the hallmark of the Kewell effect. It has been quite remarkable.

And, finally, there have been the commercial implications. Harry Kewell is the first Australian football identity to be a serious and consistent commercial property, both here and abroad. Inclusion on the Australian list of "sports rich and famous" had not been achieved by an Australian footballer. It might be a bit tabloid, but Kewell has become "Cool", and so has football, in the chic contemporary marketing stakes. He is part of the continuum of the sport's development, but he has also given that continuum the most significant and dramatic impetus to date.

Not to say that this is a good thing or a bad thing. It just is what it is.

"My parents were good to me, they never pushed me into anything. One time my dad said to me to stop playing football and to play Rugby League, so I did that for a season. I was smart and played fullback."

Kewell was born in Sydney and grew up in Smithfield, in Sydney's south-west. His first club was Smithfield Hotspurs, which played at Brenan Park, just up the road from the Kewell family home. Kewell started when he "was about Under 6s", before inquiring rhetorically, "if they go that young—it's hard to remember".

Like most Australian kids and many of his Socceroo team-mates, he played every sport possible. Anything he could realistically get his hands to, cricket and tennis, whatever was going. "My parents were good to me, they never pushed me into anything. One time my dad said to me to stop playing football and to play Rugby League, so I did that for a season. I was smart and played fullback."

There was always a natural aptitude for sport. "Once you have a natural eye for a ball, you can play any sport. Most footballers have this. I don't really know if I fell in love with football straightaway. It was something my brother did, so I ended up doing it as well. It really got interesting when I ended up making the [NSW] Academy under David Lee. That is when it really stepped up for me, learning the ins and outs of the game. I think that is when I really started falling for it. Before that, I enjoyed it, my mates played it and it was fun, but I wouldn't say I loved it."

Kewell executes technique well, but when he is really on song, he plays the game beautifully, which possibly goes to the spirit of the child in Smithfield. "I think to a certain level, you have to let kids go out and enjoy it. If you put too much pressure on them, they can lose interest early. There's a certain time frame when you can push them along a bit, or not push them, it depends. My dad did the right thing, he never pushed me hard but he gave me the encouragement. But when I did make the Academy, I was over the moon. That's when I got serious about football."

The NSW Academy program, coached by David Lee, was the vehicle that delivered Kewell to a life of football. When Kewell went, via this program, to visit Leeds United for a month, to see what it was like, he had done enough to win an invitation back to Leeds full time to join their academy.

"Homesickness was never a problem. I was lucky in a way because when I first came over, my first couple of weeks, my parents came with me. After that I had to stick it out for a year, and at the end of the season I'd get to go home. I had colleagues who could go home to Ireland or England every week. I think if you are going home to comfortable things, do you go back to training when it's bad? Do you go away from your comforts? I couldn't do that. We had bad times and we had to work through it, and I am grateful because it made me stronger."

Kewell has always bristled the moment the focus ignores the amount of work that goes into getting good at this game. "A lot of people see the great things of sport, the nice houses, the fast cars, the money, the clothes and all that, but if you took them inside and showed them how many hours are put in, and not only the players but those around them, their families etc., and how much time they'd given up. When I was young, I couldn't drive, so my family had to take me. The hours you spend are phenomenal. At the academy, it was at least four hours a day, but it was enjoyable."

It is a lot of work, but Kewell believes that everyone is born with a gift, and "when you find it, you have to finetune it. It's like a rough diamond, you have to chip away and work it until you get it nice and smooth." Of course, this leads one to inquire how far off the sparkling finish is Kewell's diamond. "I don't think you are the complete player until you finish really, because you are always trying to achieve something better. My diamond is only fully smoothed once I have finished, because I can always improve." It will be at the end of the journey, then, that Kewell will assess his diamond and it will be only himself whom he holds to account for the work done.

Football is his measuring stick for professional life. The better you are, the more he respects you. The better he can be, the happier he is. It is this hunger to be good, this devotion to improve, this need to compete with the best that has provided Kewell with the framework to play good football.

Both Leeds United and his nurturing family provided the scaffolding that Kewell needed to fly out of the blocks as a teenager. "I was brought up well by my parents, and I never took anything for granted. When I did move to Leeds, Paul Hart, the youth team coach, was very strict. He taught me a lot about responsibility and respect, particularly of the older pros.

"It may have looked like I burst onto the scene, but a lot went into it. It is a difficult thing because you play one good game and afterwards this is expected of you all the time. There is no let-up, and you get so confident you can do it, you just push on. But I have seen players come, good players, who play maybe three good games and then hit some poor form and have a couple of bad games and then that's it, you don't hear from them anymore. It is difficult, but when you do 'burst' onto the scene, then it's fantastic."

Kewell had made such an impression on the Leeds United club, that a deputation lead by the then chairman Peter Ridsdale, headed to Australia to hold various discussions with at least two NSL teams, with the view to taking control and establishing a production line that was to uncover another one like Harry. Leeds's visit to Australia came at the height of their huge capitalisation, when their ambition was bigger than their capacity. Leeds were spending big on players and looking to invest significantly on projects such as club acquisition in developing markets like Australia, to provide them with a supply line of super young Aussie talent. Kewell's performances contributed to this blood rush.

The stellar period of Kewell's football to date coincided with his entry into parenthood. He describes the birth of his children as "the best times of my life. It was hard, but one of the best things in the world, an unbelievable thing. I remember the first day I held Taylor—I had to play Leicester the next day—I was absolutely buzzing. There was no tiredness, I was just so excited."

And after the excitement, the regularity of parenthood settled in. "You do change your life [for the children] and even though I have always put my family first and football second, when your kids come it changes your ways, only for the better, I think."

This was certainly the view of people close to Kewell who offered, unsolicited, the same appraisal. Harry Kewell may keep his persona well guarded in the public domain and, as far as possible, only allow the footballer to be on public view, but there could be little doubt that the arrival of his children prompted readjustments from even this most focused of athletes.

He prefers a quiet life anyway. His work environment is so electric that he intentionally keeps the private side of his

"Once we get in the door, that's it. I don't like going shopping, there are too many people. I love my home—peaceful, the kids coming in and playing and watching a bit of TV. I love just relaxing at home, doing nothing."

life placid. "That's why I separate them completely. And my wife is in the same kind of business as me, so she kind of has it as well. We both like to step away from that. Once we get in the door, that's it. I don't like going shopping, there are too many people. I love my home—peaceful, the kids coming in and playing and watching a bit of TV. I love just relaxing at home, doing nothing."

"We have neighbours—they're nice but they keep themselves to themselves. I am not overly outgoing, I like to keep to myself. I've always been like that since I was young. When I've got to go out there and do something, I will do it, and smile and enjoy it. Once I am there, I am fine. I go out at times when I know it's not busy. I like golf, you don't get hassled on the course, unless someone sees you. A good hit-out with the lads is fun. And I am surrounded by the same kind of people, who like the same sort of things."

Whilst Kewell revelled in his domestic peace, life at Leeds United was getting less and less peaceful all the time. The club's ambitious plan to be a big player in the big time came at a heavy cost to the club, and the spending had sent the club into huge debt. The financial highrolling was all geared towards permanent Champions League participation. Almost £100 million was allocated to recruit players. After reaching the semifinals of the Champions League in 2001, they failed to even qualify for the competition the following two seasons.

When the team finished fifth in the Premiership in 2002, manager David O'Leary was sacked. There was increasing pressure to off-load players so as to reduce their huge wage bill. Rio Ferdinand moved to Manchester United, which in a defensive sense opened the floodgates. Leeds management was trying to plug multiple, gaping holes in the dam wall with only their fingers. It was all about to come crashing down.

The final ignominy for Leeds, whose financial woes were now daily discussion points, was relegation from the Premier League in May 2004.

Ultimately, Leeds's demise provided the exit for Kewell. Leeds was in free fall but Kewell was moving rapidly in the other direction. With just over a year to go on his contract, Kewell agreed terms with Liverpool. Leeds had little bargaining power. Kewell's interests lay in Premiership football, which Leeds were unable to guarantee, and if Kewell stayed to the end of his contract, Leeds would have received no transfer fee at all.

Kewell became a Liverpool player in July 2003. It was the team he had supported as a boy. But the transfer caused a huge media circus. Leeds complained to the England FA about the nature of the deal, which saw them get a reduced fee from Liverpool. To offer a little perspective, Peter Ridsdale once boldly claimed Harry Kewell to be worth £50 million on the transfer market. Although there was a significant degree of PR bravado in Ridsdale's claims, it provided another pointer as to why English clubs were falling over themselves to find a Harry or two. Actually, more than PR bravado—Ridsdale would also have been talking up his Leeds United stock so as to keep the city bankrolling his dream. Nevertheless, when Kewell moved to Liverpool, Leeds reportedly banked in the vicinity of £3 million.

Claim and counterclaim were made against Kewell's manager about the workings of the deal. Not so much column inches, but column acres, were dedicated to the saga.

This included commentary from Gary Lineker, one of England's highest profile former internationals turned football pundit. Lineker launched an attack in his newspaper column about the transfer. He may be reserved and private, but Kewell is no shrinking violet, and he took Lineker on in the courts, filing a libel case against the former England striker.

The details of the settlement are not public. However, it may be a big call, but taking on Lineker may be akin, in the Australian vernacular, to kicking a koala (Lineker is a respected national figure in the UK). What the episode reveals more is that Harry Kewell has a very keenly defined sense of fair play, of right and wrong. On matters of substance that relate to this, he will defend his ground. About the settlement, Kewell's lawyer was quoted in *The Times* of London, "Harry feels that the judge's summing up of this case vindicates his position and the reasons for bringing this claim".

If Kewell's football life is a dream come true, then signing for the famous "Reds" of Liverpool, one of England's giant clubs and the club he supported as a boy, must have been something else again. This was Kewell's first transfer move, for his entry to the Leeds first team came via the youth system. Back then, there'd been no fanfare, no press conference, no national interest. When he signed for Liverpool, the opposite was true. It set the stage for his time that followed.

"Leeds is a big club but not as massive as Liverpool. When I first signed, I was nervous, the aura about the club. Anfield [Liverpool's stadium] is a great stadium and when the Kop [the

"The first six months at Liverpool I was buzzing. It's a great club, with a great manager, who knows the game inside out. We have won games because of decisions and moves he has made. We can bring back the glory to Liverpool. It's a great challenge and responsibility."

famous Spion Kop end of the ground, a stand named with reference to the second Boer War] sing 'You'll Never Walk Alone', I don't care where you go, you will not beat that, it's fantastic.

"There is always pressure on Liverpool players to perform. To win the title, cups, Champions League, and last year [2005] was a massive boost for the club. But that's the past and that's the part of the pressure of the club—it's never satisfied, the fans are insatiable. But it is pressure that you want. You want to play for something and for people who care."

And when Kewell arrived at Anfield, he took on the number 7 shirt, but he was caught a little short on its significance. "The shirt is a famous one. When I first went to Liverpool I didn't really think about number 7. They asked me what shirt I wanted. I had number 7 when I was younger. It's always been one of my favourites. But I didn't fully realise, and in the press conference it was said to me that all Liverpudlians look at that player and want that player to be the best. It was the shirt of [Kevin] Keegan and [Kenny] Dalgleish. I said, 'That's fine, I can take that responsibility and look forward to it'. I do want pressure, I want that expectation, because it only brings the best out in me.

"The first six months at Liverpool I was buzzing. It's a great club, with a great manager, who knows the game inside out. We have won games because of decisions and moves he has made. We can bring back the glory to Liverpool. It's a great challenge and responsibility."

After Kewell's buoyant start came the injury trouble, which stretched over a fourteen-month period. Even though resigned to the knowledge that "everyone goes through it", there is the realisation that "when you are in the middle of it, you sometimes can't see your way out of it. I'd be on the phone to [Australian team physiotherapist] Les Gellis every day about it. He was a major help. 'Les, it's not working, this isn't right, that's wrong', and then I'd be on the phone to my club doctors having the same conversation. One day it would feel good and I'd be upbeat and then the next day, bang, it's off again. It was the biggest battle I have faced. Football is easy compared with getting over an injury."

Kewell, so used to flying, was feeling decidedly mortal. "It pushed me a long way. Sitting on the end of the bed speaking with Les, just thinking, near enough to tears, because this thing would not go away. We've gone through everything, you're being told, ' You just have to keep working at it', and I'm saying, 'It's just not going to work, am I ever going to play to my capability again?' It was horrible."

Injury teaches people many things. It is lonely—nobody in the world can know what you are feeling, and you look at people walking by in the street, wondering if they realise how lucky they are not to have this pain, this debilitation. For Kewell, though, there was more. "You really learn who your friends are with stuff like this. I am grateful for that. You see other sides to people." The disappointment in Kewell's voice is obvious. He'd been used to people rushing to him when he was flying, but when he was despairing at his physical state, it was almost as though he watched some of those same people retreating at equal speed.

And his frustration with the publicity surrounding his predicament revolved around what he perceived to be ignorance. "Fans come and watch and they have their opinions. The only thing I asked was that the truth be told and if the truth was told, would they still say the same thing? If, with the truth, they say the same thing, fair enough, everyone is allowed their opinion.

"I would do a job for the team, all working in conjunction with the staff and management. But people outside got frustrated because they had seen what I could do previously and suddenly I wasn't doing it anymore. Well, players don't just stop doing their thing without reason. But I have worked hard to get through it. After a few operations and jabs, I have come through the other side, though it requires ongoing management."

This 2005–06 season has seen Kewell getting back into full gear again. Chronic injuries have a treatment and recovery time and then the re-acclimatisation process. It isn't something that can necessarily be rushed, and the length of time is usually a corollary of the depth of the ordeal undergone. But, thankfully, Kewell is back enjoying his football despite, starkly, there being times when he felt like packing it all in. Given everything, there is quite a lot for him to walk away from.

The worst merged with the best for Kewell. His low point was the Champions League final in May 2005. A miraculous night for Liverpool, coming back from 0-3 at half-time to become kings of Europe, but for Kewell, whose contribution only lasted minutes before he limped off, crestfallen and injured, "It was the worst night of my life. I was so proud of my team but personally it was horrible."

In November 2005, six months after the "worst" night of his life, in qualifying for the World Cup, Kewell celebrated probably his "biggest highlight". "To come back from what I had been through and to qualify for the World Cup and play a major part in it—it was nice to celebrate. That was a relief and a big milestone. If ever there was a wall to be knocked down, that was it."

Kewell had not had a lot of football in the lead-up to the Uruguay series. He played the entire first game in Montevideo. For the second, Sydney, game, Kewell started on the bench. Thirty minutes into the game, Guus Hiddink motioned to Kewell that it was time for him to do his stuff.

Only moments later, Kewell was to dart inside the penalty area and, via a subtle interchange with Tim Cahill and Mark Viduka, had the ball sitting at his trusty left foot, with the goal well in sight. The entire stadium, trustful of Kewell's left foot, held its collective breath in anticipation.

Of all the thousands of balls Kewell has hit in the preparation for and maintenance of a professional football career, no amount of practice could have prepared him for the "miskick" that led to Marco Bresciano's goal. According to Kewell, the fact that Uruguay also braced in anticipation was probably the decisive factor in this most crucial of plays.

"It's been mentioned by the lads, they were laughing about the miskick." And Kewell, half defensive tongue-in-cheek and half logical appraisal, hits back. "Full credit to Bresh [Bresciano]. When Dukes [Viduka] laid the ball off to me and I was about to strike it, there were about three or four Uruguayan defenders around me—they all turned their head. Bresh was the only one who didn't, and look what happened. He reacted first and banged the goal in. I am happy to take credit for diverting their attention. I'd have loved to have shot the ball cleanly but the keeper may have saved it. He was ready for me too, he wasn't ready for Bresh.

Everybody's laughing about it, but it happens and what a great result."

Indeed it was a terrific result. Bresciano's goal levelled the scores and ultimately took the game to penalties and Australia through.

"I think Uruguay had the referee and the linesman, but it didn't really matter because we had 83,000 people. I know it's not nice, but it tipped it off when the anthems were played. Over there, they did it to us and Australia has never been like that. I think the whole of Australia came into this game, from whatever sport. When the anthems happened, I was sitting on the bench smiling. For once, Australians cared, I had a smile from ear to ear and I thought, 'It's going to be our night tonight'. The crowd was incredible. You still get goose bumps. But we've just started the journey. All this is nothing compared with what we have to deal with. It's a great time for us to put Australia on the map.

"I expect only good for the World Cup. Every player has got to set out into a competition to win it. If you set out to aim lower, you might as well not participate. We have something really strong here. We all want to work hard for each other. We enjoy coming into camp together, there's a great spirit."

For his part, Kewell is taken aback at the proposition that he has made such a big difference to Australia's football. And football

---

"I am happy to take credit for diverting their attention. I'd have loved to have shot the ball cleanly but the keeper may have saved it. He was ready for me too, he wasn't ready for Bresh. Everybody's laughing about it, but it happens and what a great result."

"When the anthems happened, I was sitting on the bench smiling. For once, Australians cared, I had a smile from ear to ear and I thought, 'It's going to be our night tonight'. The crowd was incredible. You still get goose bumps."

---

provides an appropriate analogy for Australia's path to maturity. The development of football in Australia has been a team game. And "whilst there may be an outstanding player, without the team, that player is nothing". Kewell likes that about football, the team thing.

And he's right, it is a team game. But many teams have a star player.

11

shirt number

"I love the game and what goes with it. Sometimes it's tough, it can be Groundhog Day. You are only in it for a short time but it's a bloody good time. You build relationships with people and there are so many players you've played with, you get back together and you reminisce and have fun."

Stan Lazaridis

Date of birth 16 August 1972

Position played Defender

Current club Birmingham City, England

Witty and jocular, Stan Lazaridis is a raconteur in waiting, whose career catalogue of stories will provide endless hours of entertainment, when the time is right to tell them. He is known to spice things up too, with "a bit of salt and pepper", which will make them all the more engaging.

The spice could have been sprinkled in another direction though, because earlier on, football nearly missed him.

"I had to choose my career path because I was close [to state cricket representation]. I was left arm pace. Going to be the next Bruce Reid. But I didn't love cricket, I loved football."

Linking himself with Bruce Reid is partly a reflection of his jaunty nature and partly a reflection of the reality. The boy could play cricket. With his running style, too, he would have had an approach to the wicket—bounding and rhythmic—sort of like the great West Indian quick, Michael Holding. Watching Holding in motion was like listening to a baroque string quartet. Completely soothing. A far cry from the hell the red ball was about to unleash. Lazaridis would have been like that.

Instead, Lazaridis unleashed himself on football, and fans of the Socceroos are eternally grateful that he did.

In this his fourth World Cup qualifying campaign, and after eleven seasons in England, "nine of which have been in the

Premiership", Lazaridis is revered because he is good at what he does, and he is good at knowing what people want of him. Fortunately for him, what people want is what he enjoys giving—it comes naturally. And over the years he has given it, both for club and country, in bucket-loads.

He first came to prominence nationally when he moved to play for West Adelaide in the National Soccer League. His impact was immediate. His extraordinarily long stride, which propelled him at breakneck speeds down the left flank, was his calling card. His weapon was that he could engage that long stride at a moment's notice. It took him no time at all to do the "0 to 100". Often, players with this style can take a bit of time and room to wind up, but not Lazaridis. A couple of quick steps, and he would be into it. It was all one could do to keep up, let alone try to take the ball from him. And with the ball at his feet, the breeze in his face and armed with the fabulous sensation of the crowd riding him all the way, he'd work his way through the gears, scorch the grass underneath, and deliver a regular supply of quality service to those in the middle, whose job it was to pick the eyes out of the Lazaridis offerings. Sounds simple, but it isn't. Sounds repetitive, but when done with the glide and grace of Stan Lazaridis, it is beautiful.

Amazingly, this entertainment and inspiration has been provided over the years by a West Australian boy who "went to London for a holiday, really". Oh, how from little things, big things can grow.

Lazaridis's parents arrived in Australia from Greece thirty-five years ago "with a suitcase, and tried to make a life for themselves". From the age of six he started chasing a ball around a field with Kingsway Olympic in Perth. This was very much a family affair for Lazaridis when his father took him and his

"I had three years in the NSL and made the play-offs all three years. They were good times, we were getting good crowds, it was really good soccer at the time, really exciting, and there were a lot of good players around."

---

brothers to the club that was also frequented by cousins and other good friends. It was natural to go to a club like this, a Greek community club. "That's how it was in those days, before the reforms came through", remembers Lazaridis.

He played most of his junior football with Kingsway before moving to another, more senior club of the Greek community, Floreat Athena. Intercity and interstate connections between Adelaide and Perth, of the Greek variety, had Lazaridis move to West Adelaide Hellas, then of the NSL.

"Playing first grade State League at sixteen with Floreat was great. It was a tough league. There were a lot of good sides around. It got me going. The next step, though, was the NSL, and at eighteen I moved to Adelaide to play for West Adelaide. That was a real launching pad for me."

The NSL was certainly one launching pad, but it wasn't the only one that gave Lazaridis's career potential a serious case of bloat.

West Adelaide was rebuilding itself for a fresh tilt at NSL glory. It had brought in Argentine Raul Blanco from his Sydney club, Parramatta. Blanco in turn brought in many top players, mainly from the eastern states, to bolster his new club. From Perth, though, he had the "young and really naive" Lazaridis. "Raul Blanco took me in—he was like my dad, really. Some of the lads used to give me stick about it."

Like a Lazaridis foray down the left wing, there is no point beating around the bush about this. “I had three years in the NSL and made the play-offs all three years. They were good times, we were getting good crowds, it was really good soccer at the time, really exciting, and there were a lot of good players around. The NSL was a really tough league. Within the first season I made the Australian team, so much happened so quickly.” A Socceroos call-up in the first season—that is quite a take-off.

Then for launching pad number two. Mission control, get ready for this one.

“There was a big off-season in those days [of the NSL]. We had, like, a couple of months break.” So Lazaridis went home to Perth from Adelaide to be with his family and friends. He was about a month into his break when West Ham United, of England, arrived in Perth for an end-of-season “tour down under”. The tour organisers were planning a game with a West Australia “select” team to play the tourists. Permission was sought from West Adelaide for Lazaridis’s participation and the player himself was asked, subsequently, if he was interested. “To be honest, I wasn’t really fussed. So I said to them, ‘If you can give me fifteen tickets so that I can get fifteen of my mates in to watch the game, then I’ll play’.”

The tickets were no problem.

“I had a really good game that night, funnily enough. They had Frank Lampard Snr, West Ham assistant coach, and Harry Redknapp, West Ham manager, talking to me on the field after the game. ‘How’d you fancy coming to London?’ Lampard was doing all the talking, Harry was in the background.

“It was massive just to be offered the chance to come over and I said to myself, ‘Well, I have never been to London, so the worst-case scenario is, this will be a good holiday. So I took that chance and I came to England for a week to trial."

After the week's trial, Lazaridis also had Sheffield Wednesday on his scent. "Harry [Redknapp] just couldn't wait to sign me and by the end of the week, I was scoring goals. David Pleat was at Sheffield Wednesday and there was a huge opportunity for me to go there. Harry said, 'No, you're not going anywhere', and he locked me up in a hotel room with the late Les Sealy [West Ham number two goalkeeper and goalkeeper coach], who ended up being my minder for that night in the hotel, and early Sunday morning I ended up signing a deal with West Ham.

"It was just so quick. I never really had time to think. It wasn't particularly a great deal, but it was a start, an opportunity. I had no agent; my agent was Les Sealy to be honest. You have to understand, I didn't plan any of this. I never planned or thought of going to England. I thought I may go and play in Greece at some point, because of my Greek background, but to think I was going to play in the Premiership was the furthest thing from my mind. I went over with no real intention that I was going to stay, I was just going to have a holiday and visit Piccadilly Circus and Leicester Square."

Lazaridis signed to stay in England for two years. "It wasn't a great deal, but not a bad one either—it was an opportunity. Les Sealy basically did the deal for me." Through the course of the first

---

"It was massive just to be offered the chance to come over and I said to myself, 'Well, I have never been to London, so the worst-case scenario is, this will be a good holiday. So I took that chance and I came to England for a week to trial."

eighteen months, though, Lazaridis "certainly wised up to the way everything works over here".

Lazaridis turned to Sealy because there was no agent looking after him. Sealy, for his part, was also keeping an eye on the young Australian. "I was young and green." But the need for an agent wasn't even a consideration. "There weren't too many other players overseas at that stage. This thing about agents, it wasn't really something that I could swallow. I was the 'agent', so I'd go to the manager and say, 'Right, I want, say for example, £500 a week to play', and that was done, when I could have got £5000 a week to play. It's laughable but that's what happened in those days. I remember after I signed my first deal in that first year, I didn't know what the rents were like in London or how expensive it was there and I think I lost money in that first year. I'd think to myself, 'What am I doing? I came here to try and make a living and it's ended up costing me money'." Like he said, Lazaridis was certainly wising up to the way things worked over there pretty quickly.

Sealy's passing was difficult for Lazaridis to handle. He had been a real support to the Australian when he arrived. Lazaridis's then girlfriend [now wife] was good friends with Sealy's wife. "It was a difficult period." Sealy died at forty-three years of age, and by all reports was a larger-than-life character who had a tremendous impact on the dressing rooms of which he was part. No wonder he took a shine to Lazaridis—birds of a feather and all that.

When Lazaridis first arrived in London for his trial, England was in summer. "It was surreal really. It felt like I was in Perth", although minus the Fremantle Doctor and the typical Perth heatwaves. "I was really enjoying myself."

He needed to return home to organise his things for his new life in London. "I went back [to London] the second time, and when I landed all I saw was dark grey clouds. And when I got to the airport, there was no-one there to see me. Then one guy turned up and said he was from West Ham United Football Club, and he was an agent and not part of the club anyway. I thought, 'What's going on here?'"

Within a couple of months of his arrival, Lazaridis fractured his leg, "not badly, but it meant that I missed the next four or five months. It was a long time. I turned to my girlfriend [now wife], and said, 'What am I doing here? Why have I left Australia to come here? I've fractured my leg, the climate is horrible, it's raining every day, it's cold.'

"Here was me, young and signed by Harry [Redknapp], at the time [he] paid almost a million dollars for me. I wasn't really taken in and that was hard for me. I expected everyone to change for me and it was me who had to change, to become strong and mentally tough. I am sure every player has this sort of story."

The learning was difficult for Lazaridis, though. The players were making life difficult for him. "It's quite daunting when you go into a squad of players that are British-based. They don't welcome you because you are a foreigner. And a foreigner from Australia—well, we couldn't even kick a ball. They thought we didn't even have running water and got around on kangaroos. We weren't taken seriously."

Lazaridis was motivated to show them the best that he had. "I'm going to get my leg right and when they see me at my best, if that's not good enough, then I'm going home."

Towards the end of that season, Lazaridis had worked his way back to the football pitch. "You have to earn their respect, but I got there. I was playing well, the fans were singing for me and I knew then that I was taken seriously and away I went. I ended up signing a new deal at the end of that first season. I had an agent by then too—you live and learn."

After four successful seasons with West Ham, culminating in the qualification for European club competition, Lazaridis moved to Birmingham City. Birmingham were in the second tier and were looking to get promoted and "I was to be the one to lead them there. Sure enough, it worked out that way."

His move down a competitive level wasn't an easy thing to accept, at first. Ironically, being part of the team that brought European opportunity to West Ham also meant that his place in the squad was going to be put under pressure. "Harry [Redknapp] had gone and brought three or four players in. I think they needed to sell me to bring in a striker or something. Originally, I thought I'd stay and fight, but when I looked at it realistically, there were players ahead of me and Harry just said to me, 'Look, you are going to be second or third in line'. I looked at it and thought, if I went to a club like Birmingham, I was going to be given my chance, I'd play games."

After his first day at Birmingham, Lazaridis thought he had made a huge mistake. It dawned on him, he had moved away from the Premiership, from a club with great players such as "Rio

---

"You have to earn their respect, but I got there. I was playing well, the fans were singing for me and I knew then that I was taken seriously and away I went."

Ferdinand and Paolo Di Canio, Frank Lampard, Joe Cole and Michael Carrick, the list goes on.

"But something was telling me that I had to make that move, a gut feeling. There were opportunities before but I didn't take them. It wasn't like Birmingham was the first club I leapt at. Birmingham felt right."

Their manager, Trevor Francis, was one reason. The club's wealthy owners "were pumping money in, too". Lazaridis had spent time analysing Birmingham's recent four or five years and they had been making progress, moving up from the second division and into the mid-table region of the first division and soon to be challenging for promotion to the Premiership. "I thought, it's only a matter of time, this club is huge. It is just one of those sleeping giants. It's like Collingwood not being in the AFL."

Lazaridis is very thankful he followed his gut instinct. His seven years at Birmingham have been the most enjoyable of his career. "It took us two years to get into the Premiership. We nearly made it the first year but lost on penalties in the semifinals. Then Steve Bruce came in and that was it.

"The people here love me, I have earned that though. I just know what they want when I play. They want to be excited. They want players to take on opponents, whip good balls in. Basically, they want to feel like the money they have paid at the gate, they've had a good time. And they let you know when you are giving that to them because they start singing your name. And when I get the ball, I just hear them and it feels as though I have them on my shoulders and I am running.

"Equally, it can be the other way, where they are against you, but for me, they've never ever been on my back."

It is the nature of the man and the style of his play to which people respond so warmly. Lazaridis says that he has had a very good relationship with both sets of fans—West Ham and Birmingham. When he returned to West Ham with Birmingham, his new team beat his old 2-0. He was substituted in the final minute of the game, "and the whole stadium gave me a standing ovation, and that doesn't really happen at Upton Park [West Ham's ground] too many times for visiting players. That was special, I'll never forget that."

Lazaridis is prepared to suggest that his eleven years, divided by only two clubs, is something respected by the fans. They appreciate the loyalty. In the modern world of professional football, with so much money floating around player transfers, clubs can become, in some instances and with some players, little more than highly lucrative transit lounges. Lazaridis's commitment to his clubs, and their fans, is not lost on the watching, and paying, public. Fans certainly accept that player movements are a huge part of football. But they love it when one of their favourites sticks around.

He is a favourite and he is one of the game's genuine good guys. He regularly "takes in" young Aussie players who hit England with stars in their eyes. He is protective of his compatriots, the young ones who aren't really prepared for the "jungle" that is

---

"That moment [the final whistle] was like a blur. All I can remember is, I am on the ground and there's a policeman standing over me. We were cruising at 2-0 up, smoking cigars and the champagne's popped, and all of a sudden it's 2-2. That's it, mate. You're walking out the stadium with a fridge on your back. It was unbelievable."

London, as Lazaridis puts it. "A lot of players who were coming over—they didn't see out the week. I had about a half to a dozen players who stayed with me, but they didn't last the week. I was just a point of contact really. You try and give the players advice and stuff like that, but ultimately it's down to them, and when it goes out onto the training field, you can't tell them how to kick a ball. You just try to help them weather the storm a bit when they first get here and settle a bit."

The lessons and wisdom of Lazaridis's career are freely offered. They are lessons that have been well learned and that are well communicated. And they come from a player whose place in the Socceroos' pantheon was cemented on that execrable night in November 1997 at the MCG, when Australia failed against Iran in the second-leg qualifier, in the quest for the final available place at the 1998 World Cup.

When the referee, Sandor Puhl of Hungary, blew his whistle to signal the end of that match, Stan Lazaridis collapsed onto the MCG turf. He lay there motionless. His tired limbs were outstretched. His chest heaved with physical exhaustion. His heart, just now broken, beat solemnly. His mind raced through the images of the match just elapsed, and then slowed as the realisation of what it meant sunk in. Then it raced again, and then it slowed. And still he stared with his nothingness, at nothing, with nothing coming back. He was desolation personified.

A police officer, on the ground providing official security, leaned over Lazaridis. "Listen, it's time to go", he said.

"That moment [the final whistle] was like a blur. All I can remember is, I am on the ground and there's a policeman standing over me. We were cruising at 2-0 up, smoking cigars and the champagne's popped, and all of a sudden it's 2-2.

"As an Aussie, you wear your heart on your sleeve and the fans can see that, they appreciate it. What I am telling you, to play for your country is the best feeling that you could ever imagine."

That's it, mate. You're walking out the stadium with a fridge on your back. It was unbelievable. You don't ever plan these things. It just happened, the reaction, the way that game was and the way it finished."

The way it was—a completely dominant display from an Australian team playing beautifully and absolutely battering their Iran opponents. Lazaridis was a principle source of Iran's torment.

The way it finished—Australia was leading 2-0 and was cruising. The score, to that point, could have been anything, such was Australia's superiority. From 2-0 up with a quarter hour or so to go, things began to go haywire. Ultimately, Australia conceded its lead and the game finished 2-2. The first game in Iran had finished 1-1. The aggregates were level and Iran progressed to the finals because they scored more goals away from home, aka "the away-goals rule".

This was a qualification lost from an unlosable position. Australia failed to qualify without losing a single match in the entire qualifying process. Iran was only the fifth best team in Asia. This was a really hard one to take. It was perhaps the most painful of all Australia's failures. Johnny Warren, in his post-match television commentary, cried.

Lazaridis was already popular because of his lion-hearted Socceroo performances. It is a fan–player relationship that has developed over many years. There have been no acts of contrivance, merely Lazaridis being himself, and the people loving it. But the MCG moment seemed to embed him deeper into the hearts of the Socceroos' faithful.

"Basically, I think from there [the MCG episode] the people realise that I love playing for my country. I play with my heart as opposed to playing with my head. As an Aussie, you wear your heart on your sleeve and the fans can see that, they appreciate it. What I am telling you, to play for your country is the best feeling that you could ever imagine.

"That's why I always make myself available for any senior game that Australia ever played. Still to this day, it's meant so much to me to get to a World Cup, but also to play in one. Four campaigns later, fifteen or sixteen years of hard work, and I want to be there. At the same time, I don't just want to be there through loyalty or because I earned it on years. I want to be there on merit and I want to play on the first eleven, mate, [firing up] because I am good enough to play—that's how I view it."

Lazaridis revealed that if qualification had come last time round, he might well have not gone for it this time, vacating his place for a younger player, "give someone else a shot". But the failures have just spurred him on. He doesn't want to have any regrets, about his life or about this game. Lazaridis, however, having missed selection in the starting line-up for the qualifying matches against Uruguay, realises he has a job on his hands to force his way back in. He respects that and is winding up for a concerted effort to win back a starting berth.

"The competition between the lads in the squad is fierce, but at the same time there is so much encouragement for whatever that first eleven is when it goes on the park to do battle. In my case, I'm up against Scotty Chipperfield, but I'm Scotty Chipperfield's best fan if he gets the shirt, and he has it at the moment. Of course I want him to do well, knowing that we are all going to do well ultimately, and the whole country is going to do well and football in Australia is going to do well. It is like that throughout the whole team and [with] every single player.

"That is why we tend to do well as Australians. We have that bonding, not the individuality that other countries have. Brazil show a similar thing, they play for each other as opposed to playing as individuals. To help the guy next to you. That happens off the field and you take it on the field too with you, it can be the difference sometimes.

"We are going to be noticed [in Germany] for the right reasons and from a personal point of view, I am looking to be a part of it. I'm not going there to make up the numbers or sit in the grandstand—that's not me. I'm going there to let Scott Chipperfield know that he's got to earn that shirt." If Chipperfield does, it would be fair to expect that the person wishing him more best wishes than anyone else, (apart from immediate family of course) will be Stan Lazaridis.

Lazaridis also has a fish-eye lens on what qualification has achieved. "It united everyone, I think. I think we have to pay credit to the likes of Frank Lowy. To come in at a time when it was down. We've had all sorts of people come in and out, the game in debt, the NSL struggling and then picking itself up and then struggling again. They've come in and revamped the whole thing from A to Z, and professionally, and it's all credit to them. He and John O'Neill have said, 'We'll honour what we say', and they have done that. In the past that had never happened.

"As a team, I think we are going to be a surprise package [at the World Cup]. Guus Hiddink knows our strength, and it is

"We are going to be noticed [in Germany] for the right reasons and from a personal point of view, I am looking to be a part of it. I'm not going there to make up the numbers or sit in the grandstand—that's not me."

---

organisation, and he's going to get us organised. He's proved that already against Uruguay and he will do that again. I think we'll go through as the second team. After that, I don't know. The euphoria in Australia is going to be incredible. I'm going to be calling Australia to find out what is happening back there. I think it's going to be buzzing."

As the European chapters of his career approach a conclusion, Lazaridis has his eyes fixed very firmly on Australia, and the new order of things is just making it even more appealing. "The game is unified now, the way everything is done. The people that you see at the game, no minorities, good for kids, there's not a problem. It's certainly heading in the right direction.

"I'd like to play in Australia for a year, depending on how the body is feeling. To put something back in and to let people back home see me playing again. My family, my dad, who watched me in every game [when I was young], but he's only come over here a couple of times because he doesn't like travelling. But he loves watching me play and my friends etc. I want to do it for the game itself and I hope other players do the same as well."

This will all come on the back of a fabulous career in England, a country to which Lazaridis acknowledges his debt. "I've got so much to thank this country for. We've settled here and we love it here, but home is home and we'll be coming home shortly. Your career is your football and it's provided a huge foundation for my family and for me personally. One of my kids was born in Birmingham and the other, although born in Australia, is raised in Birmingham. There were a lot of ups and downs along the way. Mentally, I am tough, strong, you have to take your knocks. I always believed I was good enough. When I first came here with my wife, we were just boyfriend and girlfriend at the time. She was very close to her family. She had to make the choice to stay in Australia or come on the journey with me, and we didn't know how long it was going to be or where it would go, so we took a chance. We had some homesickness. Christmas and New Year's Eve would come along and Sydney Harbour is all lights and fireworks, but you tough it out. It can't all be rosy, and there have to be sacrifices made along the way.

"It's a big stage over here. It's a life-changing thing. I love the game and what goes with it. Sometimes it's tough; it can be Groundhog Day. You are only in it for a short time but it's a bloody good time. You build relationships with people and there are so many players you've played with, you get back together and you reminisce and have fun.

"A lot of people who know me, they always say, 'Laza, whatever happens, you've always been who you are, you've never changed, you've just been a nice guy and very giving', and my mates love me for that. My close mates and family, the people who mean a lot to me, that gives me a smile on my face.

"I have played against the best in the world—Ronaldo, Rivaldo, Romario, Ronaldinho, Zidane, Brazil, France, AC Milan, Manchester United—it goes on and on. When you are walking out at [Arsenal's ground] Highbury and you are in the tunnel and there's [Dutch superstar] Dennis Bergkamp and [France's] Thierry Henry, you don't think of them as 'those' players, it's just another game that you play. It only hits you when you're back home lounging with your family and you start talking about it. You have to do a double take.

"I was once back home in Perth having a beer with my mates, and one asked me, 'What's Ruud Gullit [Dutch football legend] like?' and I said, 'He's a bloody good player', and he goes, 'I can't believe you played against him', and I said, 'Yeah, I can't believe it either'.

"Ruud Gullit was my debut. I arrived in England on the Sunday, played Monday night live on television all over England, up against Chelsea and Ruud Gullit. I couldn't believe it. I've left Perth, where the day before I was having a beer with a mate on Scarborough Beach, and the next day I'm at Upton Park against Ruud Gullit—who got man of the match that day, mind you."

All this, and more, out of a free trip to see Piccadilly Circus and Leicester Square. There are holidays, and then there are the Lazaridis holidays, the slide night for which will simply blow you away. It's one not to be missed.

12

shirt number

"I used to drive the bus from Stanwell Park into Wollongong every day. I enjoyed that job, it was a beautiful drive down the coast road from Stanwell Park. I'd meet a lot of people and a lot of them were Wollongong fans and they would want to talk about soccer on the bus. I worked there right up until I came to Europe."

Scott Chipperfield

Date of birth 30 December 1979

Position played Midfielder

Current club FC Basel, Switzerland

There are, it seems, two ways to make it to the top in football. The first, more conventional, way is to fall in love with the game, or at least the thought of being a professional, play and practise it every waking moment to the point of obsession, and dedicate yourself to improvement and progress.

There is an enormous amount to be said for this approach. It reduces the margin for error, and maximises the potential to rise high above the chasing pack and into the hearts and minds of football fans and corporate backers worldwide.

Alternatively, you can drive a bus down the Illawarra escarpment as a day job, and play football with your mates and enjoy a few beers with them in your spare time. There is a much higher risk that this approach won't morph into a career in Europe or with the national team, but it works nonetheless, or appears to have. It is called the Chipperfield Method.

Wollongong and the Illawarra have been famous breeding grounds for football in Australia. Some of Australia's oldest football clubs were spawned from the migrant populations that worked in the coalmines, steelworks and associated service industries. The appreciation of football in the Illawarra is as deep as its history is long. It was into this culture that Scott Chipperfield was born and raised.

He first became involved because two of his uncles and an auntie played football. His mum, too. His earliest football memories are of watching them play, and when he turned four, he started himself with the Bellambi Soccer Club, otherwise known as the Bellambi Rosellas. "They were a good team in the '60s and '70s. There's a bit of tradition in the club. There were a lot of mines in the area. A mine just up the road from Bellambi. Blokes would work down the mines and play for Bellambi on the weekends. There's a lot of tradition there."

But appreciation of his area's history arrived a bit later for Chipperfield. For him, as a youngster, football was just something he "played with his mates, never really took it seriously back then. Just happy to play and have a kick around."

"I played at Bellambi until the Under 14s but had to leave because there weren't enough players for an Under 15s team. I went to the next local club, the Corrimal Rangers, which also has a big history—Bobby Bignell played for them." For the record, Bob Bignell is one of football's more celebrated names. A product of the Illawarra and one of its favourite sons, he was the captain of the Australian football team at the 1956 Melbourne Olympic Games. Bobby Bignell is in Australian football's official Hall of Fame.

After a few seasons in the junior representative teams, Chipperfield moved back to the local Wollongong league. "When I was nineteen, I was still playing local league with Fern Hill. At that point, even the [NSL team] Wollongong Wolves were a long way off my thinking. But when I turned twenty, Glenn Fontana [a former player in the Wollongong, and now a development coach] approached me about playing for his then team, Illawarra Lions, in the NSW State League. I had developed a bit of a reputation in the local league. When Glenn approached me, I was a bit wary because his club didn't have a great reputation. They'd had a bit of trouble in the past. I decided to go and I went, okay, so Glenn started pushing me onto the Wolves.

“I was faced with the choice to continue playing local league for the rest of my life or try to make things happen. I had one season with the Lions and then went to the Wollongong Wolves when Nick Theodorakopoulos became coach. That was about 1996.

“There was money trouble at the Lions, they weren’t paying people, so by the end of the season I, like many players, was free to go. Glenn Fontana scouted me and then eased my way to the Wolves, he was a big support.

“I was no big deal when I went to the Wolves. I was just making up the numbers, I think. The first couple of years were difficult there. The very first year, we started well. I played a few games and got myself into the first team set-up. We had a game against Sydney United. We were running second and they were first. About 11,000 people turned up at Brandon Park, but we lost 0-4 or something pretty heavy, went downhill from there and ended up missing the play-offs.

“The next year we ran second- or third-last. But the following year we made the play-offs and lost to Marconi in the semifinal. I reckon we should have won that one.

“The last two years at Wollongong, we exploded.” Wollongong played in consecutive grand finals, winning both of them. The first in particular, against Perth at Subiaco Oval was in front of a 43,000 sell-out crowd. It was a red-letter day for football in Australia. Wollongong, playing away from home and against a vociferous, partisan and massed crowd, came back from a 0-3 half-time scoreline to level the scores at 3-3 and then win the championship on a penalty shoot-out. It was an incredible day for football. Even the much maligned NSL dished one up that day. Chipperfield played and scored, too.

"We had a good team that had been together for a few years, and then picked up Stuart Young from Singapore and David Cervinski, who came in and tightened up the defence. We had a lot of speed and attacked well.

"When I broke into the Wolves, I never had ambitions of Australia, never thought about it. Most people [who play for Australia] come through academies and youth set-ups. I had one good season at the Wolves and got called up for the Confederations Cup in Brisbane in 1998. It was an Aussie-based team. It was totally unexpected. That gave me a bit of ambition, but we lost to New Zealand, which was a disaster. I didn't see myself as a national team player, even then. I was very happy to play and very proud, but it was a locally based team and the guys were all overseas."

Chipperfield had another Confederations Cup disaster against New Zealand as one of the only overseas-based players who came back to play in 2002. Australia's loss to New Zealand immediately sent Australia into a tailspin. It would turn out to be a major catalyst for the restructuring that football has undergone in the past couple of years. It came close on the heels of the defeat to Uruguay in the World Cup qualifiers in November 2001. Soccer Australia, the governing body at the time was in a vegetative state commercially. Its big, and only, play was to qualify for FIFA tournaments and receive the accompanying fees.

Already strapped for cash, these failures put the entire structure under the microscope. This loss to New Zealand was also neatly juxtaposed with the 2002 World Cup from Korea and Japan, which was a massive event, even for Australia. In fact, there is a strong line of persuasive thought that suggests that the enormity of the impact of the 2002 World Cup tournament

"When I broke into the Wolves, I never had ambitions of Australia, never thought about it. Most people [who play for Australia] come through academies and youth set-ups."

locally, without Australia's team even being present, caused senior people within Australia's corporate and government hierarchies to ask, 'What the hell is going on here?' The chairman of Soccer Australia at the time, Ian Knopp, was also a man with political connections and it was he who, creditably, flew the white flag for football's sake by inviting the federal government's review into football's governance and structure. Something needed to be done. The failure in 2002 to beat New Zealand was, it could be argued, a blessing in disguise. There was no money to even paper over the cracks any longer. It set the wheels for reform in motion.

If football's fortunes were plummeting, Chipperfield had found himself a thermal current that was taking him upwards through the atmosphere.

For both years of Wollongong's title success, Chipperfield won the Warren Medal for being voted, by his fellow players, as the NSL Player of the Year. "It was a great honour, to be recognised by the players like that. It gave me great confidence, too. Two years in a row was unbelievable."

In 2001 Chipperfield would have a happier time of it with the Confederations Cup. "I played for Australia against Brazil in the third place play-off [which Australia won 1-0] in Korea–Japan. There was a bit of interest from the coach of Basel, Christian Gross, who was in Brazil at the time watching the game on television. They put an offer for me to go to Switzerland.

“There was also an offer to go to Lorient in France, but only with a one-year offer with an option for a second year. Basel offered four years. I went with the safety.

“It was a big change from Wollongong, which I never thought I’d leave. I’ve always been happy there with friends and family. We’d have a few beers and go out, or go to the track and have a few bets. Coming to Switzerland was a bit of a change.”

You could say that. More of Chipperfield’s characteristic “economical analysis” in evidence. The city of Basel dates back to the Roman Empire. It is a cathedral city, situated on the banks of the Rhine River. Its river position has always made it an important trade centre. Basel is also reputed to be one of the most important cultural centres in Europe. Renaissance, medieval and modern architecture abound. There are forty museums packed into a forty square kilometre area, and it boasts Europe’s oldest art museum ... But Basel hasn’t got sweeping views from the Bulli Pass Scenic Reserve down the escarpment to the ’Gong! You couldn’t get that piece of art into any museum.

“The first season I was really homesick. Those first six months were really tough. I went back home for Christmas [to Wollongong] and when it was time to go back to Switzerland, I was nearly in tears going back to the airport. I didn’t want to go back.

“It was snowing and freezing and minus ten degrees. I went with my girlfriend at the time, from Wollongong. It was difficult for her because she couldn’t get a work permit. It was a tough year for her. After a year she went back to Wollongong. We’ve moved on now, it was a difficult time but we’ve moved on now.

“I wasn’t enjoying it much, but as time passes, you settle. Fortunately enough, we won the League that year and qualified for Champions League for the following season. Your thoughts [and preoccupations] change a lot when you start playing against good teams like Liverpool, Manchester United and teams like that, so it was a great experience."

Chipperfield now says that he is comfortable living in Basel—"it's a beautiful city, a German city". Although after spending the last five seasons there, he isn't yet speaking German.

"The standard is not a big step up from the NSL. Training was the most different. Here it is twice a day for four days a week and once a day on the others and then games on the weekend and recovery after games, everything. I was very tired the first few months because I wasn't used to it. That took about four or five months. The travelling and hotels before every game too, even for games in Basel, took a lot of getting used to. Once you do, though, you don't mind it."

Chipperfield's performances for Basel have attracted regular interest from other European clubs, including Bielefeld and Monchengladbach in Germany and Millwall and Charlton in England. Crystal Palace was the closest he came to leaving, last season, when they were in the Premier League. But Chipperfield is happy where he is. "Basel is a good club. When clubs have come in for me and they [Basel] have rejected offers from clubs, they have adjusted my contract instead. They are good fans. I get good money here. We play in Europe every year. One of the

---

"It was a big change from Wollongong, which I never thought I'd leave. I've always been happy there with friends and family. We'd have a few beers and go out, or go to the track and have a few bets. Coming to Switzerland was a bit of a change."

reasons I have stayed here is because I play. The coach is a big fan and has been very supportive. Only one or two games I have been on the bench in five years. That is important for me.

"My wife is from Basel and we are happy. Her family is here and they look after our baby if we go out somewhere. I am happy off the field as well. I enjoy the life here—it's nice, nice coffee, and ski fields are only an hour away. We have a little apartment in the mountains and we go there to relax a bit. I am learning snowboarding, but I have to take that easy."

Not that his current comforts indicate a long-term life in Basel. "I think I am winning the argument at the moment about where to live. My wife likes Wollongong. She likes the beach and the sun. She has met my friends and is happy there and is looking forward to living there. She fancies the Gold Coast, and Perth too. My contract finishes in 2008. Maybe we'll come home then to the A-League or the local league in Wollongong again. I'll be thirty-two then."

Those next two years sound like they will see Chipperfield done. He has horses and dogs in Australia, of the racing kind, that he is "missing, and I want to watch them race". That will take his European adventure to seven years "and that's a long time. I am looking forward to going back to Australia to live."

Chipperfield is genuinely perplexed as to how this has all come about, or at least genuinely humbled by the whole thing. One would suggest the latter is closer to the truth. "I am not one of the greatest players. I have just been lucky. We had a great team at Wollongong and it suited my style." Indeed, this Wollongong team was one out of the box. Chipperfield benefited from it, true enough, but he was a big reason why it was so potent. There was hardly an opposition team in the league that could contain the

"My wife is from Basel and we are happy. Her family is here and they look after our baby if we go out somewhere. I am happy off the field as well. I enjoy the life here—it's nice, nice coffee and ski fields are only an hour away."

Wolves in those days, with Chipperfield in open field absolutely devastating. The only pity was that more Wollongong people didn't savour this and Chipperfield whilst they had the chance, because it was a special team.

Chipperfield made his own luck. It was his prowess that won him a Socceroo shirt, and it was his performances in that shirt that attracted Europe. The luck thing, well, everyone uses at least an ounce of that every now and then, but it isn't fuel that will last for ever. It wasn't luck then that got him to Basel and once there he has thrived. "Basel is a big club, I have learned a lot, and playing against top teams improves your game.

"But at nineteen I wasn't setting the world on fire. I finished school to Year Twelve and sat around for four or five months doing nothing. My dad was a mechanic and he spoke to his boss and I got a job there. I was like his apprentice and then qualified as a mechanic. After a couple of years, I got a licence to drive the buses.

"I used to drive the bus from Stanwell Park into Wollongong every day. I enjoyed that job. It was a beautiful drive down the coast road from Stanwell Park. I'd meet a lot of people and a lot of them were Wollongong fans and they would want to talk about soccer on the bus. I worked there right up until I came to Europe. I am thinking about going back to it. I certainly wouldn't mind. It was pretty relaxing and you meet a lot of people."

"Going into the Uruguay game was the most pressure I have felt—there was a lot at stake. All of Australia watching. The biggest thing I was worried about was if I made a mistake. And they'd score or something. I didn't want to have a shocker that I'd have to live with for the rest of my life."

Even to have come this far, from schooners of VB at Fern Hill to Lindt chocolate and Champions League in Basel, is remarkable. One almost has to shake one's head and clear some space, because the fact that Chipperfield is now one of those "overseas guys" bashing down the door for a place in the World Cup squad almost requires a double take. But not only in line for the squad—because on most recent evidence, he is a starting eleven player. Blow the froth off that one.

For Chipperfield, "the biggest change was making the Confederations Cup last year". And here we go with the Confederations Cup again. If he wasn't playing the role of Jonah—part of Australia's repeated doom against New Zealand—he was either winning himself a contract in Europe or branding himself in the eyes of the national coaching staff as a serious contender for a Socceroos position. If ever there was a love–hate relationship between a player and a tournament, this would have to be it.

"I was fortunate for that tournament [2005 Confederations Cup]. Stan [Lazaridis] was injured and I was able to get a start. I had a good game in the warm-up match versus New Zealand, and at the Confeds Cup I went well. Now I have been in the starting line up under Guus [Hiddink]. It has been an incredible twelve months."

That included of course the Uruguay matches of November 2005. "Going into the Uruguay game was the most pressure I have felt—there was a lot at stake. All of Australia watching. The biggest thing I was worried about was if I made a mistake. And they'd score or something. I didn't want to have a shocker that I'd have to live with for the rest of my life."

This provides interesting context to that first game, in which the team did so very well, and the 0-1 score that they brought back to Sydney was eminently assailable. But given Scott Chipperfield's "concerns" pre-match, it is ironic that the Uruguay goal came from a free kick conceded by Chipperfield. Actually, most people who watched the game are of the opinion that Chipperfield should have received the free kick. But the referee, in his infinite wisdom, supported by his assistant referee (linesman) who seemed to be having enormous difficulty even holding his flag at the time, gave the free kick to Uruguay.

Nevertheless, the free kick was taken and Uruguay scored. "I was disappointed. It should have been my free kick. It took me a few minutes to recover after that. I was shaking a bit. It took me a little while to get back into the game, but I got a few touches, good ones, and I was right after that.

"For the second game, we were all pretty confident. The flight back was good and we felt fresh. We thought they'd be suffering a bit. The crowd was great.

"When we did the warm-up they had on the big screen a tribute to Johnny Warren. That was pretty emotional. Most of the players were watching that and a lot of the players were a lot more pumped up after watching it. It was fairly emotional after everything that he has done for the sport."

"When we did the warm-up, they had on the big screen a tribute to Johnny Warren. That was pretty emotional. Most of the players were watching that and a lot of the players were a lot more pumped up after watching it. It was fairly emotional after everything that he has done for the sport."

Not even Johnny Warren could have scripted penalties for this one. Or, on second consideration, this whole adventure has been so incredible that there was very possibly non-material energies taking control. What we know to be true is that the penalty shoot-out brought incredible drama to the climax of the battle.

"I was number ten in the queue. Arnie [Graham Arnold] said to me, 'Do you want number six' and I said ,'Nah nah nah, I'm not confident at all'. So Arnie says, 'Okay, you're number ten then'. That was the most nervous I have ever felt. I don't know if I could have kicked the ball far enough if it got to me. I couldn't feel my legs after the game. They were numb. I do not know how I would have kicked that ball if I'd had to take one. I took three practice penalties the day before and I missed two of them. Not for the World Cup. Na-ah. Just glad Johnny [Aloisi] stepped up and put it away. It was a big relief.

"It was a massive reaction too. My club gave me five days off, so I stayed until the Tuesday of the next week. In Wollongong everyone was talking about it. The publicity was amazing and the interest incredible. I didn't think it would be that big. People out partying and dancing. I didn't really associate it with any sport in Australia, there was so much media."

Chipperfield's job is to get himself ready for the World Cup. He spent two weeks in hospital with bruised kidneys when the Swiss League resumed after the most recent winter break. That was after falling on a frozen ground. He has had his time off and now aims to be fresh for the tournament in June-July.

Not much has changed for Chipperfield, despite the amazing time he has had. He likes to have a punt at the track and catch up with his mates in Wollongong for a beer or two. "I have mates from when I was four or five years old who I have grown up with and they are still my best mates. That's important to me."

One kind of expects he would say that.

"I try to enjoy the game still, go out and have a kick"—against Manchester United, of course, what else, a kick and giggle. "If we lose, I'm not going to go around sulking for a week. Life goes on. I try to enjoy it as much as I can."

It is a very fresh perspective.

And when it finishes for Chipperfield, the boomerang will have him return from whence he came. He has more than a heart for Wollongong. It is in his blood. He wants to develop football there and, heaven help us, start an academy. One wonders if the academy will employ the Chipperfield Method, where the prerequisite for study is bare-boned down-to-earthness, and graduates receive a PhD in understatement.

Or if it isn't the academy, keep your eyes out for the Stanwell Park to Wollongong bus. If you see a Swiss cowbell swinging from the rear-view mirror, you'll know things are really back the way they were.

13

shirt number

"I love this job. I love this sport. I love everything about it. It was a dream to do it, and I never take it for granted, never. I train when I have to train, and rest when I have to rest. I am not a priest and enjoy myself when there is something to be enjoyed, but never take it for granted."

Vince Grella

Date of birth 5 October 1979

Position played Midfielder

Current club Parma, Italy

If ever you are to meet someone who is just so hopelessly besotted with what they are doing with their lives, Vince Grella is that person.

"I haven't thought about it too much, not playing football. I love this job. I love this sport. I love everything about it. It was a dream to do it, and I never take it for granted, never. I train when I have to train, and rest when I have to rest. I am not a priest and enjoy myself when there is something to be enjoyed, but never take it for granted.

"The margins at the top are too tight. I know my limits, and for me to stay where I am playing, I have to train seriously. Italy, the first two and a half years was a shock to the system. You never play if you don't have enthusiasm and spirit. To hold down a spot in Italy, at twenty or twenty-one years old—you are holding out experienced campaigners—it's tough. And the position I play, I can't just get the ball and dribble two or three players. I can't razzle. For me, it's about getting continually involved in the game, so if you are not razzling how do you continue to be involved? People have to hear you, see you, feel you, and they are not going to do that if you are out of the game."

We are hearing and seeing you Vince, but …

"That's why I stuck out the first two and a bit years there. They were very hard, the fact of playing against Juventus etc, that can sometimes give people the wrong idea, because they think you go there and play Juve and you are a superstar."

So, Juven ...

"Because when you do well against Juventus, they expect you to do it all the time and you don't have the experience or the personality to do it all the time. The only way to build it is every day, working and understanding your position. Sometimes I don't even think people understand their position, and if you learn how to play your position properly, then it gives you a big advantage in the future—like every week you are going up against the old wolf that's ready to teach you a lesson."

Sounds as though it has been quite ...

"I have been lucky to have good coaches in Italy. Sometimes they overdo the tactics, but for us, coming from Australia, we grow up with a different mentality, so that stuff was good. Maybe in Italy it is too much. They can sometimes suffocate a player with all the tactical crap, but for someone who doesn't know enough, it's good. They help you read the game better and get into the best positions. It's about positioning and timing. For midfielders and defenders, they are brilliant. In Italy they are brilliant with defenders—they are the best. But sometimes they suffocate quality players with these tactical cages.

"Now, sorry, what was your question?"

It hadn't yet been asked!

Suffocated, Grella certainly isn't. Well, tactically he may feel constrained, although it seems as though he is loving the football education he is receiving. But suffocated by Italy?

Not on your nelly. Football, Italy, achieving, striving, competing, all of it, the love for it, oozes out of Grella, from the top of his blonded head to the tip of his right toe, which does its share of letting opponents know he is around, or in Grella-speak, "feel him".

Grella's football started at Springvale City, in the southern part of Melbourne, "out Dandenong way, where I grew up".

From the age of "about ten or eleven", he was always in the Victorian state team. He had two years with Ernie Merrick at the VIS (Victorian Institute of Sport) from fourteen, and two years at the AIS. "That period from fourteen to seventeen was very important for me. It gave me a great grounding, good information. It's hard to drum into players at that age what it's all about for a player." Some of it must have permeated.

"But when a player gets to twenty-one or so, it is time—there are no more excuses. If you don't learn the lessons, you are going to start sliding away, the years pass. Then what? The information the AIS was giving was great. There was no pressure there, but not enough of the people listen to the lessons. Many players slip away, but what they were saying was right. What I learned from them is still true, even though I have learned more since Italy, but it was a great grounding."

Grella is a great learner of football, a great student of professionalism. He wasn't much of a student, in the normal sense, though.

"Australian people would have no idea about my life now. And back then, a lot of people close to me had always heard and known about my dream of becoming a footballer. When I was a kid, they wouldn't take me for crazy, but nearly. They'd say, 'You are a nice boy, it's better that you go to school', and I'd say, 'I'm not going to school, I am going to training'. I used to catch the bus to school, about thirty-five minutes, and a train into the city after school, into Richmond. I'd get changed in the toilets, school clothes off and VIS tracksuit on, and get a tram out to Burnley. Then on the way home Ernie Merrick used to drive me halfway home and we'd meet my mum. I used to leave home at about seven in the morning and get home about eight o'clock at night. And then do homework? No chance.

"I had every excuse under the sun. I used to leave my books purposely on the tram. I lost everything except my training gear!

"Late letters for school, I had them all. My mum was probably the best, and dad, I don't know if it was a gut feeling, but they never really put a lot of pressure on my schooling, whereas my brothers and my sister, my parents were really on their back. We went to private school, St Bedes, so they had to pay. A big school and the demands were high. But they never said much about me. Even when I went to the AIS, Steve O'Connor [Head Coach] used to nail me because I became his responsibility. I wasn't doing my school work so he spoke to my mum, 'Vince isn't turning up for school, blah blah'. He used to sit us all down and say, 'Lads, you know that out of this AIS team, three of you players will make it—do you want to be one of them?' 'That's a bit harsh, Rocks, we're all pretty good, mate', I remember thinking. We were pretty cocky. But he was right."

To be a footballer has always been an obsession for Grella. "Those crowds, the big players, the game itself, it is hard to explain really, the atmosphere and the feeling when you step onto the pitch, that opponent you have to beat, playing against the best and winning."

Football was always a family thing for Grella. His father "loved it" and his brothers played. They used to "eat, live and breathe soccer. It would be dinner table conversation. We'd play in the backyard. I'd play at home by myself. I always stayed late after training—I could never get enough. I was like a kid in a candy shop with football, and I can't really believe it is happening, but it really is."

Both Grella's parents are migrants. "Mum came over when she was eight and basically grew up with the Australian schooling system. She has all the Australian traditions. She speaks and writes closer to Australian than Italian."

His father was twenty when he arrived in Australia from Naples. "That bit older, with stronger Italian traditions.

"My background was a wog upbringing, which surprisingly didn't prepare me that well for Italy. My Italy from Australia was a big difference from when I moved to Empoli, which is in Tuscany. They are very classy people. My wife is from there. They dress well, they look after themselves, their hair is always perfect."

Grella wasn't really into that sort of thing. At Empoli the guys used to look at his jeans, with Grella feeling the stares and the insinuated questions, "'Where did you get those, Springvale? Don't you have jeans in Australia?' At the start it was a pain in the arse, but I like all that stuff, the style, the class, the way they move.

"Those crowds, the big players, the game itself, it is hard to explain really, the atmosphere and the feeling when you step onto the pitch, that opponent you have to beat, playing against the best and winning."

Half the time, they play it big. But I had nothing like that at home. My parents came from the south of Italy. It's a lot harder to get by there and that's why they came to Australia. If they were doing well there, they'd never have moved to Australia."

Grella came to Empoli via Carlton in the NSL. Before Carlton, Grella's AIS graduation took him to Canberra Cosmos. Grella was in the squad for the Sydney 2000 Olympics and as part of the warm-up for that, the team had a three-game series against Brazil's Olympic team in Sydney, Adelaide and Perth. He sent a video of the series to Empoli, and it served to secure him a week's trial. Empoli agreed to take him on loan for a year from Carlton, and agreed a fee with his Australian club to keep him at the end of the year if they chose. Before that season ended though, in the January transfer window, Empoli finalised the deal, fearful that if he did well in that next six months, someone else would snap him up.

When most people think of Tuscany, they think of romance, summer holidays, villas, food, wine, life's finer things. For Grella, Tuscany was his Italian launching pad to a dream realised.

"The football was immensely difficult early. It was difficult to keep up the training standard. There was so much physical work. It wasn't the stereotype that I had of Italy. A lot of running and gym sessions. And when a young kid comes in, every time you make a mistake it is made out to be a major stuff-up. That is the start of personality development, or at least that is where it has to come in. Do you get on with it and push yourself, or do you become the victim because they are picking on you? If you feel like that, you are better off packing your bags and going home because they will eat you for breakfast. As soon as they see you drop your head a little bit, you're gone. So you have to just get on with it. And all the while you have to coach yourself too, because it's not like when you first get there they really help you that much. You are on your own. They chuck you out there and see what you are made of."

It was three or four months before Grella started coming to grips with his "dreamlike" surroundings. "I was watching them like a hawk from the start, putting the picture together, looking at the tricks of the trade."

Grella ground away for a year and a half before being "sent away" to a lower league team—Ternana—in the second division, near Perugia. This was Grella's worst time in his journey so far. It wasn't at all to do with being loaned to a second division club, because that is quite a normal thing for a club to do, to get more games in senior football for younger players who are not quite ready for the top team in the top league yet. "At Ternana, we had a team that was built to win the second division. I left Italy for the 2000 Olympic Games and when I got back, the team was in second place on the table. I hadn't had a good Olympics. I wasn't in great condition when I went there—it was a disaster in fact. When I got back to Ternana, I found myself not even getting changed with the first team. It was like I didn't exist. I had to start all over again. I was right out of the twenty-man squad. I had five midfielders before me in the pecking order. I wondered where the hell I was going to go and what I was going to do.

"I was struggling. There was no light at the end of the tunnel, nothing. We used to play eleven against eleven at training and I was still on the bench. They tested me alright. Those three months of torment will probably cost me two years at the other end of my career, from the stress. I live football and take it to heart—I was suffering. But hanging on paid off, and the ball always bounces to those who do something extra. The more I go through my career, the more I see that pattern."

"I got it into my head that this could be my last three months. So I just knuckled down to the point that every single day at training was like a cup final for me. I was chasing people everywhere. Doing whatever I could to 'be seen, heard, felt'."

Ternana, already in the second division, forced Grella to crystallise his thinking on exactly what he was facing. "I couldn't drop down another division to get games. I looked at other options, but I didn't really have the world knocking at my door. Also, this was at the start of October, or thereabouts, and there would be no chance of transfer anyway until the transfer window opened in January. Those couple of months probably changed my whole career."

If Grella was a determined, grateful and respectful trainer prior to this potential career derailment, he flicked the switch to another level, to try and resurrect the dream that was in danger of etherising. "I got it into my head that this could be my last three months. So I just knuckled down to the point that every single day at training was like a Cup final for me. I was chasing people everywhere. Doing whatever I could to 'be seen, heard, felt'. My luck came in a couple of midweek friendly games, where I did really well. It's always fate that gives you a chance—an injury and a suspension—and I got back on the bench for the first team. When I came on, I made sure I did really well and have played consistently ever since. This happened the second last game before the Christmas break. In Italy they have a Christmas break—on 1 January I would have been looking for another club, but there was no need to move now."

Grella stayed with Ternana for another year and a half, achieving what he was sent there for in the first place. Ternana won the second division. Grella moved back to Empoli and ever since has been a regular in the first division.

For Grella it was, and has been, about development of personality and character. The approach to training more so than games, because his training at this level is what provides him with the background for his approach to the game. "There are only five or six of the top players in the world, the very top, who don't have to adhere to that. And even them, they work incredibly hard or if they don't, they will pay for it. The way the new-age coaches are studying the games, a player who is not in the top physical condition will not be able to perform at the top level consistently."

Physicality is one thing, but there is also the football for which Grella is responsible. He has a very clear view of his game and his ability, and he works to mould that for the good of his team and the longevity of his career. "My strength is simplicity, moving the ball, staying involved in the game, being available. I am not able to do huge things with the ball, but for me it is the amount of balls touched and the simplicity. Low errors and consistency of the passing, and I take a lot of pride in that. It is often commented about my game, 'Yeah, but they are only five-yard passes', but if there are twenty-five of these in a game, clean and accurate, it keeps my team moving, ticking over, and helps people to move into position to attack, or regroup. It is about providing my team with position and time to do things. I used to love getting the ball and dropping it in behind the defence, every time, but if our team has just won the ball back, it is physically difficult for them if I keep launching the ball into an attack that they have to support. Sometimes people need a breather, and we have to keep the ball."

That is the essence of Grella's game, the simplicity and the decision making. Does he launch it or play it easy? "It is about reading the game, it isn't necessarily about that one play. Reading the game is a lot harder now, with the speed of the game."

Grella is paid to make these decisions and that's a big responsibility, particularly in Italy, where tactics are everything and the scrutiny is microscopic.

He does it well enough to have earned a move to Parma, a bigger club in a bigger city. "Parma is a livable city. It is a cosy city. The weather's not the best; it's a bit foggy. For the kids it's not the greatest of places to be, so they suffer a bit more than us. But it's a club with a great playing history and it's a shame to see what is going on there now."

What is going on at Parma is the fallout from one of the world's worst corporate meltdowns in 2003–04. In fact, the scandals at Parmalat, the huge Italian dairy conglomerate, reverberated around the international corporate world. Parmalat, the multinational, had a 45 per cent stake in Parma, the football club. When the red ink from Parmalat's books began to flow like lava from a Vesuvius re-eruption, the regulators stepped in.

"No-one really knows what is going on. It's fixable, but it is going to cost a lot of money. The club is under controlled administration of the government. It is owed a lot of money. Of all the debts, the government is the biggest creditor. They are trying to sell the club to get the money back, and not let it go bankrupt in the meantime. There was a deal, supposedly, on the table from Lorenzo Sanz, the former Real Madrid boss. It was going for about three or four months and then he seemed to just pull out." Negotiations between Sanz and Parma's government-appointed president Guido Angiolini and government-appointed administrator Enrico Bondi stalled over the government's €27.5 million asking price.

It was Grella's coach from Empoli who took him to Parma in September of 2004. Empoli had just been relegated to Serie B. "It was all a bit protracted. The coach was told there was no money for players because of the financial situation. He started pre-season without me, but kept beating the drum that he wanted a midfielder and wanted me to be that player. Meanwhile, Empoli were playing silly buggers over the transfer fee and were being stonewalled at the other end because Parma was now in administration and the money wasn't there. It got complicated, but in the end, thankfully, I signed five hours before the transfer window closed—sweated it right out to the last minute. If I went down a division with Empoli, that would have changed a lot of things."

Parma was a good move for Grella because he was wanted by the coach and he played a lot. Although at first, there were problems. "I went to play for Australia against the Solomons. The game was at one in the afternoon, it was 45 million degrees there; I was knackered when I got back to Italy. I don't know how much weight I'd lost. He threw me straight back into the team on the Sunday and I had a shocker."

The coach then began to doubt Grella physically, which riled the Australian. "I played eight games in four weeks, including the international travel and the tropical Solomons adventure. 'Any chance of giving me a breather?' I asked, as I needed to recover. I should never have opened my mouth. He left me out altogether. The team started doing well, then the people started to doubt, and when they start thinking like that, they start crucifying you. Every time I got on the park, it was like I was cursing the team."

Strangely, for Grella, it was an injury that saved him. A medial ligament tear in his knee was enough to get him away from the pitch for enough time to have a general rest. He could rest up, then train. "It probably saved me. When I returned I did really well again. Mate, this is a high-stakes game, everyone was so nervous. If we lost and got relegated, the club might have gone bankrupt."

Parma's situation has been difficult for all concerned. Naturally, the fans are worried about their team, but also it has been very testing for the players. It was having a particular effect on the team's performances. "It's difficult on the players because mentally, he [Sanz] was getting in our way and filling our minds with all the wrong stuff. We met with him twice, as a player group. He came and offered us a bonus to beat Juventus, at our ground. We lost and we never saw him again. His son then came and watched us and said to a journalist that we'd need to change the coach and probably six or seven players. This was all in the media. We didn't know what was going on. There was nothing constructive. And if he did take over, how did he think the players were going to respond? Anyway, it appears he pulled out. It is in flux to the end of the [2005–06] season."

Sharing this dilemma is fellow Socceroo Marco Bresciano. The two have become the umbilical brothers of the national team. Having known each other since childhood, they moved to Carlton together, then to Empoli together, and now are at Parma together. Grella moved first to Empoli, but it was Bresciano who headed to Parma with Grella following. "I hope fate has us at Milan together. I'm hoping he moves to one of the big clubs and I can slipstream him."

"If you don't like where you are staying, it will come out in your football. But I really love Italy. I love being there. I am really getting into the Italian way of living."

But if the chance comes up for Grella to move now, he will. Parma's future is so unclear there is a chance anyway that they will be looking to move players to stimulate, or save, their economic situation. Grella would even consider changing countries, depending on the opportunity. "Not every place is going to be like moving to Tuscany. It was a beautiful place in a great area. I met my wife and settled down there. I lived well there, which helps the football. If you don't like where you are staying, it will come out in your football. But I really love Italy. I love being there. I am really getting into the Italian way of living. Having an Italian wife has made it easier. I have a house in Tuscany, so I can go there anytime. But Empoli is part of my past and a move will have to be a bigger club than Parma, especially if I was to move to another country."

England is a country that appeals to Grella, but with the shrewdness of mind that understands what has to be done for him to survive, he only wants to go there as a "good player, with everything in place." That includes knowing how to look after himself physically, diet—everything. He hasn't wanted to go there without being comfortable with this knowledge because "from what I have heard, they have a beautiful mentality in England—they live soccer—the Italians should learn from them because the English live it beautifully. But the Italians are very particular in certain things—their training methods, eating, rest. In these types of things, in Italy, they never make a mistake. They are obsessed."

There's that word again, obsessed. Perhaps Grella has learned it from Italy, or perhaps he has made it in Italy because it is in his own DNA. Dreaming and obsessing, the keys to Grella's career, as well as being the key to World Cup success. Grella's first dream was to play in the World Cup for his country. His second dream was to play in Italy. He knows how lucky he is. "I'll make sure I honour the shirt every time I play."

"There were five and six pages in the newspaper. We only used to get the column next to the obituaries. Every time you'd read the soccer, you had one hand covering the death notices because you didn't want to get sad with the news of the dead people."

"The World Cup was everyone's dream. It's not like the guys before didn't dream it and it's not that we have any more right than anyone else. I don't want to pump him up too much because I still have to work with him, but the timing of Guus was very important. He knew how to organise; that was the big thing, tactical organisation. We've always had good players; tell me we haven't. I remember that game against Iran at the MCG in 1997. I'd never seen Australia play that well. It was beautiful football. But we still didn't get through. But this time we had very good tactical awareness. It made a big difference. It was a good learning experience for me too, because I have been moulded in an Italian sort of way, and Hiddink's way of thinking and seeing, I have learned something from that—another way to see the game."

Unfortunately, Grella had to leave the day after qualifying over Uruguay. But his family was ringing him giving him updates. "'What's going on here? It's unbelievable, the people have gone crazy'," they'd bellow (if one bellows in Italian) down the phone. "There were five and six pages in the newspaper. We only used to get the column next to the obituaries. Every time you'd read the soccer, you had one hand covering the death notices because you didn't want to get sad with the news of the dead people."

Grella is positive about the team's chances. "We've got a good guy in charge. We have a good blend of experience, too, of guys playing at the top level. We can get through the first round. We line up, possibly, alongside Italy in the draw for the second round [Australia's group crosses over with theirs]. I played against Italy in the Sydney Olympics and we lost, and that hurt. Don't get me wrong, I am very proud of my background, but I love Italy. My kids were born there and the chances of me living in Italy in the future are growing every day. But I want to write something for Australia. This 'you are only an Aussie' stuff we get in Europe is really starting to piss me off. The only way to shut them up is to beat them, that's the only way they hear you. Playing Italy and beating them—they'll see me walking down the street and they'll be ducking into the first available corridor. For them, it would be a disgrace. For us, we have nothing to lose.

"We also have enthusiasm, which is like a drug. If they tested for it, it'd be banned, because enthusiasm is more than any drug and if you have it, you'll kill anyone. We've got it."

Seeing you, hearing you, and feeling you, Vince. Loud and clear.

14

shirt number

"I love doing the football, always. Not many people get the chance to play and experience the things we get to experience and to have the life that we have, too. The money is great. It is only for a short time, but I am loving it at the moment."

Archie Thompson

Date of birth 23 October 1978

Position played Striker

Current club PSV Eindhoven, the Netherlands

When the Frank Lowy–John O'Neill axis at Football Federation Australia anointed the new domestic competition, the A-League, part of their plan was to have some of Australia's foreign football legion return to Australia and play. Actually, at that point it wasn't so much a plan as a platitude. The launching of the A-League was more "announcement" than "launch". There was an enormous amount to do and, perhaps before things were really ready, positive inertia had to be effected. Things needed to get rolling. Late in 2004, at Darling Harbour in Sydney, the A-League officially became Australia's newest sporting competition.

It couldn't be all things to all people, but the A-League was constructed with the view to providing the two things that all leagues must—commercial stimuli to keep the sport liquid, and a more viable career for talented players. It was, as it must be, envisaged that the A-League would slow the drain of talent to overseas destinations and would give fans in Australia the chance to enjoy the best possible for as long as possible. It needs commerce (funding) and credibility (as a football product) with both working in unison, to achieve this.

When Melbourne Victory formally commenced operations in the A-League in November 2004, they were a chairman (Geoff Lord), a football manager (Gary Cole) and soon after, a coach (Ernie Merrick). Amidst everything that needed to be done to get ready for the first competitive game in May 2005, Victory set about finding some, one, football names to excite their new market, to stimulate some interest, to garner some support, to rally the troops. They could not have pulled a better rein than they did.

Since 2001 Archie Thompson had been playing his football in Lier, a small town of about 32,000 in the Belgian province of Antwerp. He'd always been an exciting type of player, and during his time in Belgium's top league, the Jupiler League, with K Lierse SK, he had played ninety games and scored twenty-seven goals.

In fact, just before Thompson left for Belgium in 2001, he came into the international spotlight for setting the world record for the number of goals scored by one player in a single, officially sanctioned match. It was April of that year, and Thompson helped himself to thirteen goals in his team's thirty-one-goal demolition of American Samoa. It was a 2002 World Cup qualifier. The record had apparently stood since John Petrie scored a hatful in a Scottish Cup tie in 1885. Thompson's effort made world news and caused a bit of a stirring locally, but American Samoa probably received more sympathy than Thompson did praise. It was a record, and it was notched up on a football field, but it was really more like a re-enactment of the Battle of Little Big Horn, with the American Samoa goalkeeper doing an Oscar-quality impersonation of General George "where have all these Indians come from?" Custer.

Anyway, Thompson didn't need a record of any sort to have people notice him. Anybody who has watched him play immediately forms their own impressions. Most often they are favourable. Melbourne Victory's people certainly hadn't forgotten, and when it was time to build their team, they made a beeline for Archie Thompson.

It was an inspired choice. Thompson returned from Belgium to assist in establishing Australia's new competition. It was a bold move by Thompson, jumping into a club and a competition that were, effectively, names only. But fortune favours the brave, and history will record of the A-League's first season, that Thompson took the place by storm. In fact, it was Thompson as much as anyone, in the singular sense, who helped deliver the A-League dream to Australia.

Organisers couldn't have planned it better or imagined it more completely. Archie Thompson, an Australian football product (though born in New Zealand), was everything the present and future is to be about. His effervescence, his common touch, his on-field charisma, his footballing quality is everything that the Australian sports marketplace needs football to deliver.

Thompson was such a success that before the first season was over, he'd be wooed back to Europe's Low Countries as a fully-fledged member of Australia's national team, in pursuit of the World Cup dream. It has been an incredible and energy-packed blitzkrieg. Far from spooking the horses that the A-League will suffer the same talent haemorrhage as the old NSL, the "Thompson exercise" will actually push greater investment and belief in the domestic product. This is a pivotal achievement.

"It has been an unbelievable six or seven months. Once I returned to Australia, I thought my time was up in Europe. I was more concentrating on doing well in Australia, without any real idea of the national team or anything."

The relocation to Melbourne was more of a family than a football decision, although for a professional footballer neither consideration ever strays too far from the other. "I had the opportunity to stay [in Belgium] but the Victory offer came up and I really wanted to be part of that. My wife had our second baby and it was the right time to move back to my home city. It was unbelievable, the A-league. I was happy to be there.

"I was happy in Melbourne. I loved it. We had just bought a house. My little one was just getting to know her family. Because she was born in Belgium, and on my wife's side of things she was the only grandchild, she was getting totally spoilt from the time we landed. Also, things like being able to go outside in shorts and to go to the beach, enjoy the weather, things that you really do take for granted living in Australia. The transition back to Europe was harder on my family, as they were settled in Melbourne. For me and my wife, it is just so cold outside, it just seems like a hassle getting the clothes on and off the kids.

"But the opportunity came up with Guus [Hiddink], and he has given me a whole new outlook on things. I want to achieve, and now that I am back in Europe, in one of the biggest clubs in Europe [PSV Eindhoven]—it's amazing really. It was just so hard on the family [moving again so soon], but this is such an important year and my wife knows what this means to me. I am hoping that my daughter won't grow up hating this and will appreciate what I have done."

Thompson was born in New Zealand but left the Shaky Isles as a newborn, even before his posterior fontanelle had closed. "I was three weeks old when I left New Zealand. My dad was an electrician and so we moved around a lot, from country towns mostly. He loved football, but he didn't really have the opportunity in New Zealand because it was all Rugby. Also, he wasn't from a wealthy family, and they were really religious, so

---

"I just sort of lost interest a bit, the travelling was a bit hard and I said to my dad, 'I don't feel like this anymore'. All my time was gone, my weekends had disappeared. I decided to just play local league in Bathurst."

he didn't really get a chance to excel in sport. Dad just wanted the best for my brothers and sisters, for us to achieve what maybe he didn't have."

Thompson's country town life took him to Albury–Wodonga and then Bathurst. His first football team was the Lithgow Rangers. "My dad was working in the mines at that stage." From Bathurst, he was in the NSW Academy team, "trekking back and forth over the Blue Mountains, getting to training".

Thompson came to the Academy via country soccer. Playing in local club and representative teams, he ascended to the NSW Country team, from where he was cherry-picked for the Academy program. "I started playing with Emmo [Brett Emerton] and Harry [Kewell] in the Academy."

But the drain on a youngster, and the family, of travelling regularly from the central west of NSW into the western suburbs of Sydney for training got too much. The Bathurst to Sydney round trip for training would easily be five hours on a good run, not including the training session. You'd be forgiven for thinking you had swapped your life for that of an interstate trucker. All this to kick a ball around.

"I just sort of lost interest a bit, the travelling was a bit hard and I said to my dad, 'I don't feel like this anymore'. All my time was gone, my weekends had disappeared. I decided to just play local league in Bathurst."

Stop press! Imagine, if you will, that Archie had been lost to football at this point in his life. Imagine what the A-League wouldn't have had in this case. Imagine what the national team wouldn't have had. Imagine what possibilities our country would be missing if Thompson wasn't around to sell Australia, like only footballers can, with his personality and style. Imagine how much joy Thompson wouldn't have brought to so many lives, through football, if he hadn't returned to the game. Imagine if Thompson hadn't resurrected himself. Organised football in Australia has a lamentable history of expecting people to come to it, rather than taking it to the people.

Imagine how many other players the game has lost because of this.

Thompson wasn't lost to football, but the road back was long and winding. "A friend of mine called out of the blue—an old coach of mine called Carlo Villani. He said that I would have a chance down in Gippsland with former Socceroos coach Frank Arok, if I wanted to have a crack."

At the time, the Morwell Falcons were in the NSL. Arok has always had an uncanny knack of finding gold in disused mines, and Thompson was to show Arok, the alchemist, enough specks for him to think something might be done.

"I'll give it a shot and see how I go", was Thompson's mind-set. "This was in 1997. We trained in a gravel car park down there. I wanted to do so well. I was sliding in for tackles, everything. At the end of training, my legs were all cut up but it was worth it. Frank Arok saw something in me. I have a lot of respect for Frank. I owe a lot to him. He pulled me from nothing and gave me opportunity. He believed in me and it skyrocketed from there."

It is a golden word, "opportunity", but it doesn't come from nothing. Nor had Thompson gone from totally nothing to Morwell. It was one of his current Socceroo team-mates who inadvertently re-lit Thompson's fuse for football.

"The spark from watching Harry got me going. I had put on a bit of weight and wasn't training. I thought I'd start running home from work. It took maybe fifteen or sixteen times of stopping and starting and I finally made it home in one go. I remember thinking I'd had a major breakthrough."

"I was watching the Premier League on television. I saw Harry Kewell, the way he was playing, the way they were talking about him, the money he was getting. I just thought to myself, 'I used to train with him and was at least at that or a similar level back then'.

"When I took that time out of the game, I was probably hanging out with the wrong crew. Though I still consider them to be some of my closest friends, I was doing the wrong things. I was working in a Chinese restaurant in Bathurst. It was a crappy little job but they were good people.

"The spark from watching Harry got me going. I had put on a bit of weight and wasn't training. I thought I'd start running home from work. It took maybe fifteen or sixteen times of stopping and starting and I finally made it home in one go. I remember thinking I'd had a major breakthrough.

"I got back playing in the NSW leagues with Bathurst '75, and about a year later the call came to go to Gippsland. From that point on, it keeps going up. I know at some stage it's going to come down, but until then, I am going to keep riding the wave."

After a highly successful time with Morwell, Thompson moved through NSL clubs Carlton and Marconi before leaving for Lier. His career shows that he has scored goals wherever he has gone. His references would likely suggest that he is a crowd favourite too.

Thompson's appeal is, apart from the goals, the character that he takes onto the field. He doesn't leave himself in the dressing room, as some players do. The same things that make Thompson appealing off the field are exactly those that work for him on it. He is one of those players who plays his personality. He is one of those players to whom fans adhere because, when they watch him play, they get a sense of him as a person. Not all players are like this, nor should they be. Different things work for different people. But this is one of the key ingredients to Thompson's success.

This same style has dumped him in trouble from time to time though. "I had a bugger of a coach once in Belgium. He didn't know the Australian mentality. We want to win, of course, but if we don't win, then okay, we'll win next time. That's my way of doing things. We lost one particular game. I can't remember it exactly. It wasn't a Cup final or anything, and the next day I was laughing with the guys. He saw that and he didn't like it. After that, I didn't play in the first team and went to the second team and was training with them for nine months. I learned a lot from that, when to be myself, and when to toe the line and say to myself, 'Hey, I have to focus here'. I get on well with everyone. I like to have a laugh. Just got to pick the right times."

To be back in Europe provides Thompson with a terrific opportunity. To have been taken back there by Guus Hiddink, one of the world's most highly regarded coaches, is huge vindication for Thompson's potential. To be at PSV means that he will be noticed, and from there anything could happen. "I am speechless really. I am grateful for Guus, I have a lot of respect for him. The PSV fans don't really know me yet—they are still trying to work me out. I am taking it pretty quietly." One would expect the PSV fans to be similarly smitten by Thompson once they do get to know him, supposing of course that his football is good.

Thompson's incredible 2005–06 has reunited him with Jason Culina, with whom he played in the Olyroos (sobriquet for Australia's Olympic team), and the two are now together in the national team and at PSV. And his national team status has also forged him a spot back next to Harry Kewell and Brett Emerton, rekindling those days of the NSW Academy. Life's cycle, circles turning a full circumference, going around and coming around—it has just fallen nicely into place for Thompson.

"I have had to make a lot of sacrifices. I have had to work harder than some. Some players are established in big clubs. I was in and out of the national team and didn't really feel part of it. I was just looking forward to a [training] camp where my name wouldn't be 'stand-by', but would be in the squad, up front and of its own accord. Now it is and it feels good that I am getting recognition. If you work hard, you get the rewards.

"I love doing the football, always. Not many people get the chance to play and experience the things we get to experience and to have the life that we have, too. The money is great. It is only for a short time, but I am loving it at the moment."

Coming from out of the blue and into the World Cup qualifiers, how could Thompson be anything other than ecstatic? "It's still a blur to me when I see photos of me lining up in the Centenario

---

"I have had to make a lot of sacrifices. I have had to work harder than some. Some players are established in big clubs. I was in and out of the national team and didn't really feel part of it."

[Montevideo]. The players and the fans. I still have to pinch myself that I started that game. He [Hiddink] had faith in me to do the job and it gave my confidence a huge boost. I would have liked to have had more time on the field, and the chance to do more, but it was incredible.

"The return game, wow. Still when I watch the video and we are sprinting off the bench [when John Aloisi scored] gives me goosebumps. Unbelievable, once in a lifetime."

It was, in fact, Thompson who led the charge from the bench at that moment of the winning penalty. There were great pictures of him, champing at the bit, waiting, hoping, expecting, anticipating ... and then, bang, catch him if you can. Even though he didn't play in that game, he still managed to provide great memories for everyone watching.

Without having played in the English Premier League, Thompson's "seal" has already made it that far. Australia's friendly game against Jamaica in London, in October 2005 in which the Socceroos won 5-0, featured a performance by Thompson, and a goal to boot. Thompson made his way to the corner flag where he unleashed seal, his trademark celebratory flurry of kicks and punches on the hapless flag. It wasn't a new sight. Fans of the A-League had seen Thompson let loose regularly throughout the season. It is his signature.

Tim Cahill was Thompson's team-mate that day against Jamaica. When Thompson scored his goal, Cahill became a very interested spectator. Being a regular goal scorer himself, it was something new for Cahill to take in.

"Tim saw the celebration against Jamaica. He said to me, 'Arch, can I please take this [celebration] to the Premier League? Once

"The return game, wow. Still when I watch the video and we are sprinting off the bench [when John Aloisi scored] gives me goosebumps. Unbelievable, once in a lifetime."

---

they start seeing it and asking me about it, I'll say it was you'. I said it was okay and that 'if this is how I have to get my name out there in the UK, then go for it. I'll have a copyright on it though.' His has a little more jabbing, whereas I put the kick into it."

The motivation for Thompson's celebration came from Claudio Canosa, a team-mate at Morwell, who also worked on the coaching staff for the 2000 Olympic Games campaign. Canosa had taken Thompson under his wing. "He said that I needed something that makes me stand out. So I thought, 'I'll kick the corner flag', and it has just grown from there." It has, and it certainly will from here. Expect to see young players across the country scoring and then mauling the corner flag, in exactly the same way that a generation of Australians grew up wiping sweat from their brow with an index finger and a flick, à la cricketing great, Dennis Lillee.

And never mind Tim Cahill delivering the message to the UK about the Thompson goal celebration. There's the small matter of the FIFA World Cup approaching and Thompson is working hard to ensure he can deliver the "autograph" in person. "I want to be in that squad, and do really well. I reckon we can progress—it's realistic."

If that comes to pass, there will be the game against Brazil that the whole world will be watching. A goal against Brazil will show the world what Thompson is all about. "If that happens, forget the corner flag. I might have to punch and kick myself."

15

shirt number

"It's been brilliant and I wouldn't swap it for the world because I love the game and I want it to go on forever. I enjoy playing in Europe—it's a great atmosphere. It has always been a dream to play in such big leagues, with such good football against such big teams and such big players."

John Aloisi

Date of birth 5 February 1979

Position played Striker

Current club Alaves, Spain

John Aloisi didn't really need to "show" anybody anything. For him, pride is very much an individual thing and isn't reliant upon what other people think. But he did get a bit irritable, sick of this whole football thing being a secret in Australia. Four years ago, preparing for the 2002 qualifiers, he was intent on showing Australia what he could do and who he was. Four years ago, because of the failure, John Aloisi and "this football thing" remained a secret. The frustration only grew. Aloisi returned to Spain to resume his work, which was to take on the biggest names in football against the likes of Real Madrid and Barcelona in the Primera Liga. Meanwhile, Australia withdrew into its shell and continued its national sport, navel-gazing.

Four years later, Aloisi's wish came true. Football was no longer a secret in Australia. The players were no longer invisible, and there was no need for him to be irritable any longer.

And by 17 November 2005, there wouldn't have been a person drawing breath under the Southern Cross who didn't know who John Aloisi was and what he had done for his country the evening before. For John Aloisi, "that penalty" has drawn back the curtain on a trek through European professional football, particularly through the three biggest leagues in the world, England, Spain and Italy—something that no Australian other than Aloisi has yet achieved. His decade-long journey through the cold and isolation, the joy and elation of top-flight football and onto Sydney's Olympic Stadium has culminated in catapulting

Australia to only its second appearance at the finals of the World Cup.

"I knew it would be big if we got through, but I didn't ever imagine it would be this big. I can't explain what it has done for me and how it makes me feel, to have helped Australia get to the World Cup."

Aloisi hasn't just arrived at the front door of Australia's sporting consciousness. After knocking politely for many years and being refused entry, he's now stormed his way straight in, strode up the hallway and taken his place on the lounge—for as long as he damn well likes. There won't be a moment when the consciousness will be without him, or be free of him. He is there, now and forever. It is quite ironic really, because Aloisi himself is very self-effacing, quietly spoken and not at all presumptuous.

Aloisi had a stirring in his loins that he was going to do something significant that night, like score the winning goal, for example.

"The whole two weeks leading up to it, I was saying to Lucas Neill that I was going to get the winner. More joking than anything at that stage." Many a true word is spoken in jest.

His wife would frequently get sick of him predicting goals by himself, in significant matches, such as the 2005 Copa del Rey (the Kings Cup in Spain, Spain's "Cup" competition). Aloisi scored in that, too. There was a two-strand pattern developing here.

"I knew it would be big if we got through, but I didn't ever imagine it would be this big. I can't explain what it has done for me and how it makes me feel, to have helped Australia get to the World Cup."

"I was pissed off, like any player would be. I think that is healthy anyway. I spoke with my brother, who said, 'What does it matter if you play ninety minutes or fifteen minutes, and you score the winner that gets us through?' And he was right of course. But I still wanted to start."

Aloisi discovered the day before the game in Sydney that he would not be starting the game. "I was pissed off, like any player would be. I think that is healthy anyway. I spoke with my brother, who said, 'What does it matter if you play ninety minutes or fifteen minutes, and you score the winner that gets us through?' And he was right of course. But I still wanted to start."

At training that day before the game, Aloisi grabbed Lucas Neill to go and take some penalties. He took him to the end of the ground where he thought the penalties would be taken, if it got that far. "Lucas asked me how I knew we'd be this end and I said because our supporters who sing most are down this end and I am sure they will put us down here. I don't know why I thought this, there was no basis." But he would turn out to be correct again, another premonition to come true.

Neill and Aloisi put the third keeper, Ante Covic, in goals. They hit five penalties each. Aloisi had his run-up marked. He hit his first four penalties well. He knew where he was standing, lined up the ball, his position and the post, and repeated it each time, the same thing. He figured that if he was going to take a penalty, he'd only get one chance so he'd perfect that one penalty that he was going to take. For his fifth penalty, he went for a little more oomph. I skied it a bit, it rammed off the crossbar and went into the goal. Neill turned to him and said, "Nice one". Aloisi turned to Neill and said, "Too close for comfort".

The beautiful thing about history is that two people can recall the same event in different ways. Lucas Neill's recollection of that fifth practice penalty goes like this. "For Johnny's fifth penalty, he said, 'I am going to aim a bit higher this time'. He hits the crossbar, it goes in, I say to him, 'Please don't do that tomorrow night'."

Aloisi knew that he had to practise penalties because he'd played with Uruguayans Pablo Garcia and Richard "Chengue" Morales at Osasuna, the club of Pamplona. They had seen him take penalties at club level in training. He believed, quite rightly, that if you hit the ball well enough, the keeper shouldn't have a chance anyway. Aloisi thought, "I'll stick to my guns. If the keeper moves, he'll have to move early to get it and then, if he does, fair play to him.

"When we'd finished taking our penalties, we were on the field stretching down. I asked where our families would be sitting because I wanted to know where I would have to run when I scored the goal, but at that stage I was thinking about the goal in normal time, not the penalty shoot-out. I was half-serious and half-joking.

"At the end of the actual game, prior to penalties, we were huddled together, milling about, having a drink, stretching, trying to relax. Arnie [Graham Arnold, assistant coach] was asking who was confident taking penalties. Straightaway, I put up my hand. Arnie suggested I take first penalty but I said, 'No, put me fifth', because you have more of a chance of hitting the winner—but you can be the devil too. People remember Roberto Baggio from USA '94.

"Gathered on the halfway line, we had our arms around each other, close and together, people in different states emotionally, but the 'we are going to win' energy was circulating. It was very strong.

"I looked over at Lucas and asked, 'Are you taking a penalty?' and he goes, 'Yeah'. He was talking a bit, confident, the normal sort of Lucas. And Lucas asked me and I said, 'Yeah, I'm taking the fifth one, the hero or the villain.' Lucas couldn't help himself and asked, 'Which one's it going to be?' and I said, 'The hero' and we had a bit of a laugh, although I'm not sure if it was a nervous or a confident laugh.

"Harry [Kewell] stepped up to take his penalty, no drama. Lucas, well, I knew he'd be okay. Then Tony [Vidmar] stepped up and I realised I had never seen Tony hit one before, but he'd had such a good game—I can't remember him having a better one actually. When I saw Tony's penalty I thought 'brilliant', because Schwarzie [Mark Schwarzer] had already saved one.

"And then Dukes [Mark Viduka] stepped up and missed. That's when my legs went a little bit. I looked over to Uruguay and saw Chengue Morales, my mate. He was struggling and drained—it made me feel a bit better. Schwarzie saved the next one, too.

"Then it was me. While everyone was jumping up and down at Schwarzer's save, I started to walk to the spot. All the way up I was thinking, 'We're going to the World Cup', because I just knew my penalty was going in. Of course, players can miss, the best in the world can miss. But those penalties the day before—'everything the same, just hit it where you are going to hit it and if he gets there it's a great save, and if he doesn't, we're through to

---

"And then Dukes [Mark Viduka] stepped up and missed. That's when my legs went a little bit. I looked over to Uruguay and saw Chengue Morales, my mate. He was struggling and drained—it made me feel a bit better. Schwarzie saved the next one, too."

the World Cup'. All I was thinking, on that walk up, was, 'You're taking Australia to the World Cup. Come on, just go and do it'.

"As soon as I saw the net move, it was all over from there."

It all started for Aloisi in Adelaide. He and his brother Ross were very keen sportsmen. Both played soccer. They'd play one against one in the backyard. Ross also played cricket and John did a lot of athletics. When John was by himself, he'd practise football alone in the backyard.

"When I was younger, I always felt that I was never going to be brilliant, but I wanted to be good. I loved scoring goals and I trained hard."

Both Aloisi boys were with the Adelaide City club; dad Rocco was the coach there too. John made his NSL debut with Adelaide City when he was fifteen, which was when he first felt he had a chance of doing something with football. "When I cracked it so young, training with the likes of Aurelio Vidmar, who himself was nudging for a move overseas, I wanted to do the same."

The NSL debut is the sum total of his NSL experience. And what an experience. Entering the fray late in that game, Aloisi got in a tangle with an opponent, upon whom some local fans wanted to exact retribution, and an affray ensued. The papers went to town the next day. Aloisi has always been a headline act in Australia. Whether it is a goal on debut or a riot on debut, he usually dishes up something.

Aloisi soon moved to the AIS, where he teamed up with Mark Viduka, Josip Skoko and Craig Moore. He returned to Adelaide and was included on the bench for a couple more games, but patience, or lack of it, got the better of him.

"It's funny how things work out. In Adelaide there was a Serbian player, only there for a short time. He had an agent and he put me in touch with him. He suggested that I go over for a trial. I went with my dad to Standard Liege in Belgium just before Christmas that year. I was sixteen. I have never been so cold in my life; it was minus four degrees. It was uncomfortable—December in Adelaide to Belgium—it was quite a shock to the system. But the clincher for me was the game we went to see on the weekend. We were put up in a box. They treated us well. Watching the game I thought 'This is what I want. I don't care how cold it is, and I don't care if I have to leave my family, this is what I want to do.'

"I was in the reserve team and training with Standard, not the first team. I was still young, just turned seventeen. I didn't know the language, and French, I never really got for the whole time I was there. The first day was the worst. I was a shy kid. I was put in an apartment at the training ground, it wasn't really much. There was a cafeteria at the training ground and I went there to eat. I returned to the apartment and I couldn't get in the door. I didn't know what to do. I was locked out of the apartment but I couldn't tell anybody because I couldn't speak the language. I had no-one with me. I sat there, lonely and embarrassed, and after a couple of hours—strangely, the door wouldn't open itself—I went and got someone from the club to let me in.

"Standard wanted me to stay for six months to see how I went. I wasn't going to be in the first team, so they let me go to Antwerp, where I ended up staying for two and a half years."

Royal Antwerp is a big, supported club. It is in a Flemish part of Belgium where English is more widely spoken. "I didn't play a lot when I first got there—mainly in the reserves. I made my debut when I was eighteen, and scored. It was hard to break through because there were so many players, a lot of African players, Brazilians and Yugoslavs. It was so congested."

Aloisi's chance to break in with the first team coincided with a camp for the Young Socceroos. He approached the coaching staff to discuss the qualifiers and the predicament he was facing with his club situation at Antwerp. The Young Socceroos team was a good one and the qualifiers were to take in the Oceania members, Fiji, New Zealand etc., and there was no realistic threat to Australia qualifying. He'd be away from Antwerp for four weeks. Aloisi stated his case. "I am just breaking into the first team at Antwerp. I will be away for qualifiers for four weeks and then for the World Cup for another five or six weeks. I want to play in the World Cup, but that will mean something like ten weeks away from my club. I was the only player in Europe at the time—all the others were either at Australian clubs or the AIS, so it didn't really affect them. I asked permission to miss the qualifiers."

The request fell on deaf ears. "I was told I had to come. I was put right on the spot. I wanted to play so much for Australia, but I couldn't miss so much football with Antwerp. I was young, very upset. I didn't know if I would get another chance to play for Australia at a big tournament."

From Antwerp, Aloisi moved to Cremona, Italy. Playing for Cremonese in Serie A, Aloisi became the first Australian to score in Italy's top flight. "The Italian League is tough for a striker, especially when you are young and in a poor team. At the time, clubs were allowed only three foreigners, and even though I had an Italian passport, I was classed as a foreigner. There was a lot of pressure on the foreigners. That was probably the hardest time in my football life. We got relegated; the supporters were unforgiving. I managed to score on debut again, against Padova. But it was a really hard slog. We got a lot of stick and at the time

I didn't know how to take it. Reading the papers, what they write about you. On debut I was their saviour, and then I'd be reading that I was the worst player they had ever signed. That was the whole sentiment over there. I couldn't really handle that. I wasn't enjoying soccer, not enjoying training, not playing happy.

"Cremona is only a small town, but it's a nice area. My parents are Italian so it was nice to be in Italy. Being Italian in Australia didn't prepare me at all though. They are different types of Italians, those who live in Italy and those who went to Australia. My family is from the south and there is a bit of a clash in Italy between the north and the south. I didn't really speak Italian—my parents always spoke English to me. Italy was good for those cultural reasons, but the football was very difficult."

Meanwhile, there was to be a change at Socceroo headquarters that would signal positive things for Aloisi. Englishman Terry Venables became the coach of the Socceroos, replacing Eddie Thomson. It was Venables who contacted Aloisi when he accepted the post to check his availability for the international program. Until then, since the 1995 Youth World Cup episode, Aloisi had been estranged from the national team set-up and he leapt at the chance offered by Venables. He has been involved ever since.

It was Venables who also called Aloisi to offer him a new club experience. The Englishman was taking an interest in Portsmouth in England, and he'd approached Australians Craig Foster, Robbie Enes, Hamilton Thorpe and Paul Harries to move there. Aloisi was looking to get out of Italy, and although Portsmouth represented a step back because of its status as an England second league club, he saw it as a chance to get some regular football. "At that stage it was very important that I consolidate and prove that I had what it takes to play at the top level."

Venables's interest in Australian players for his English club was causing quite a bit of heat in Australia. As coach of the national team, there was a whiff that he was using that position to leverage his club's position. Apparently, there was heat in England about it too. "Portsmouth was difficult because of all the stuff Venables went through. The Aussies copped it there, copping it because of Venables's trouble."

Venables departed Portsmouth and was replaced by Alan Ball. Ball wanted to clear the club of the Australian players. "I was the only survivor. I was the team's leading scorer, but I didn't play much under Ball. They wanted to get rid of me but from the time Ball started I hadn't scored enough goals to get anything better and I didn't want to go to anything worse.

"During the pre-season of the next year, I just fought really hard. Ball still wanted me to leave, but I was determined. I was banging goals away during friendly games and he couldn't ignore me. I wanted to show him that Aussies weren't there just because of Venables. I was scoring goals, the only one who was, so he had no choice but to play me."

By the November, Aloisi had scored seventeen goals in both league and cup games and was the first division's leading scorer. "Ball couldn't ignore me, but he wasn't liking it either." Coventry, then in the Premier League, came in for Aloisi and Portsmouth needed the money, so he was sold. For Aloisi this was fabulous news, a move away from Portsmouth and a move up to the top division.

"Osasuna isn't a big team but they had just got back to the top division. The four years I spent there probably ended up being the happiest I have been."

The Coventry chapter started very well. "In the seven games I started, I scored five goals. But the following year I got injured and never really recovered during the rest of my time in Coventry. In my third year there, coming back into the team and scoring goals, I got injured again and the manager went to the transfer market. I fell out with Gordon Strachan [manager]—things happen in football. The club got relegated. But I was happy to stay, play hard and help the team get promoted, but then Spain came up."

Spain was always a huge attraction. Osasuna, in Pamplona, also provided Aloisi with the chance to pick up the hat-trick of big leagues, although this is not something that Aloisi would have focused on. "Osasuna isn't a big team but they had just got back to the top division. The four years I spent there probably ended up being the happiest I have been."

Happiness in Spain would take time to evolve, however, because Osasuna didn't start terribly well either. "The club didn't pay me for the first year. In Spain, they pay wages on a monthly basis, which are fairly small amounts and then two large lump sums, one in January and one in June. In Spain they have a knack of not paying on time. When they told me that, I thought a week or two perhaps. But when I went back to pre-season training for year two [July] I still hadn't been paid the January wage. I asked Osasuna what was going on."

Aloisi's agent advised him of one of the options that he had. It was a risky one that would involve taking the club to the Spanish Football Association, at which point Osasuna would have one week to pay money owed or else get relegated. Nobody had done this at Osasuna before. It was a situation where one player could bring an entire club down.

“So I did it. I wasn’t going to let them take advantage of me, and if they did it then, unchecked, it would have got worse later. But didn’t I cop it from the supporters, the press, the new president, everyone. The new president particularly, because I was the purchase of the former president, Osasuna’s biggest purchase, and now this was happening.

“I had three years at Osasuna with a president who didn’t like me. The first year was a very tough year. But I was playing, and the coach, Mexican Javier Aguirre, liked me. I liked him too—he is the best coach I have ever had.”

Over time, Aloisi won back the press and the supporters. Never quite the president, however. By the end of his time at Osasuna, “they were completely with me, the fans and the press, and they turned on the president.

“I had a really magic time with Osasuna. In my last year there we made the Spanish Cup final, the Kings Cup. I scored in that game. It is a career highlight for me—second to the Uruguay game—55,000 people, great atmosphere. One half of the stadium green and white, the other half in Osasuna red. Our fans were brilliant. We lost 1-2, but for the supporters it was like they’d won. I couldn’t really celebrate because I had to leave for the Confederations Cup, but it didn’t really matter because I kept scoring there, so the party continued.

“After the final, I was asked if I was staying with Osasuna, because my contract was up. It was the first time I have had a tear in my eye over football. I said that I didn’t know, but that I thought this was my last game for Osasuna. It seemed to touch everyone. It was the realisation that it was over. I was so happy to have helped this club make a final and do something, but it was time to move on.”

Aloisi's form at the Confederations Cup of 2005—two goals against Germany and two against Argentina—earned him rave reviews. Out of contract and in demand, exactly the way a player wants it. Greek giant Panathinaikos were one such party. Aloisi was interested because this is a club that regularly challenges for the Greek title and plays in the Champions League. It is a massive club and it wins things. Of course Aloisi was interested.

In Greece, Aloisi was "greeted like a star. You can imagine, after the Confeds Cup and being on the scorers' charts with [German star] Ballack and [Brazilian] Adriano. There was press everywhere, it was a bit of a circus."

Aloisi did his medical, did some press interviews and headed straight back to Spain. Greece was a day trip only. He then gathered his family and escaped for a brief holiday. Whilst at Coventry, some years prior, Aloisi had picked up a knee and hamstring injury. He'd passed a medical to get to Osasuna four years earlier, and played regularly since, so there shouldn't have been a problem. Aloisi himself was very confident, and hadn't really given the knee of years past much thought at all. Upon his return, he was shocked to hear that Panathinaikos had "come back saying my knee was no good. I couldn't believe it."

Not only was the disappointment acute, but Aloisi was now faced with the "what am I going to do now" question. The Panathinaikos decision had dragged on for a week or so. "The on and off stuff got a bit ridiculous. But the bad press damaged me. People became a bit stand-offish. The longer it dragged on, the harder it would be to get a club. Then Alaves came in for me. It was a pretty easy choice. I love Spain and wouldn't have to move far, only about forty minutes from Pamplona.

"To play the best players, to beat them, is just fabulous. Sometimes they do things on the field and you just think, 'Wow, how good is this?'"

"I am very settled in Spain. My family love it. The first year here was unbelievable. Playing at the Camp Nou [Barcelona]. We beat them 1-0 and at the end of the game the Barca fans were clapping us off the field. That was an amazing experience.

"Then, four years ago, my first game back from the Uruguay defeat was to play Real Madrid at the Bernabeu [Madrid's stadium]. To walk out there, wow, what a place. We were down 0-2 and then I scored, what a feeling, my God.

"But we topped that. Not only have I played there every year since, but a couple of years back we beat them at their ground 3-0. The supporters in Pamplona went berserk—it was like they'd won the Cup. They hate Madrid, for political reasons. The Basques hate Madrid. We beat them two or three times at our stadium. It's a great atmosphere because it means so much to the supporters. They are the best games to play in and win because the whole country is watching Madrid on television.

"To play the best players, to beat them, is just fabulous. Sometimes they do things on the field and you just think, 'Wow, how good is this?'"

Of all the good things Aloisi has done—scoring on debut, scoring in cups and qualifiers—he has an astute capacity to compartmentalise things, contain them and move on, all to be looked at and enjoyed in retrospect when he has finished playing. Now is not the time to get bogged down in achievements and experiences. Experiences are to be enjoyed in the moment and then bottled, perhaps, for later consumption. There is always a new challenge and hurdle and experience in football, and time is too short to sit dreaming.

"Even the goal against Uruguay, I can't dwell on that because I have a job to do and that is help Alaves avoid relegation. I have more goals to score too—it is like an addiction, scoring. There is nothing better than that. I am a bit embarrassed by the shirt celebration against Uruguay, but you can't plan for it, it just happened. It was ecstasy. Did you see the players run? Where does that energy come from, after what they had been through? Only a goal can do that.

"I knew where my family was and I wanted to go and celebrate with them. They are the most important people in my life. They deserve it as much as I do. They've been there the whole way. Leaving the family when I was so young was difficult and keeping going when things are tough and you are so far away from everyone. There's been many times I felt like packing it in. I left home at sixteen, and have a sister who is ten years my junior, so I have missed watching her grow up. There's a lot of ground to make up."

Aloisi subscribes to the "it's time" theory of qualification. "This is a dream of mine to play. I am very fortunate. A lot of players before me were so close and never got there and they had the same dreams. I am representing all those who couldn't go. All the disasters and heartbreak.

"It was just our time. We had to beat Uruguay to show the world that we aren't qualifying easily. We've earned it. People know we have a good team now. My Uruguayan mates at Osasuna didn't say that four years ago. They said we were good in Melbourne but we 'bottled' it in Montevideo. That was their impression."

Now the focus is definitely on doing well. Brazil traditionally start slowly and build towards the end of tournaments like the World Cup; they are tournament-play experts. “Anything can happen. Argentina, Portugal and France didn’t get through the first round last time. You never know.”

And Aloisi is getting the mind going again. “Why not create history? See how much we can create. Why not be the first player to score for Australia in the World Cup finals?” Given the personal notches on his totem pole, one can just see him adding some World Cup achievement to that also.

Whatever happens from this point, nobody can take from John Aloisi that for which he has worked so hard to achieve.

“It’s been brilliant and I wouldn’t swap it for the world because I love the game and I want it to go on forever. I enjoy playing in Europe—it’s a great atmosphere. It has always been a dream to play in such big leagues, with such good football against such big teams and such big players. Well, actually, if you could play with, rather than against, it would be better, specially for a striker. I’d score more goals.”

John Aloisi

18

shirt number

"Some days, when I get to training, I watch these players, the same ones I used to watch on TV. Champions League nights were the only nights I wouldn't go out, watching these guys on TV from Kerkrade or Perugia. I was transfixed. And now I am here, participating with one of the world's most successful clubs in that competition, at one of the world's biggest clubs."

Zeljko Kalac

Date of birth 16 December 1972

Position played Goalkeeper

Current club AC Milan, Italy

From the peak of his two-metre frame, Zeljko Kalac has a good view of things. It is a view that has taken in some remarkable sights over the years. Stories of globetrotting and of a full life. Perspective that, unlike oxygen, doesn't thin with altitude, but only gets clearer. Normally, someone who stands at two metres is casting the shadow, not being cast therein. Zeljko Kalac's frustration and motivation have been to find his own, international sunlight.

Kalac is part of Australia's golden era of goalkeepers. The battle for the national team shirt was, for a long time, a three-way tussle. But since the personal difficulties encountered by Mark Bosnich over recent years, that struggle has come down to two—Kalac and Mark Schwarzer. All three grew up in Sydney's western suburbs and, because they are all of similar age, have been jostling each other since their earliest days.

It is a competition that has been intense but respectful. It is not a competition that Kalac will ever concede, nor to which Schwarzer will yield. In many other forums this could be quite a combustible potion, but both have too much respect for the job and for each other for that to happen here.

Kalac's is a story of parallels. A club career that has soared to incredible heights and an international career that has never been given the opportunity he believes it deserves. It is what keeps pushing him along the road to the World Cup. Always available, always there and always ready—that has been Kalac's call sign. His football operates from under the umbrella of one of Australia's real characters. Unaffected by pomp and unmoved by circumstance, "Spider" Kalac is the man to play it, and call it, as he sees it and, like dipping into a mineral spring, there are few things quite as refreshing.

Luddenham Croatia, a small junior club in St Marys, was the starting point for Kalac. At six years of age he began playing football as a striker, where he stayed until he was "nine or ten". His father was coach of the team. Kalac, competitive even from these early days, recalls being "gutted after we lost a game, so I said, 'We can't lose like that' and went into the goal. That was that."

Junior representative football beckoned and Kalac headed to Nepean to engage this higher level. It was here that at "ten or eleven, me and Schwarzie were playing at Nepean together. He was my reserve keeper. Schwarzie moved to a smaller club in a lower division, Blacktown Association. I went from the Nepean Under 13s and ended up at Sydney United from the 14s on."

Kalac began to train with the first team at Sydney United when he was fourteen. It was about the same time, probably because of it, that he recalls starting to dream of being a footballer, seriously and properly. There isn't a great deal of meat on Spider's bones now, but then, "There was nothing of me. I was tall and skinny. When [Zarko] Odzakov used to hit the ball, I'd dive the other way so it wouldn't hit me—he'd have broken me in half."

Graham Arnold was a senior player at Sydney United (Croatia) at the time. It was he who gave Kalac his nickname Spider, which has remained to this day. It has become as much apart of his kit as are his gloves and boots. Ron Corry was coaching Kalac, who speaks of him with serious affection and respect. "He was a massive influence on my career. For all of us, he was always keen to play the youngsters—me, Popa [Tony Popovic]. At sixteen we were playing in the first team."

Kalac looks back over his time since then and likes what he sees. "It's gone absolutely perfect. I have stepped up, every club I have gone to has been a step up the chain, not many people can say that. At thirty-three [currently], I am still heading up whereas most players are heading in the other direction."

It is a club career that has taken him from Sydney United to Leicester City in England before boomeranging back to Sydney. Then it was off to Roda JC in the Netherlands, Perugia in Italy and now, incredibly, AC Milan—one of the world's top half-dozen clubs.

It might have "gone perfect" on balance, but along the way there were glitches for Kalac. His time in England with Leicester never really kicked off because of his inability to secure a work permit from the Home Office.

He had the chance to go to Leeds or Celtic at that time but didn't, which he says now "was a mistake. I should have gone for the biggest club. I went where I was going to play, where I was going to be more comfortable and at a young age not be under too much pressure.

"It's gone absolutely perfect. I have stepped up, every club I have gone to has been a step up the chain, not many people can say that. At thirty-three [currently], I am still heading up whereas most players are heading in the other direction."

"Plus Mick Hickman [coach from Australia] was there at the time, too. I could have also made a lot more money if I'd gone elsewhere. I am a little disappointed that I never had the opportunity to demonstrate what I had in England, because I had the quality to become one of the top keepers there. To this day, I can't work out what went wrong with the paperwork. [Terry] Venables then wanted to take me to Portsmouth with him. I wasn't even getting a response at all from the authorities."

Kalac had his first season at Leicester and was part of the team that won promotion to the Premier League. "I walked up the Wembley stairs to get my medal for that and went home for a holiday. One week before I was to return to England, I got the message that I couldn't get a work permit."

England was a real test for Kalac. He spent five months trying to secure his initial work permit, which made for a very interrupted season. He arrived after the season was already underway, so he didn't get much of a chance to get to know any of the players. He went to the smallest club on offer, thinking that is where he'd be happiest, a corollary of playing the most. "It just didn't pan out that way." The England experience had dented him. He had what he believed England was looking for—young, tall, authoritative—but bureaucracy bounced his ambitions.

Kalac ended up back in Sydney and at his old club, playing and enjoying football again. His Sydney United team of the day was a special one. Coached by Branko Culina, it stormed the NSL, playing one of the most fluent and attractive styles of football seen for quite some time. It easily won the minor premiership, only to be beaten by the Brisbane Strikers in the Championship match in what was a famous day for club football in Australia. Brisbane's Lang Park was a 43,000 sell-out, packed to rafters, with, it was estimated, another 5000 fans turned away. One would defy

Kalac not to enjoy a team and a season like that. His football was good; he was home and comfortable. Kalac even considered doing the work-and-play combination, and making Sydney his football home again, more permanently.

Kalac knew, though, that he could, should, have another go in Europe. Australian players from far and wide were making their way to the continent and winning contracts of significant size. Towards the end of the 1990s, money from television began to pour into English football in particular, care of the digital television roll-out. ITV digital, following the BSkyB example, saw large subscription numbers if they could secure football content. With the Premier League the property of Rupert Murdoch's empire, the next league down was where ITV sent its money. The clubs responded to the cash injection by committing incredible amounts to player salaries. It was orgiastic. Many got in way over their ability to service, with the fallout, just a few years later, quite ugly as clubs in financial free fall looked to refinance. Many went into administration. Famous clubs held public fundraising rallies. It was a sad chapter in British football and one that has not yet completely worked itself out.

Kalac had nothing to do with any of this. However, he was witness to the rush of Australian players, who were both sought after, and attracted to, the huge money that was on offer in the UK. Understandably, Kalac was again pricked to the possibilities of overseas. The highway to football fame was congested with every sort of beaten-up jalopy you could imagine. It was as though England had lost its mind. With so much money coming in so quickly, that's not so surprising. For Kalac, a football thoroughbred, it just wouldn't have been right for him to sit roadside watching the stream of football traffic gush past him. "I had all the right ingredients for another club to get me, but not in England. I didn't want to go through that hassle again.

"Holland was fantastic. Roda was a great club, a lot of spirit. It had great fans and great players. I had a great lifestyle there. I was just the right age. I enjoyed my football. I enjoyed life. I couldn't have picked a better place to start a European adventure."

"After the season with Sydney United, I got a call from someone I'd never met in my life. I'd never heard from, or of, him. 'I've got a club for you here in Germany', he said. I was very dubious. I had just bought a house here in Australia. I was going to play football and go back to work and enjoy life. This guy was adamant that he had something for me—Borussia Dortmund—a massive club in Germany. 'What do you want from me?' I asked him. I had to get to Germany.

"I jumped on a plane and headed over. Dortmund had a problem with their first-choice keeper. I stayed for a month. They looked at me and I at them. They couldn't settle their contractual problem with their number one keeper and would have to keep him for another year. They still wanted me, but for the intervening period would move me to Vitesse in Holland for the next season and would bring me back into Dortmund when this guy's contract expired. That seemed okay to me."

Whilst on the way to Vitesse, the phone in Kalac's car rang. It was the president of Roda JC, another club from the Dutch first division. "I hear you have an Australian goalkeeper with you", he said to the agent who was accompanying Kalac. "Yes", the agent said, "a very good one". Roda's president, there and then, offered more money and the guarantee of football.

"So we turned on the highway and went to Roda, simple as that. They finished fourteenth that season, and were almost relegated, they'd used three different keepers and they were adamant that something needed to be done. The next season, my first, there was one other new player too, we finished third in the comp. It was a whirlwind for me. From Dortmund, I was heading to Vitesse and ended up in Kerkrade with Roda JC, and flying."

Dutch football is dominated by the big three—Ajax, Feyenoord and PSV. Roda, from the south of the country, is famous for being the "best of the rest" in a country that is committed to football. It is absolutely fitting that Kalac would end up at Roda, a club with a very convoluted history.

In 1954 Roda Sport was formed by the union of SV Bleijerheide (born in 1914) linked with SV Kerkrade (born in 1926). Meanwhile, also in 1954, Rapid JC was formed from the union of Juliana (1910) and Rapid (1954). In 1962 Roda Sport merged with Rapid JC to form Roda JC (Juliana Combinatie). The "Juliana" strain appears to be quite a strong recessive presence through this club's genealogy. Roda JC won promotion to the Dutch first division in 1973, just a few months after Zeljko Kalac was born, and has not been relegated since. Neither, metaphorically, has Kalac.

"Holland was fantastic. Roda was a great club, a lot of spirit. It had great fans and great players. I had a great lifestyle there. I was just the right age. I enjoyed my football. I enjoyed life. I couldn't have picked a better place to start a European adventure. After all the problems I had in England, where I really lost a couple of years of my career, Holland was great."

Kalac signed a five-year deal with Roda, but in the fourth year of that deal, Italian club Perugia came into the equation and whisked Kalac off to the Serie A. "Perugia was an easy decision. Italy, you can't get your foot in. The Serie A—you can't get your foot in. People don't understand this, how hard it is to get into Italy."

The icebreaker for Kalac was a quarterfinal UEFA Cup game against AC Milan at the San Siro in Milan. Roda lost the first leg 0-1 in Kerkrade but won the return in Milan 1-0. They did it with only ten men, too. Kalac was "on fire. We eventually lost on penalties. I saved two but our team missed three and we were out. The Italians noticed me. Milan has never forgotten that game. They remember it forever, because when I just signed with Milan, Vice-President Adriano Galliani remembers it like it was yesterday.

"Perugia is a beautiful city; it was a great experience. I started to enjoy the food more, dinners and lunches became longer. My lifestyle became slower, compared to Holland where I was out a lot, enjoying myself. Holland, for me, it was the time to do it. Football and enjoyment match themselves. Holland—open-minded people, I was there from twenty-five through to twenty-nine. The team was very competitive but without pressure to win the League. We made UEFA Cup every year, won the Dutch Cup one season without conceding a goal—first time in that country's history that a club achieved that. I was loved by the fans. It was perfect. But it was time to move on.

"My career was always blossoming at club level, but I never got the respect that I deserved because I wasn't playing in England. That's disappointing. I was always playing when sometimes others weren't, but because people weren't seeing me on the English highlights program at home, they didn't know where I was or what I was doing. That was frustrating. When I went to Perugia, playing in Serie A, it still wasn't good enough for people. Perugia is only a small club, granted, but every week I was playing. My peers know what's what."

Perugia also meant an introduction to Saadi Gaddafi, son of Libya's President, Colonel Moamar al Gaddafi. Gaddafi junior was a contracted player at Perugia. He and Kalac hit it off and the friendship, which has endured post-Perugia, was to provide Kalac with a litany of lifetime experiences. "You couldn't imagine the stuff we did. We had a party in Milan one evening and I called some of the [national team] boys to come over. Saadi organised the hotel, all the rooms for the boys, everything. They walked in, their jaws dropped. You have to see it to believe it. When he does something, he does it properly, and people everywhere to do it for him.

"Just before Christmas break one season, he said to me, 'We go to Milano for the night, just tonight, we come back tomorrow'. We flew to Milan, had a night out and stayed in a hotel. He says, 'Let's go somewhere warm, we've got ten days off', so I asked him where we were going to go, what'd he suggest. 'The Bahamas', he said, 'let's go the Bahamas'."

As you do.

Kalac had no clothes other than what he'd worn to Milan for the night. Gaddafi was not fussed. "Let's go, don't worry, we get on the plane [private jet] and get stuff there." That afternoon Kalac was in the Bahamas and nine days later returned to Perugia for training, tanned and relaxed. Naturally the team-mates wanted to know where they'd been. He could offer only one answer—"Bahamas".

"He liked me because of my personality—direct— I always told him what I thought. He was surrounded by people all the time. It was a bit of a circus. Perhaps he liked me because I didn't respond really to all that. I never told him what he wanted to hear, only what I thought. He just seemed to like that. He's a good friend; we keep in contact. It was a hell of a lot of fun. He could play too, but probably didn't have the physical strength. He had the brains and love for football and the desire. He trained really hard.

"He lives in a different world. It's incredible to see. He called one day and asked me to fly with him to Venice to have dinner with him and Nicole Kidman. I told him I was at training. He wasn't fussed, said he'd have his jet at the airport waiting for me straight after training. So I finished training, went to the airport and was flown down to have dinner with Nicole Kidman and Saadi Gaddafi in Venice.

"He's friends with her, loved her movies and her personality. He also loves Australia, loves Aussies. The things that I have seen, I have been privileged. With Gaddafi, it's all organised before you get there. Nothing but the best. He has a huge heart. He's just a good person. I get on well with him, simple.

"People at home couldn't comprehend. My mum and dad have no idea. To be fair, I couldn't have imagined it. I landed in Sydney once, with Saadi, and I called Dad. 'What are you doing? Who are you playing?' We weren't playing anyone. Perugia hadn't paid our wages, so we went to Australia for a bit. Perugia was going bankrupt. They hadn't paid us for a year. It was one hell of a roller-coaster ride."

There'd be more to tell, no doubt. And more adventures to have, if Kalac wanted, but Kalac says that he doesn't have the energy for it now. "Four years in Holland and three in Perugia, fantastic. I had a dream ride. Now, though, I am actually living like a professional. Previously, I was always in good form and happy. Any coach who wants to change your life is going to hurt you. If you are happy, people understand you and you are playing well, then the best thing to do is to keep it on track. If you are happy you'll give your best. If they want to break your routine, they run the risk of messing things up."

Perugia was always interested in signing the Australian. They were a club more likely than many to give foreigners a chance. Because of the attention that foreign players receive in Italy, clubs are very wary of exposing themselves to potential risks. The majority of Italian clubs leave the recruitment of lesser known foreign players to smaller clubs, who are lower profile than the bigger clubs, which suffer terrible PR when an import doesn't work for them. The bigger clubs then allow the smaller clubs to parade their foreign talent. People then wait and see who shapes up, who acclimatises, who survives in the greenhouse of Italian football. Perugia would then do business in passing the foreigner up the chain. For Kalac, Perugia provided the forum for him to show Italy what he was about. It worked well for Kalac, but not so well for Perugia.

Ultimately, Perugia didn't get to sell Kalac. Their financial problems resulted in free agency for players and also saw them relegated to Serie B. Kalac was free to move to a club of his choice.

Kalac had multiple offers on the table when his time with Perugia ended. At each of those clubs he would have played regularly. "But I said to myself that I want to go and train and play with these guys at San Siro. I didn't think it would be this full on. I watched these guys play; they are not normal. I thought they'd all be full of themselves when I first arrived, but they are top people. Paulo Maldini was the first one up to shake my hand. Italy and Milan legend, he just didn't hesitate.

"Milan knew everything about me. They knew where I was and what I was doing. They couldn't bring me any earlier because they were full. They don't go and get someone for the sake of it.

As soon as room was freed up, last year Christian Abiatti asked to leave, and they came straight in for me. Abiatti wasn't playing, hadn't played for three years. They remembered me from five years ago, and came straight in for me. For Perugia, I played eight times against Milan, they remembered all of it."

For Kalac, Milan is a totally different mind-set. He is at a different stage of life, too. He'd played at every club to whom he'd been contracted and felt he had nothing to prove to anyone. He went to Milan in full knowledge that he would be number two keeper at the club, behind Brazilian Dida. He was offered more money than anyone else could offer and, for Kalac, it was an obvious choice. Milan is one of the world's mega clubs. Kalac has arguably broken new ground for Australian players by moving there. This is the football big time; this is football Hollywood. It does not get any bigger than AC Milan.

Quite understandably, Kalac finds the whole thing difficult to believe himself. "Some days, when I get to training, I watch these players, the same ones I used to watch on TV. Champions League nights were the only nights I wouldn't go out, watching these guys on TV from Kerkrade or Perugia. I was transfixed. And now I am here, participating with one of the world's most successful clubs in that competition, at one of the world's biggest clubs. They don't sell players, they only buy, and they only buy the biggest.

"There is someone or something for everything you need at Milan. You want it, or need it, they do it. We have our own hotel rooms here at the training ground. Every person has their own room with computer, DVD, TV—everything to make you comfortable. If there is anything wrong, you let them know. The remote control doesn't work on your television, you let them know. By the time you have come back from training, the remote is either working again or it has been replaced."

"They don't sell players, they only buy, and they only buy the biggest."

As a sign of his developed years, Kalac goes home after training nowadays. Training sessions are usually televised. "I can't be going out at night and coming to training under the whip. People are watching and making opinions. The scrutiny is too much. It's okay for me, I'm not [Andriy] Shevchenko—for him it's impossible. He can't even go out for an hour shopping in peace. They break my balls enough, but him, his life is ludicrous. But what a player."

Kalac waited months to play in the League with Milan. When he did, he received rave reviews for his performance. "I am competitive and want to play, but I know what it's about here. They know I want to play and they know what I am about. That is one of the reasons they like me. I got heaps of accolades for the things I have done and I was very happy, but I know that when Dida is fit he'll be back in. That's how it works at the big clubs. The number one plays until he drops and then it'll be my turn."

AC Milan is an all-encompassing life. Kalac sleeps in his own house and bed "twice a week", because the rest of the time, the team is in camp or travelling. "They are nice guys, good companions and work-mates but enough is enough. We all need time to get away from each other and the job."

For Kalac, his success in the job has been because he has kept it, for as long as possible, as a game. His attitude and spirit are what has won people to him, and his steadfast determination to enjoy this life that he has been given and that he has crafted is the footnote to his life.

If ever a scene sums this up better than anything, it is one described by Johnny Warren from the 1991 Youth World Cup in Portugal. Warren was in attendance in his capacity as a TV commentator. Australia had qualified for the semifinals of the tournament. Kalac was then understudy to Mark Bosnich. Young players, eager to impress, hoping to be noticed for a European contract, played against host Portugal at the Estadio da Luz in Lisbon, with 80,000 in attendance. Quite a tense atmosphere, one would imagine. With both teams taking the half-time break, the field was left for the substitutes to perhaps get ready for a second-half inclusion in the game. Kalac, according to Warren, "was performing overhead scissor kicks as his half-time warm-up". Warren would have no reason to gild the lily. Moreover, it fits with the Kalac philosophy, "to always live life the best you can live it, you never know what tomorrow is holding for you".

For Kalac and the rest of the team, there is a big "tomorrow" looming.

"I expect to get past the first round in Germany. The third game against Croatia is nothing [special] to handle, we have to beat them. I want to win so the people in Croatia realise what Australia is. It will take us to win on the big stage for people to believe us.

"We believe we can do it. We got this far because of that. I don't think we really believed it last time. There was a lot of positive talk but the vibes weren't right. Inevitability doesn't happen in football, if you don't put in, you don't get there. Hiddink was

---

"I can take criticism, I have taken pain, I have taken disappointment and accepted it all without spitting the dummy."

massive. He woke us up with his charisma, his character and we responded to him. He was so calm, it went through the whole team. There were too many mistakes in the past.

"The crowd was brilliant. I can't remember many nights in Australian sport as big as that. We are used to seeing other Aussie teams win. We were used to seeing the Socceroos lose the big game. Well, didn't that change. The mentality was right, the moment was right. The Federation has to take credit for the platform they laid."

It has been a Promised Land experience for a committed servant. Kalac has been sustained by his strength of mind. "I can take criticism, I have taken pain, I have taken disappointment and accepted it all without spitting the dummy." His character and will to win have kept him plotting this course until now, where he is with one of the biggest sporting clubs in the world and preparing to partake in the biggest sporting event in the world. Luddenham would be, should be, proud of him. "I missed the Barcelona Olympics at the last minute, that hurt. I have had to take stuff on the chin, be strong, beat it. You can't go spitting the dummy. How many times could I have 'retired' from international football? I was playing every week. What else did people want? Because I didn't play in England? No, I wasn't going to spit the dummy. Where would that have got me? This all means too much to me."

Zeljko Kalac is no dummy spitter, in case you missed his point. He's an Aussie who believes in himself and is prepared to have a go. He just makes sure that he enjoys himself along the way, and bravo to that!

19

shirt number

"I am looking forward to playing a role in the development of Australia's football. It is so exciting to be part of this. I look forward to the day when the sport is recognised in Australia as it should be."

Jason Culina

Date of birth 5 August 1980

Position played Midfielder

Current club PSV Eindhoven, the Netherlands

One of football's great mysteries is how players who make the game look so rough have such smooth careers, whilst players who glide around a field looking so smooth have such relatively rough careers. There can be no answer to this, other than life can sometimes be a funny thing.

Not particularly funny, however, when you are the subject of such a tale. Jason Culina is one such player. So easy on the eye is Culina, that watching him play can transfer a viewer to another state, where time has no meaning and gravity doesn't exist. As a youngster learning his game in Australia, there were many who commented that Culina took too many touches on the ball. One's response to that might now be, too many isn't enough. Granted, like any player, there is a maturation process required to understand, in the fuller picture of football, what is required and when. This resistance to what he was offering is perhaps a reason why it has taken so long for Jason Culina's career to really blossom. However, like a desert flower waiting patiently for rain to arrive, Jason Culina is now, however belatedly, in full bloom.

Like many of this Socceroos team, Culina is a product of Australia's Croatian migrant community. And like many of those same players, his first club was with a Croatian community club. Jason Culina is from Melbourne, and he started playing football with St Albans Dynamo. From Dynamo he moved to the Melbourne Knights until his father, Branko, took the family to Sydney so that he could take on the coaching position at Sydney United.

Culina moved into the club's Colts team, and then the Reserves, and by sixteen, his father had put him in the first team at Sydney United. During his time with Sydney United, Culina was offered a scholarship with the AIS but turned it down, because "I thought playing with Popa [Tony Popovic] and Spider [Zeljko Kalac] and these guys was a better learning opportunity for me".

The coaching merry-go-round saw father Branko move across town to Sydney Olympic. Jason packed up and followed suit, having a brief time with Olympic—which coincided with the 2000 Olympics—before the he moved to Europe.

Jason had obviously been doing enough to earn his place in the national youth teams, but otherwise his time in Australia was unremarkable. He was never, and still isn't, one to look for the spotlight or a soapbox. His focus, which becomes obvious the more one watches him play, is football, and getting as good as he can at it.

Perhaps part of his "problem" as a young player was that he was the son of Branko. Branko, the coach, was busy forging his own career in the Australian game in a full-time sense after taking a break from his career in publishing. Branko himself had made enough sacrifices to chase the first love of his professional life, football. There can be little doubt that Jason learned, by observation, what dedication to football is all about.

But football in Australia has been a fractured organism over the years, where suspicion and jealousy have reigned supreme and individuals who try to make their way are often castigated or maligned. Whether this environment was problematic is a moot point, because Jason is now sailing the seven football seas with a full spinnaker, and his father, Branko, has continued to be in football, full time, in Australia. Suffice to say, the local scene probably caused its share of grief for the Culina family.

The observation that one feels comfortable to make at this juncture, however, is that of all the influences father may have had on son, the way Jason plays football is a testament to growing up in the close confines of a culture that appreciates the simple beauties of the game. Those simple beauties are to be admired of themselves, but they are also the building blocks to an effective football philosophy. One can feel safe making such an observation about the Culinas because teams coached by Branko have always played a nice, entertaining and fluent style of football. And as Jason Culina goes about his business, with his own specific interpretations on situations, the cultural hard-wiring that has taken place is equally obvious. In this sense, it has been a good union.

But father promoting son is never an easy thing to manage in a professional environment, particularly in sport and particularly when that sport is football, in Australia. Nepotism is rarely an easy sell, irrespective of the bona fides of the individuals involved.

Jason is full of praise and gratitude for his father's influence, though. "I wouldn't have got a chance when I was sixteen and I know he got a hard time when he gave me my chance, not only by spectators but also by players. It was only later that they began to see I was serious about what I was doing, and they started to believe in me. But now I am very grateful to him and my family."

Whatever else is true, there are not many players who can go home after training and talk football with someone who has put so much time and effort into understanding it. Whose chosen path in life is then to communicate that knowledge and organise for its dissemination within a team environment, and who then has to juggle the multiplicity of issues that arise when managing people and players in a football club. For Jason to have this insight so close at hand could only have helped.

"It has helped me more than hindered me, definitely. His [Branko's] experience and knowledge. Everybody knew the Culinas as Branko, but over the last couple of years I am starting to get my own space. The national team and other things have helped. I am very grateful to my dad and what he has done for Australian football. He has helped greatly.

"There are still jibes about it all. But I think everyone likes him and they are grateful too for the input he has had into their careers. A lot of the players in this national team. He gave Mark Viduka his first chance at the Melbourne Knights."

Jason Culina always wanted to be a footballer. Not such a surprise, given his family and the communities in which they mixed. Most kids probably wanted to be footballers. "School was no good for me. I never took it seriously. When I started playing for the Joeys [Australia Under 16/17s] I was away from school a lot, and with Sydney United too, the travel took too much, and halfway through Year Eleven I quit school. Football was something I always wanted to do."

From Sydney, Culina was to go to Brondy in Denmark, a club with a good reputation for developing young players. "I was about to sign there and the coach got fired. I'd left to go to the Youth World Cup in Nigeria, with the Under 20s and Ajax [of Amsterdam] was at the tournament."

Ajax, perhaps the biggest club in the Netherlands, has become synonymous with football development, and its reputation, based on the procession of high-quality footballers who have gone on to play for the Dutch national team as well as the big teams in Europe, is second to none. When Ajax expressed interest, Culina sat bolt upright.

"At the time, my father also received a call from Italy. I went there for a quick spell, but I got injured at training and only had one session in the two weeks I was there. Afterwards, I went to Ajax to have a look around. Hamburg, from Germany, also got interested and they approached me. By the end of the week I had to choose between Ajax and Hamburg.

"I had always seen Ajax on television and knew of their youth system. I decided to go there. It was a bit daunting. I was nineteen, walking into the dressing room, and it wasn't even the coach who took me to Ajax. It was very difficult because they expect a lot from you.

"It took about a year to get used to things and I am not very patient, because I wanted it to be straightaway. When I realised things weren't going my way, I started to get frustrated. You have to be mentally strong to go to a big club like that. Maybe I should have stayed in Australia for a bit longer to get a bit tougher mentally, physically too."

In fact, Culina's move to the Netherlands was not turning out well at all. It was to take him literally years to find his feet. Years to get to a position where he could do what he always wanted to do—play football with regularity and freedom of expression.

To get into the mind of a young athlete in this situation, if possible, is instructive. The degree of self-doubt must have been significant. Culina left Australia in 1999 to take up his place with Ajax, a dream club and a dream destination. To be seven years into that journey and turn around and say, "The first three or four years were very difficult, it really wasn't working out" is a very stark realisation. Away from family, away from friends and barely playing. Culina's dream of playing at Ajax, even after all that time, was stillborn. Playing action with Ajax came in the youth and reserve teams. Ajax also loaned him out every second year, firstly to Germinal Beerschot in Belgium and then to De Graafschap in the Netherlands. It had been a very disjointed period for a player who was looking to actually bed down some footballing foundations. It speaks to the character of the individual to have persevered through this. One wonders what did keep him going.

"It wasn't until the fifth year when I really started to play well. That was under the guidance of Van Basten." Incredibly, the one coach who has been able to put air in Culina's tyres is one of the all-time great strikers, Marco Van Basten, himself a product of the Ajax youth system. Van Basten won universal admiration for his achievements on the football field, with Ajax, AC Milan and the Netherlands. Here was Van Basten admiring a product of Australia, and a withered product of Australia at that. But there was something about Culina that pressed Van Basten's buttons.

"I think he liked my determination. I thought it was my last contract at Ajax. For me, it was all or nothing. I was resigned to going out and enjoying myself. The worst thing that can happen is that I go back home and play in Australia. That wouldn't be bad either."

To do well under Van Basten did wonders for the Culina stocks. When Van Basten speaks, the Netherlands listens. Actually, that is true literally, as he is currently the head coach of the Dutch national team and will lead them to the World Cup finals in Germany. "Fortunately, it went really well. To have Van Basten talk about you well to other clubs really pumps you up. It was perfect." It was Van Basten who moved Culina forward from his more traditional midfield role and played him as an attacker. As they say in the trade, Culina was "banging them in for fun", goals that is, under Van Basten, and it was this more than anything that lit the torch on a career that was only surviving off promise to this point.

From the period of renaissance under Van Basten in the Ajax reserve team, Culina moved to FC Twente in the border town of Enschede. "The coach believed in me there and even though I didn't play every game to the best of my ability he kept giving me a chance. I was fortunate because not every coach would do that."

Culina is perhaps being a bit humble with the truth. He shot out of the blocks at FC Twente, almost as though he let loose with all the anguish that had built up throughout his troubles at Ajax. Culina was a headline in the Netherlands during the 2004–05 season with Twente. Now it was not just Van Basten and the Twente coach, Rini Coolen, who were taking notice.

"The coach persevered with me because he realised my determination. I never give up. I am good tactically, although I could be better, but I have improved dramatically. And I started scoring goals. Van Basten must have rubbed off on me!"

Another significant personality in Dutch football also took notice of Culina. Guus Hiddink, football boss at PSV Eindhoven, also

---

"I think he liked my determination. I thought it was my last contract at Ajax. For me, it was all or nothing. I was resigned to going out and enjoying myself. The worst thing that can happen is that I go back home and play in Australia. That wouldn't be bad either."

"I was very close to coming home. A lot of phone calls between Holland and Australia were had. Close to tears with the frustration. You know that you are a good player. It's so hard to express yourself when things aren't going well, and the more you try, the harder it gets. I came to a point after five years, I'd just had enough."

liked what he saw of Culina at Twente, and six games into the 2005–06 season, Culina moved to Hiddink's club. Guus Hiddink is also coach of the Australian national team. A soaring club career, a new contract with one of the big clubs of the Netherlands, and the interest at both club and international level of one of contemporary football's sharpest operators, Culina must have wondered why he was ever worried.

"I was very close to coming home. A lot of phone calls between Holland and Australia were had. Close to tears with the frustration. You know that you are a good player. It's so hard to express yourself when things aren't going well, and the more you try, the harder it gets. I came to a point after five years, I'd just had enough."

"So I started putting in my mind that I missed my family, that was a reason to come home, making excuses for myself. But deep down I knew that I should be staying, that I had come overseas for a reason. It was just too easy to pack up and go home. That's where the mental toughness kicks in, I suppose. Some players have it easy in their careers. Some have it harder. I used to watch other players, exasperated, thinking 'He is nowhere near as good as me. He is playing at this club, or that club, and here I am and I can't even get a game in the youth team. What the hell is going on here?'

“I don’t regret the Ajax experience at all. I went there because I chose to go there. Good or bad, you learn from these things. It definitely made me stronger and when, if, things go bad from here, I have a compass to steer my way out of trouble.”

At least Culina is now familiar with his surroundings. The pincer movement for young Australians going to Europe is the difficulty of the football and lack of familiarity with the surroundings. Individually, they are both big tests, but lumped together, they become a significant burden with which to deal.

“Being in Amsterdam helped when I first came because it is very multicultural—a bit like home really. You get used to Holland after six years too—time helps. And I have learned the language, to an extent. I can speak it if I really want, but I hate making mistakes and getting laughed at, so I sometimes don’t try too hard. Then Enschede, it is a very small town and it can get a bit frustrating, but because the football was going well, it was okay. It might have been a bit much otherwise.

“I miss this place [Holland] when I go back to Australia. It probably took two or three years to stop missing Australia. You always miss your family and that never fades, but I always know that I am going to be back there when I finish here.”

Culina’s club form sent a signal to Australia that perhaps he should be looked at for the national team. As part of the development system in Australia, through all the various youth teams, Culina had been earmarked for further involvement. But his slide into the nether leagues of the Netherlands made it impossible for him to be considered for selection. It has only taken that one real season with Twente to get Culina back on the screen.

"I never really expected to be in the Socceroos. I had to prove to people and to myself that I was good enough and durable enough. Then, I did start to wonder when I was going to get the call. It was frustrating because I was told on a couple of occasions by Frank Farina that he was coming to watch, and he never turned up."

"I had to refocus. I wasn't doing this for anyone else, only me. It's not my team, it's their team. I can't control anything, I will just keep going. Eventually, he came to an away game in January [2005] against Willem II. I scored one and set one up, and from that time I have been included in the picture."

The picture included an international debut against South Africa in Durban, February 2005, which finished one goal apiece.

"A debut for your national team is always special. But the team really didn't go that well and it wasn't a great period for the national team. They were difficult circumstances, too. I came in the day before the camp, after a long flight, from the cold of a European winter, and arrived in Durban in an African summer. And I went straight into the starting line-up. But I was so happy to be part of it."

Of Culina, it couldn't be said that his has been a meteoric rise. But it could be said that 2005 was, for him, an incredible turnaround.

"It's been a long road to hoe. Then it happened all so quickly. It's been an incredible eighteen months and it still hasn't really sunk in. But I don't take anything for granted, at PSV or with the Socceroos. I treat every day as though it could be my last."

"There will be a lot of hype surrounding our game against Croatia. It will be quite emotional for a few of us in the Aussie team, as well as it will be for the Aussies in the Cro team. But when the game starts, it will be just football."

"It's been a long road to hoe. Then it happened all so quickly. It's been an incredible eighteen months and it still hasn't really sunk in. But I don't take anything for granted, at PSV or with the Socceroos. I treat every day as though it could be my last."

The value of appreciating and being happy is a key to Jason Culina's success. It was a key to his survival before the success came. A clear picture of what he always wanted to do, and what he wanted to be, never left him for any serious length of time, even considering the time his football took to get rolling. He is a quiet man, considerate and neatly presented, still-mannered and respectful. He needed all those attributes to sift through and make sense of his situation.

His circumspection, a result of the union between his personality and his experience, will be a handy tool when the World Cup comes around. "We have difficult opponents, but as Aussies we always go out in every game and try to win. We will go out to enjoy ourselves and to play our best. There is no point putting too much pressure on ourselves.

"There will be a lot of hype surrounding our game against Croatia. It will be quite emotional for a few of us in the Aussie team, as well as it will be for the Aussies in the Cro team. But when the game starts, it will be just football."

One of those "Aussies in the Cro team" is Joey Didulica. Didulica, a goalkeeper from the Melbourne Knights, spent time with Culina at Ajax before moving his football to Austria Vienna. He was to be a groomsman at Culina's wedding in Sydney but missed a connecting flight from Los Angeles and missed the ceremony. Didulica tired of waiting for a call-up to the Socceroos; instead, he has become a Croatia international. That exchange, should it come to pass, will be an emotional one.

Culina's preoccupation, at least outwardly, with the World Cup qualification is the impact it will have on the sport in Australia. Overwhelmed by the outpouring of support from the Australian community, for Culina it was heartening to see Australians supporting football the way it is supported around the world. For him, apparently, this was a breakthrough. "Montevideo was fantastic; that is where you see the real football fans, what it means to people, and to see a similar thing in Sydney was fantastic.

"But we need more good results. And the World Cup will lift the profile again and that is good for football. We still have a fair way to go in Australia, one or two games isn't going to do it.

"There is a fantastic feeling in the national team now. The best since I have been involved. And on the field we know what we are doing, it's fantastic.

"I am looking forward to playing a role in the development of Australia's football. It is so exciting to be part of this. I look forward to the day when the sport is recognised in Australia as it should be."

Culina's grand plan is to enjoy himself. That has been his lesson so far—getting paid for what he loves doing. Every day he wants to step on the field smiling and up for the challenge, so that when he gets back to Australia, or finishes football, and wherever his career has taken him, he will be grateful and happy for the experience.

Along the way, he will have provided many people with much pleasure. Jason Culina is happy that he persevered, and so too is football's viewing public. There's hopefully plenty more to come.

23

shirt number

"I can't lose. I always have aims and I don't stop until I get what I want. I never give up. I could easily have given up when I was younger, never making those rep teams, thinking I wasn't good enough etc., but I believed in myself."

Marco Bresciano

Date of birth 11 February 1980

Position played Midfielder

Current club Parma, Italy

Marco Bresciano was born to build things. Were it not to be a football career, it would have been bridges, computer processing units or chemical concoctions for the multinationals. You see, even though his focus was football, his contingency plan was engineering. Or he may have diversified slightly into the world of explosives and demolition, because bursting through the midfield of a football pitch and shooting at goal, you'd swear he had dynamite in both feet. To date, the twenty-six-year-old has combined the two interests in his life—the subsidiary with the primary—and engineered a football career that has been built methodically and assiduously from the ground up. By the time he's finished, Marco Bresciano could well become the grandest building in Australian sport's entire architectural range.

The only impression one can get when speaking with Bresciano is that everything is completely under control. Manifestly in charge of his own destiny, he is rolling out each of the chapters of the plan only when the time is right. Much thought has gone into the roll-out. Not a lot has been left to chance. Each upward step is only taken when he is assured that the ladder is securely affixed to terra firma and won't topple over—too high, too fast is not the way to go. The tensile strength of the supporting structures has to be guaranteed before additions are made. Vertigo isn't a problem, because he refuses to look back and see how far he has climbed—you can't get the wobbles if you don't know your altitude, and anyway, the lessons learned along the way have provided the necessary material flexibility to withstand sudden changes or unforeseen circumstances. Besides, the view is better from the top, once the climb has finished.

There are a lot of stories in contemporary Australia that reflect the way in which migrants have worked their way into the fabric of Australian society, by their sweat and toil, to make a life for themselves and their families. Modern Australia has been built on the back of these people, folk who have arrived here without anything really to their name except rolled-gold integrity and an iron-clad commitment to work. An inkling of an opportunity for a life better made was the only consumable in their baggage.

Marco Bresciano is the fruit of such labour. Humbled by his parents' daring and bravery—for emigration is a brave and daring option to take—Bresciano is an Australian-born-and-raised example of why, and how, multiculturalism works. He is a gracious man with a laid-back exterior and an elephant-like memory of where this all came from and what it's all about.

"My family is not an educated one. It's not a football one. Both my parents migrated in the 1970s. My dad from Potenza in southern Italy and mum from Istria, which is Croatia now but was Italy before the war [World War II]. They came here with nothing and provided everything for us, the three of us, including private schools, the best that they could give us. Like a lot of families, they struggled and worked hard to send us to good schools and to get us an education. Most of my success, I owe it to them. People who came with nothing and made good lives for themselves with their sweat. It's not an uncommon story. It's the hunger, with nothing, the only way to survive was to work hard and do your job."

For someone working to enter the cut and thrust of professional football, these are salient observations to make. Football, the most popular sport in the entire world, is full of people who dream of making the top. Football, the passion of the people of the world and plaything of the rich and the famous, is also a boulevard of broken dreams. Football has the capacity to inspire and unite, with those who scale the summit bestowed with untold riches, both mercantile and intangible. But it takes a lot of work to get there. By his parents' example, Bresciano learned good lessons from his earliest days and is reaping the rewards now.

His appetite for the fight in football was created early when he couldn't get selected for Victorian squads, which for Victorian kids is typically the most direct route to a career in football. "I always seemed to get cut at the last stage of the Vic trials and I wasn't involved with the VIS [Victorian Institute of Sport]." Not because he didn't want to be there, desperately; it was just that what he had wasn't wanted back then. If only they "knew" then what can be readily seen now.

Instead, Bresciano was a one-club junior man. As a youngster, he joined the Bulleen Veneto club, "which is called the Bulleen Zebras I think now", and played with them through the junior ranks up to the reserves team. He was selected to play in the Australian Schoolboys team, from which Ron Smith (currently technical manager for Australia's national teams) recruited him to the Australian Institute of Sport.

"I was a bit lucky, I guess, because the Schoolboys program isn't historically a really big part of the football culture. But I had a good tournament at the championships and was happy to accept a scholarship to the AIS.

"I wanted to be a footballer as a little kid. I was concentrating on both school and soccer. Non-selection in things didn't really faze me, although there were tears, but it was the best thing that

"I was very excited when Carlton took me in. Vince Grella was there too, which was good. I still think and reminisce about Carlton days. They were very good memories."

---

happened to me. I remember seeing a lot of the boys who were getting the nod at the time and I thought they were pretty good, but now, I don't even know where they are or even if they are still playing."

The effect of non-selection gave him the hunger and aggression to go further. "I was always on this track but I was taking my schooling very seriously if football didn't take off. At school, I wasn't bad with maths and sciences, I was looking at engineering." But in what is a common refrain from players in this Socceroos team who've been through the national institute, "It was the AIS that really fired me up about the possibilities" [of a career in football].

For Bresciano, the possibilities were always going to be explored in bite-sized measures. From the AIS, he moved to the now-defunct Carlton in the NSL. "I like to take things step by step, never doing a big jump. I knew that from the AIS I wanted to go to the National League in Australia, and from there I wanted to go overseas. But I didn't want to go into the high leagues, I wanted to work myself up. I always knew the steps I wanted to take.

"I was very excited when Carlton took me in. Vince Grella was there too, which was good. I still think and reminisce about Carlton days. They were very good memories."

Which gets on to a recurring theme in the Bresciano story—Vince Grella. It's also a recurring theme to the Grella story—Bresciano.

"Vince and I first hooked up in the junior regionals. We then were at the AIS together, had time at Carlton together, then Empoli together, and now we are at Parma together. It's a bit by chance and a bit by design. We both have the same manager."

It is more than that, though. The two have variously described the brotherhood that exists between them. Theirs is more than merely coincidental careers.

"Vince went to Empoli first and I followed a few months later. We knew that Empoli would be a good club for us, a good schooling club for young players. Because of our management, we were both getting the same advice, so that put us together. Vince left for Empoli about six months before I did."

In one sense, Grella's earlier arrival provided a sort of bulwark for Bresciano. "When I first arrived, I sensed a big difference in Vince, the seriousness and the focus, he was much more aggressive. It was very hard to break in over there. They look at you as very much a foreigner trying to take a local's position. They weren't too happy. But we just kept quiet and worked. The Italians like the Aussie mentality, though. We are part of the furniture there [in Italy] now. I've been there for seven years. They respect us a lot more and kind of look at us as Italians, though in the back of their minds we are always Australians. Now they are a lot more open and make us feel a lot more comfortable.

"For me, it took about two years before I settled really; the third year I started to feel comfortable. Not so much what people are thinking of you, it's more on the park. My life is what happens on the park, in training and in games. You can sense it when you are on the pitch—the comments and the tackles. We got the worst tackles when we first went over there. That's all part of the test. In the third year, when they realised that I was good, finally, and I was fair dinkum, life became a bit easier."

It is, by any measure, a long examination to have to sit and a difficult one to pass. But pass it one must, if progression is going to be achieved. There is nothing for nothing in this environment, particularly at the start of the voyage. It is very much a throwback to the gladiatorial testing ground, where only the few survive. In an uncoordinated sort of way, "everything" is heaped on the young hopefuls to see exactly what they are made of. Talent gets them through the door, but talent itself won't be enough to survive the introduction. And the feeling is, if one can't survive the introduction, then it is better found out earlier than later, for the crux of a key game in a packed stadium with a title or survival or a cup on the line is no place to realise that a faint heart has been contracted. The attention is so relentless for the players in Italy, that the introductory pains are a necessary part of the process, a rite of passage. To the extent that some careers are destroyed by this before they have even started, they could be considered mercy killings.

Despite Carlton receiving other offers, none matched what Empoli offered Bresciano. "It isn't a big city, only about 50,000 people. They are renowned for their youth. They produce players and sell them to the bigger clubs. That is their business model. That's how they survive. It was good for my development." Given the general difficulties of adjustment, the passage was smoothed significantly by making a good choice of club. "Empoli fans aren't

---

"We got the worst tackles when we first went over there. That's all part of the test. In the third year, when they realised that I was good, finally, and I was fair dinkum, life became a bit easier."

“It’s tough, sometimes the Italians can take the fun out of football. In Italy, it’s so stressful and they don’t help themselves. In fact they create it. Home and away games, we are always in camp, always having meetings. They seem to perform better under stress.”

---

very aggressive. Some clubs have troublesome fans, not Empoli. In your personal life, the fans left you alone and let you live your life. At some clubs that isn’t the case. It is a more middle-class area. The fans were happy to see us in the top division, but there was no pressure to win things. Really, there weren’t enough people to cause us trouble anyway. The facilities weren’t the best, but we knew we were going to get the chance to play.

“The NSL was a million miles from where I went. It was totally different. In Italy, football is their life. In Australia we have a lot of distractions and we enjoy ourselves in other ways. The people there [Italy] look forward to the weekends just so they can see their team play. There is more money involved so there are more businesspeople there, more business oriented. I noticed that when I came here.

“It’s tough, sometimes the Italians can take the fun out of football. In Italy, it’s so stressful and they don’t help themselves. In fact they create it. Home and away games, we are always in camp, always having meetings. They seem to perform better under stress. For me, it hasn’t taken the fun out of the game. The training and the game, I still enjoy it, but the environment can be a bit much. A lot of the boys playing in the English League, they love it there. Over there, it sounds like it is more of a sport and they have some down time. In Italy, it’s full-on the whole time and it is totally all-consuming.

"Everyone sees the good bits, the fame and money, whatever. Behind the scenes that people don't see ... our lives change. Our family and friends suffer from the sacrifice. We don't live a normal life. That's the price we pay, and I'm okay with it, but sometimes people like to have their own private space and that can be difficult to find. Players do go through depression when things happen."

Football can be a difficult thing to control. There are many variables, but because the atmosphere is so intense, and because of the nature of the people who make it to this level anyway, football governs the other aspects of their life. It is not something that is turned on and off like a tap. When things aren't going well, the pressure can be enormous.

"Australia has no idea what my life has become. The AFL is the only thing that is closest and it's still pretty far away from it. Italy is pretty bad, I'd reckon South America is like it, too, a bit. It's not 'bad'. I wouldn't be doing this if I didn't love it. I love all that pressure, maybe that is what gets me going as well. But it is full on."

Bresciano's real Italy is totally different from the Australian version in which he grew up. "I thought I knew Italian when I came over here. Aussies speak with a mix of English and Italian. It is much faster here, too. The culture shock was significant. Simple things like realising the shops go from nine o'clock to one o'clock, then it is siesta in the arvo till four. The whole city is dead. It took a little while to get used to. Italy's a different world, a different lifestyle."

And Parma, from Empoli, was different again. "It's a bigger city, a bigger club, bigger expectations and a bigger history. Parma is actually a good city, wealthy and civilised, and the people aren't too bad."

Bresciano transferred from Empoli for a big fee, for $20 million or thereabouts, making him the most expensive player in Australia's history. When you achieve the status of being a top goal-scoring midfielder in the Serie A, which Bresciano did in the 2003–04 season, your worth on the transfer market does tend to shoot skywards.

Parma, though, was heading for a "big" degree of trouble too. In December 2003, the rug was pulled from under the huge corporate fraud that centred on Parmalat, the Italian dairy giant that held a significant stake in the Parma football club. In fact it is the biggest bankruptcy in European history. The depth and brazenness of the fraud, as it has been revealed, is outrageously breathtaking. The quagmire that resulted has placed the football club under enormous pressure. Unfortunately, the players haven't been shielded from the tension.

"The problems of Parmalat affected the football operation significantly. The club is very different now, as opposed to when I arrived [2002]. It is the third year now that we have been playing with no president. It's run by the government, and is in administration. It's a big change. There's no structure, it's all a bit of a mess. [Lorenzo] Sanz [ex-Real Madrid boss] was going to take over and buy the club. It was actually a negative for us. Each week, there was a date made as to when he was going to come in and take over, and each week it changed again. Then he was going to bring in his own coach and staff and players. Most of us were concentrating on when and who, and not concentrating on the games, and perhaps there was a drop in respect for the coach who was there at the time. We were all thinking that he was going to go. That's why I think we struggled at the start of the season. This went on for five or six months and then we just said, 'Forget it, let's just get on with it'. Nothing happened since then, but we did start to pull ourselves up the table."

"It is hugely flattering. All your hard work is being noticed and people are interested. It's a confidence boost. It helps you train."

Parmalat's effect on Parma hasn't unduly affected Bresciano, it would seem. The big clubs have already been hovering. Inter Milan was widely reported as one of those. "I could have gone to a bigger club than Inter two years ago." A bigger club than Inter! "[AC] Milan, Inter [Milan] and Juventus [of Turin] are the big three. You work it out. I put it off then, because I wasn't ready, it wasn't the right time."

It is with those dynamite feet that Bresciano is attracting so much attention. Goal scoring has always been a feature of his game, and to have risen to the standard of the Serie A is hugely gratifying. "Scoring goals at training is good—imagine what it is like in the Serie A or the Cup or UEFA. It's an incredible rush. I usually celebrate, the statue stance, like I did against Uruguay. It's just natural. It's a buzz." The "buzz" has made its way around the entire Serie A. A move to one of the giants of Italy, which would really be a remarkable achievement, appears to be edging closer.

"It is hugely flattering. All your hard work is being noticed and people are interested. It's a confidence boost. It helps you train. Living in Italy is week by week, you win and you have a good week, eating in restaurants etc. You lose and the introspection is almost unbearable. News like that boosts you a little bit more.

"I am getting close and I am almost ready to move to a bigger club. You have to be careful in Italy, because there's a lot of hatred between clubs' fans. You have to be careful what you say in the press, keep a low profile, and when you are interviewed just answer in general. You can't afford to give them much. You have to be very guarded. But they understand that the players have ambitions. When players come back to Parma and play against them, as long as you are focused on playing for Parma [now] they'll respect you [then]."

Bresciano thinks quickly, but is slow to speak. He measures his words with the same precision that he has planned out his career, the same consistency that he passes the ball and the same accuracy that he shoots for goal. The key to his success, he says after some contemplation, is, "I can't lose. I always have aims and I don't stop until I get what I want. I never give up. I could easily have given up when I was younger, never making those rep teams, thinking I wasn't good enough etc., but I believed in myself. I will find goals to achieve, to play World Cup and move to a big club. It's hard to stay at the top and be there as long as possible, that's a challenge in itself, which I am looking forward to. It's a dream to move to one of the big ones.

"Everything has gone okay. Step by step. There have been no dodgy agents, no real politics, no major injury. There is a bit of fortune along the way, but I have sought and received good advice about where to go and who to trust, so that takes the luck out of it a bit. And I am happy with the way things are going. The people I am involved with are people I trust. There is no-one else in that circle at the moment."

"I will find goals to achieve, to play World Cup and move to a big club. It's hard to stay at the top and be there as long as possible, that's a challenge in itself, which I am looking forward to. It's a dream to move to one of the big ones."

Part of the "small steps" philosophy of Bresciano is that it has enabled him to build his confidence, as much as build his learning, as he went. Growing up and playing in Australia, European football is full of stereotypes and perceptions. Those perceptions tend to be skewed somewhat because of the distance between Europe and Australia. The television highlights packages—the diet that feeds the perception—are not always an accurate picture of what is actually what. A ninety-minute game edited down to a couple of minutes of highlights is, by definition and necessity, going to look spectacular. Superimposed over all this is the negative press that football and footballers in Australia receive. It is no wonder that young Australians who go to Europe, apart from the difficulties of assimilation, realise that in technical football terms, they aren't as bad as everyone, and seemingly everything, has been making out.

"Once you get involved and see the players, well, it changes your view. When I went, I initially thought Empoli was it for me. But you get to see the players and realise, 'Hey, I can do this'." The training ground is a great leveller and benchmarking exercise. Relative abilities become obvious and there is no reason why things can't be done. "I wasn't really thinking about the big club thing. I was just hungry, was putting everything on the line for this. The only thing I was doing was training and playing. The last couple of years at Empoli were when I started believing, playing, scoring goals and being noticed."

Big clubs and big stages—there are none bigger in either category than Italy's big three or the World Cup. He's not that type of person, but to the selectors of those junior teams that Bresciano never made, it's not a bad "I told you so".

Australia versus Uruguay was a big stage, too. Perhaps the biggest stage Australian football has been on. The four years since the

2002 Uruguay qualifiers have seen a lot of changes, another positive sign of the times perhaps. "The crowd really sticks out this time round. Four years ago my memory was the Uruguay crowd, but this time it was our crowd. We were much more prepared this time, and knowledge helps. We knew what to expect this time from four years ago. There was a lot more confidence."

Bresciano was a little miffed by the penalty shoot-out. "It's a bit of a luck-of-the-draw thing and that's where I was a bit upset because I wanted to beat them on the park in ninety [or however many] minutes. I thought we were a better team and when it gets to penalties it was anybody's game. But the best team did win."

An unjust way to get a just result—it does sometimes pan out properly in penalty shoot-outs.

"Although the shoot-out does give you more of a celebration. I mean, Johnny [Aloisi] scores that goal and finally we can all just jump out and enjoy it and go crazy, there was a lot of relief."

Bresciano believes there is a good chance of Australia progressing to the second round, where reassessments will then take place. There is the potential for an encounter with Italy at this point. "That can't be just another game. We'll live it differently. We're going to play for the Croatian boys in that [Croatia] game, it'll be the same for them in the Italy game if it comes around."

Italy has been an official opponent for Bresciano previously, at the 2000 Olympics. It was one of the few low points in his career thus far. "I didn't have much game time. I was expecting to play, and just before the game, the day before the game, I was told I was out. I was gutted. When I think about it, I still get angry. I always respect a coach's decision, but I didn't like it."

It was only a minor setback, though. Bresciano has moved on and into a career that just keeps pushing ahead. "I will just keep going. If I win something, I want to win it again. I want to last as long as I can. I love this sport so much, I want to keep doing it. Yeah, it's a happy life. I always have been, and always will be [happy]. I just want to enjoy life and what I am doing is a joy. Be easygoing, have a laugh and play good football."

Bresciano has one more year to run on his Parma contract beyond the 2005–06 season. Parma spent a lot of money on him and they will be eager to recoup at least some of that via a transfer fee. If they wait, or Bresciano waits, until the contract expires, they will receive nothing for him. For a club in a financial pickle, such as the one in which it finds itself, this may be untenable for Parma. It will make the period after the World Cup very interesting. A case of "watch this space".

Whatever is next in store for him, potential suitors will know that in Bresciano, they certainly acquire a talented and determined footballer. But they will also know of and be attracted to his temperament and character. From his earliest days, Bresciano has been involved with four clubs. In the mix-master life that can be football and transfers and clubs, that is notable. "I had three years at Empoli and now five at Parma. I can give the most to any person, not just a club, once I get to know them and feel comfortable. That's when I give my best."

His best is good. He has become the hottest property in an Australian team that is full of hot properties. He scores goals,

---

"I will just keep going. If I win something, I want to win it again. I want to last as long as I can. I love this sport so much, I want to keep doing it."

excites crowds and is worth a lot of money. And he does it with a very unassuming disposition. But you can see the soul of the being when he does score, standing solid in his statue pose, radiating poise and strength, and taking in the atmosphere. But it's more than a statue; these are more than goals. This is the story of a monument in progress, a representation to Australia of what we are and what we can become.

assistant coach

"When I look back from 16 November 2005 and the months preceding it compared with what we went through as players for all those years, from 1985 even right up to 2005, everything was done on luck. We simply weren't ready. For 16 November, we had all bases covered. Nothing was left to chance."

Graham Arnold

Clubs played Sydney Croatia, Australia; Roda JC, the Netherlands; Standard Liege, Belgium; Charleroi, Belgium; NAC Breda, the Netherlands; Sanfreece Hiroshima, Japan; Northern Spirit, Australia

Teams coached Northern Spirit, Australia (Head Coach); Socceroos, Australia (Assistant Coach)

He started in football as a purple and white gladiator and has since, for the most part, marked his life in green and gold. Sylvania, New South Wales, was the epicentre of his youth, but in adulthood he became a citizen of the world. Cricket was to be his pathway to fame, but football came like a thief in the night and stole him away. His vantage point overlooking Australian sport's greatest train wreck has become a seat at the right hand of the Most High sporting moment for Australia in many years, possibly ever. Twenty years since it first began, Graham Arnold's association with Australia's national team has finally reached his (and everyone else's) Holy Grail—the FIFA World Cup.

Graham Arnold is the assistant coach of the Socceroos, but he is also a former Socceroo. He is a player's coach. His own career on the field allows him to know, as well as anybody, the precipice on which the players walk. He knows of the World Cup pain, because he has lived it. He knows of the European adventure, because he was one who pioneered that track. He anticipates the frustration because he has watched the dismemberment of Australia's football at regular four-yearly intervals since Australia last qualified in 1973. His career has pre-empted, in some cases created, the current Socceroos players' careers. His story pre-empted their stories, and both reached a glorious rendezvous on the night of 16 November 2005.

Arnold's involvement with the team has been almost unbroken since he made his debut in 1985 under then coach Frank Arok. It had been a meteoric rise for the "Shire boy" who started with the Gwawley Bay club in the Sutherland Shire, in Sydney's south.

"I started in the Under 6s. I was four and a half. Played for Gwawley Bay, the purple and whites, for about fifteen years. My old man was the coach—this was the old days when you didn't have coaches who were football people. My dad wasn't a football person. I got sixty-eight goals in my first year in the Under 6s. I played in the Sutherland reps, state school boys and state teams and stuff."

Although Arnold's father wasn't into football, his elder brother was, and it was he who provided the conduit for the younger brother to play. "I used to kick the ball around the backyard with him. But what Johnny Warren used to say about the mentality against football back then is true. I went to Sylvania High School, which is a Rugby League school. I played Rugby League at school because the soccer ball was never seen. I went to a twenty-year school reunion recently and nobody knew that I played soccer [in those school days]. They had no idea. I left school and worked as a builder. They'd seen me on TV or in the national team playing soccer, but they had no idea I ever played as a kid. I never talked about it. I wasn't proud of it because the Rugby League was so strong."

Typical of his time, football didn't provide Arnold with huge focus. There were no real opportunities to go and play overseas. There wasn't really a market for it and not really the conception even that this sort of thing happened. There was really no career path, even locally, that could justify players dedicating themselves to the sport. It was normal for players to work in other areas or develop other careers, whilst they played football. This wasn't reserved only for football; most athletes at the time, across all the "major" sports, were juggling sport and work careers.

Full-time professionalism was still little more than a concept, really, in Australia back then.

But there was to be a brief hiatus in Arnold's football progress. As with anything, particularly at formative stages of life, one decision here or there could have completely changed the course of a life. "I gave football away when I was sixteen. I was rejected from the Sutherland third grade team because I was too small. The year I was away, I shot up and started playing first grade cricket with Sutho [Sutherland]. I was a wicket-keeper and batsman. I used to replace Steve Rixon [Australian test wicket-keeper] when he was on state duty."

Thankfully for football, thankfully for Arnold and thanks to Australia's climate, he found "cricket was too hot and long" and the football hiatus was bridged. He was collared by Max Groll, who was for a long time the director of coaching in New South Wales. Groll was at the Canterbury Marrickville club but he knew of Arnold's activity with the Sutherland teams. He wondered about Arnold's absence and invited him to Canterbury to play. It was the off-season from cricket, so there was no clash and Arnold accepted the invitation.

Within that first year at Canterbury, Arnold had moved to the first team, where Ron Corry was the coach. He was leading scorer in the State League that season. In the first game of the following season, Canterbury played Sydney Croatia, then also in the State League. Playing in the centre of defence for Sydney Croatia was Bruno Vidaic, who, whilst marking Arnold, also asked him, "What are you still doing here [Canterbury] and would you like to come and play with us [Sydney Croatia]?" In those days Sydney Croatia would commonly get 10,000 spectators to a State League game, although according to Arnold, "It was more to fly the flag than support the football.

"Two weeks after that game, I was at Sydney Croatia. I remember turning up at Canterbury training one night and the coach said to me, 'What are you doing here, we sold you last night for $10,000'. So then I was out to King Tomislav [Edensor Park, south-western Sydney], which is miles away from Sylvania. I ended up staying with the club for eight years."

If Arnold thought the King Tomislav club was miles away from Sylvania, it was a mere pimple on the proverbial compared with the places this sport was going to take him, although he was none the wiser at the time. Even National League football wasn't really the plan. Sydney Croatia was a State League team when Arnold moved there, and at the time, that was as far as he could see. "I was seventeen, eighteen years old and just having fun." During his time at Sydney Croatia, Arnold enjoyed promotion to the NSL, was NSL Player of the Year and top goal scorer in 1986 and made his Socceroos debut in 1985. "I was happy playing for Sydney Croatia and the national team. It was only as I got further on, I thought I wouldn't mind trying [Europe]. I didn't go away until I was twenty-six, which is late, but I'd had enough international experience with the Socceroos to know that I could handle the step up. The higher I got, the more aspirations I got, but I didn't have any dreams to do anything. Eventually, I ended up in Europe, but it wasn't a dream. It just sort of happened."

Without getting misty-eyed about it, these are the most enviable stories. Things in life do sometimes "just sort of happen" and they often end up being the most rewarding. One's not exactly sure how this matches up with the mantra of "career planning and goal setting". Our lives, in modern, western, developed, civilised societies, are basically very ordered. We consider, we plan, we plot, we strategise. Many hours are spent with the "butcher's paper", comparing and contrasting, mixing and matching the "pros and cons columns". And then like a gust of wind through your neatly built house of cards, the entire thing scatters asunder. Random tangents become the new direction. It is surely the stuff of life.

Graham Arnold's passage to Europe is one such random tangent. "I wasn't even thinking about it", which, as far as the butcher's paper goes, is a pretty definitive starting point.

"I had my own business as a builder. I was getting paid well at Sydney Croatia. I was captain of the club and got on well with the people. The Croatian people helped build my house. I was happy there and proud to play for Australia, so I never really had any ambition. But Robbie [Slater] was always wanting to go, and he had about a hundred tapes of himself floating all over Europe at the time."

Robbie Slater is a former Socceroo and a long-time friend and team-mate of Graham Arnold, stretching way back to these Sydney Croatia days. Slater went on to pursue his professional ambitions in Belgium, France and England. He forged his own legend in France, with Lens, joining them whilst in the second division and becoming part of the push to take Lens to France's top league. In England, Slater won a Championship medal with Blackburn Rovers. His persistence in getting to Europe certainly paid off.

"I was happy playing for Sydney Croatia and the national team. It was only as I got further on, I thought I wouldn't mind trying [Europe]. I didn't go away until I was twenty-six, which is late, but I'd had enough international experience with the Socceroos to know that I could handle the step up."

Whilst Slater was agitating, Arnold was reclining. His club and country activities were enough to satiate his competitive and, at the time, life ambitions. "We went to South Korea to play in the President's Cup with the national team and played against Fortuna Sittard, a Dutch professional club. Not long afterwards, I received a call from the chairman of Roda JC, another Dutch club, who said they wanted me to go over on trial."

Roda called at an inopportune time for Arnold, who was about to take his place in a combined Australian club side to visit Croatia. The team was a blend of the Melbourne Croatia and Sydney Croatia NSL clubs. The Australian Croatian communities sent the team back to Croatia regularly, as a form of ceremonial and cultural linkage between the homeland and the new country. Arnold told Roda that he couldn't go to the Netherlands. Undeterred, the Roda coach travelled to Croatia to watch Arnold play. "I was two weeks on the drink so I wasn't in the best of shape, but he said, 'If you come across now, we want to sign you'."

Arnold must have found this all very strange. Europe wasn't a big destination for Australians. Frank Farina and Slater were having a crack there. Eddie Krncevic and David Mitchell were also soldiering their way through it all. But Arnold seemed to have been happy with his lot in Australia.

Happy except for the interest rates, the famous "banana republic" and "recession we had to have" days of the Keating Labor government. "I ended up going over because the interest rates in Australia went from 6 per cent to 18 per cent. I was struggling to pay off the mortgage on my house. Frankie [Farina] had gone away and Robbie [Slater] too, and they said I should try it. So I went over there to sign with Roda."

Arnold ventured to the Netherlands to meet with Roda, still otherwise quizzical, "I had no idea how they knew who I was or where they'd seen me play. But the guy in the office there had Slater's video from Sydney Croatia. And here's this red-headed guy [Slater] running down the wing, crossing all these balls, and there was a curly-headed bloke heading them in all the time. They said, 'We don't want him but who's the number 9?'"

The "number 9" was Graham Arnold and that was him off to Roda JC. His European career was "just sort of happening" from this point on.

Arnold had two years at Roda, followed by two years in Belgium with Standard Liege and then six months with another Belgian club, Charleroi.

"I had a great time with Roda and then two great seasons with Standard. Towards the end of the time there, I got a minor ankle injury that required a small operation. After that, the interest in me was less. I was thirty-one at the time. Charleroi came in for me and was prepared to pay good money. I didn't even go and have a look, I just agreed to go. Within three months, I was hating it.

"Over a football career, everyone makes one bad decision and Charleroi was mine. I didn't even check out the city. It's a French part of Belgium and I had been living in St Truiden, a Flemish part of Belgium. They speak English in those parts and my Dutch was good enough to understand Flemish—which is a softer form of Dutch really. I used to drive the twenty-odd minutes from St Truiden to Liege, which is a French part of Belgium, but I was only training and playing there, not living there. I couldn't speak French and they weren't friendly. The training facilities were amateur. It was a lot less than I had become used to.

"Out of the blue, Dutch club NAC Breda called me. Their striker, Pierre van Hooijdonk, was about to leave and go to Celtic in Glasgow and they wanted me to replace him. I jumped at it and stayed for two years."

On the relative Australian scale of linguistic dexterity, though he ain't no Tower of Babel, Graham Arnold is bilingual. His Dutch is fluent, which is very handy given the relationship he now has with Guus Hiddink at the Socceroos. One of the bonuses, surely, of European football careers is the chance to learn about other cultures, and particularly languages other than English. For Arnold, with Dutch, his hand was somewhat forced, but he is thankful that it was.

"Roda is in the south of Holland. Everyone spoke English to me until the day I signed the contract, and afterwards it was all Dutch. The coach made me have Dutch lessons four mornings a week before training for about four months. It was great in hindsight, but it was a pain in the arse while I was having to do it. But with the training environment, and everyone talking Dutch, I picked it up quite quickly.

"We had an assistant coach there, Willy van der Kuijlen, the highest ever goal scorer for the Dutch national team. Because the level of training in Holland was more than I was used to, I was very tired. Totally knackered, actually. When I was learning the language, he kept on saying to me after training, asking me in Dutch, 'How are you?', and I would try to say, 'I am so tired'. So he said to me, 'This is how you say it, in Dutch—*ik ben lelijk*'."

Dutifully, Arnold used the phrase he had been advised to, when and where relevant. Unbeknown to him, however, the correct Dutch phrase for "I am tired" is "*Ik ben moe*". Van der Kuijlen had actually armed Arnold with the phrase, "I am ugly". "I was even using it in press conferences after games, 'I am ugly'. I was the laughing stock of Holland."

When Arnold first went to the Netherlands, the "three-foreigner rule"—stipulation of the number of foreigners each team was permitted—was in force. The competition for access to European countries was very hot, and with the player market regulated in this way, potential talent had a very difficult time securing contracts. It speaks loudly for those who were able to do so.

For Arnold, the language lessons provided an ongoing appeal between himself and the clubs. "At the time, there was me, the Polish goalkeeper and a Nigerian. We were going into their world and into their environment. Instead of changing the whole environment, we had to become one of them. That is why I am still remembered now, ten to fourteen years after I played in Holland, because when I was here I was one of three foreigners. We stood out for that reason, but also because you had to go into their world and it wasn't easy. You were going to take the position of a Dutchman, and unless you could add something to the team, you were gatecrashing their party. It took a while to prove yourself, when you first went over there, in friendly games etc., because you'd be in a good position to score and they wouldn't give you the ball. You'd feel that they wanted to give their mates a chance first. But you break down the barriers and after a while you show them that you are not a nasty person and you want to fit into their environment. That was the good thing about learning the language, they could see that I was trying, and once you start scoring goals and playing well, they realise that you can add something, help them etc., and it went from there."

But settling in was difficult. "Naturally the first year was the toughest, with the homesickness and cold weather, which hangs

"It was a great experience, in all, for the family. I had two kids born in Holland and they see their passports now and ask about where they were born. My only regret is that I didn't do it earlier, go earlier."

around for about six or seven months, living an indoor life, where in Australia it is an outdoor life. But you are only there to worry about playing football, so you get over it. It was much harder on the families, mainly because they lose contact with the outside world. I'd go to training and there would be people around but not so for my wife. Roda helped out a lot here, and it was quite a unique club like this. They used to have social functions through the year that were geared to having the families comfortable and mixing. They'd have a creche at the games so the kids could have fun and the mums could watch the game. They were about having a good time and fitting everyone into the club situation.

"It was a great experience, in all, for the family. I had two kids born in Holland and they see their passports now and ask about where they were born. My only regret is that I didn't do it earlier, go earlier."

Which is all very well to say, but they don't play much cricket in the Netherlands or in Europe generally, if at all. And it should be remembered that cricket was chasing Arnold well into his ate teens, when many of these overseas ambitions were germinating. Hindsight provides interesting angles, but you can't want for something you don't really know exists. Keeping wicket for Sutherland on a hot and steamy Saturday afternoon is a long way, in every respect, from football in Europe. The former was his teenage reality, the latter another universe.

For Arnold too, going that bit later in life, as unplanned as it was, enabled him to avoid the youth and reserve team circuit over there. He had played many internationals for Australia by the time he left, which had given him the "step up" experience that the NSL couldn't.

When Eddie Thomson's time as coach of the Socceroos concluded, or perhaps because of it, he took up a position coaching Sanfreece Hiroshima in Japan's newly formed J-League. Thomson moved quickly to add some Australian steel to his new team's scaffolding, and he called Graham Arnold in the Netherlands to canvass his interest.

At the time, Breda also offered Arnold an extension of three years, the third year of which would provide a transition into the coaching staff. Also of consideration to Arnold was his children's schooling. His eldest was reading and writing only in Dutch and the siblings were following closely behind. It was really time to decide whether to move back home or sink some roots more seriously and deeply in the Netherlands.

Thomson's offer provided Arnold with another life experience, and after a degree of deliberation, he was off to Japan for the final chapter of his overseas playing career. Arnold signed for the Hiroshima club and stayed for a year and a half.

Japan's league was in its infancy and Arnold found the environment amateurish compared with the Netherlands. "It was a bit of a setback, there was nothing in the papers, there wasn't a focus on football and my motivation level was down because my family had moved straight back home to Australia."

No matter, because compatriot Tony Popovic had moved to Japan and the two were living in their own apartments but in the same block. "It was like we were married for a year and a half."

The end of Arnold's time in Japan coincided with the start of a new NSL club in Australia, Northern Spirit, based on Sydney's lower North Shore. Not sure exactly what he was going to do when he got back to Australia, Spirit's offer of the player–coach role was both agreeable and timely. However, the Northern Spirit exercise was to become a bipolar experience for Arnold.

"What I learned out of the Spirit, you could never replicate. A lot of good things and bad things. In hindsight, I should have probably come back and played for a year to get to know the players. I came back cold, I'd been away for six years and I didn't know any of the players.

"I certainly learned a lot about what not to do. Club structure was one, but also in the way I handled things. I probably didn't coach as much, but tried to lead by example because I was still a player. I didn't have a problem with the tactical side of coaching, but my man-management skills were crap. I am the first to admit it. My frustration of being a player carried across onto other players, my expectations of some of those around me were unrealistic. It took me time to learn it.

"The sad thing about it was that the club was only around for a short time. I actually believe that the Spirit had a big part to play in the new A-League. People saw what could be done—big crowds, non-ethnic clubs, well-promoted, good hype. There was a market there.

"As a coach, I took too much on my own shoulders and didn't delegate enough. I played, coached, tried to do everything around the club and I was only young at the time—thirty-five, thirty-six.

"Whilst the first year was successful—we had big crowds and made the play-offs—the second year was not good memories. The

"As a coach, I took too much on my own shoulders and didn't delegate enough. I played, coached, tried to do everything around the club and I was only young at the time—thirty-five, thirty-six."

---

club was in a bad position financially and I had to release players. The results weren't good and I got worse as a person, which was the biggest disappointment. It really tested me. I became angry and bitter and I am not that type of person. I let myself down."

Everyone needs a test in life. By his own admission, Arnold had pretty much escaped his until the Spirit, which came in his mid-thirties. That's a pretty successful running of the gauntlet. As a player, he only ever had one small injury and that only put him out for a month or so. He had nothing that had really tested him mentally. Coming back from injury shows a lot of character, but his good fortune in not having to go through anything like that had left him without the scar tissue that makes one stronger, or at least better prepared, when trouble comes.

The difficulties at Northern Spirit pushed Arnold to the limit. But coming through it, he became much tougher for it. Tests such as this are almost a mandatory part of the voyage. He saw a side of him develop that he didn't like, the opportunism of uncharacteristic traits, almost like mutating viruses, which started dictating his views on things and people. He has grown because of that and believes he is better equipped now to not go there again. "I look back on that—I learned so much. That's why I am a lot more confident in my own ability now than I was."

After two seasons with Northern Spirit, Arnold moved into the national team set-up as assistant coach to close associate

Frank Farina. Apart from their closeness, Arnold's CV made him Farina's ideal choice as number two. As a player, he knows acutely the disappointment of not qualifying and has been close enough to understand some of the reasons why. Having lived the life of a European pro, he could also talk the talk with the new generation of players.

His reunion with the national team, albeit in a new capacity, has meant that there have been only two World Cup campaigns since Australia last qualified that have not involved Graham Arnold—1978 and 1982. For every campaign since, in one form or another, he has been as close as anyone to it all. His views on the reasons why Australia didn't qualify, and then why it did, should be noted.

"When I look back from 16 November 2005 and the months preceding it compared with what we went through as players for all those years, from 1985 even right up to 2005, everything was done on luck. We simply weren't ready. For 16 November, we had all bases covered. Nothing was left to chance.

"Previous to that, we never had the right preparation. The governing body never had the money behind them and it never had the organisation to do what was needed.

"Frankie [Farina] probably had the most tumultuous reign that any coach could go through. He had something like five chairmen and five CEOs during his time. Very difficult to work in that environment. This was all during a time when the life cycle of a team is rapidly evolving. In 1985, when I started, the national team was based at home—none of us had careers in Europe. In 1989 there were one or two. In 1993 it was mainly home-based, there were four or so players overseas. By the time it got to 1997, it was 90 per cent, and in 2001 it was 100 per cent of the team based overseas.

"To fit and mould a team became harder and harder. There seemed to be fewer resources to do it. And less structure. In the '80s and '90s we used to get through on team spirit. Then we had to get people back from all over the world to try and mould them into a team. It was very difficult.

"For the 16 November game, we had everything covered that we couldn't do or couldn't afford in 2001. This time round we scouted the South American opposition for sixteen games, we had comprehensive video analysis and we knew exactly what they were going to do, even right down to penalty-taking technique. In 2001 Frank went across to watch the last game. That is all they [the governing body] could afford."

Things cost money, granted, but in the scheme of things? Really and truly. The international humiliation that comes from failing like that in football is, make absolutely no mistake, serious. Only for a lack of resources! It has all been so unnecessary.

Arnold looks back at the 1997 campaign, his last as a player, with anger as much as anything now. "I am angry that we didn't do everything properly. In '97 for example, [Terry] Venables didn't even go and watch the last game of Asia qualifying, Iran versus Japan, in Singapore." Australia had to play the loser of the match in a two-legged play-off for the last spot at the 1998 World Cup. Australia played Iran and failed to qualify.

At least Farina was able to one-up that; he got to scout his opponent once. From 1997–2001 there was improvement then.

"That result in '97 against Iran put us back ten years. It hurt a lot as a player, but losing against what was the fifth best team in Asia then put us right back down the international pecking order. It allowed us to be lumped back in with South America in qualifying. If we'd won that, our path would have [probably] gone through Asia for 2001, which is much easier.

"In the 1993 game against Maradona and Argentina, we just had no chance. The organisation said we had to play at home first because they didn't want us to get smacked away from home. They wanted to avoid the financial pain of a dud gate in Australia. Then after we played in Sydney, the European players had to go straight back to Europe to play the next weekend, then get a flight to play in Buenos Aires the following Tuesday. We got to the airport in Madrid, we were knackered, shot to bits. We had to fly economy class, seated down row 54 and beyond, whilst the Argentina players were swanning past us in the aisles on their way up to business class to relax. We just had no chance."

And yet the game against Argentina was lost by a single, deflected own-goal by Alex Tobin. "That team, that game, was a great performance away from home and it was predominantly a home-based team."

Even playing against the might of Maradona, the margin was small. Back then, Australia didn't count the small things well. In 2005, it was very different.

"There was the video analysis and the scouting. We had a chartered flight from Uruguay to Sydney, which allowed the players to stretch out and get physiotherapy, massage, whatever.

"If you prepare right off the field and in training, you have a good chance on the field when it gets down to performance, and I knew we had good players."

"I felt for Dukes [when his penalty missed in the shoot-out] because I thought, 'Jesus, don't let this go down on one of our best-ever players, for the rest of his life to cop this. That would be unfair.'"

It was the sum of the small things, which ended up tipping the scales.

"I went into the game against Uruguay very confident. We had the players who had individually carved out their careers, but they needed to become a good team. I was so relaxed because we had covered everything. If you prepare right off the field and in training, you have a good chance on the field when it gets down to performance, and I knew we had good players.

"The people involved now are doing a wonderful job and have given us everything possible to qualify. We cheated ourselves for so long, we tried to do it on the cheap. We used to cut every corner possible and hope we'd qualify, and when you look back now, there was never any chance."

When you look back, when you look at anything, the manner in which you prepare for something is a reflection of the respect you have for it. Regarding World Cup qualification, Australia, the country not just the football body, didn't respect the prize enough to win the prize. It's a basic life principle. It's been a lesson learned very slowly by this country.

For 2005, however, things changed. "The preparation and the pre-planning went right down to the penalty taking. The night before, at the last training session, we did a ball skills session in the centre circle and the players had to then do the walk-up to the penalty spot—a simulation. Mark Viduka did exactly the same penalty in practice as he did in the shoot-out, it was an exact double.

"I felt for Dukes [when his penalty missed in the shoot-out] because I thought, 'Jesus, don't let this go down on one of our best-ever players, for the rest of his life to cop this. That would be unfair.'

"I look at this squad and I was very positive because I've always believed in these guys. It would have been an injustice for them not to qualify for the World Cup. I look at my era, we were a good side, we'd roll our sleeves up and we'd play. But we weren't a good footballing team. We had good players in and around, but these guys now are top-class players and it would have been a real injustice to them if they'd gone through their career and not gone to a World Cup.

"I was really happy for them. They've all gone overseas and made their careers. There's a lot of talk about the money they make. But they are wonderful blokes. They are good people. They are down to earth. They have a lot of pride in the jersey and they've copped a lot of criticism over the years. But people don't know what it's like to go through what these guys have to go through. The travelling, playing top-class football at your club. Putting their careers on the line. They are out of Australia for one reason only and that's to play football. Sometimes, often, it's not appreciated.

"I had a feeling right through the whole game that it was ours, even up to the penalty shoot-out. I had it before and during the game. I don't know why but I had this feeling that it's ours—it's time. There were four main things, really: the work we did off the field; the last fifteen minutes in Uruguay where they threw everything trying to drive the final nail through us, but we got through; the chartered flight; finally, Recoba's missed chance. I felt at that point, this is our night."

Alvaro "El Chino" Recoba is one of the world's top players. He has one of the most delightful, and deadly, left feet in the game. Midway through the first half, Recoba chased down a ball that was flicked on by his strike partner. Australia's defence was breached. Recoba was charging down the inside left channel, eyeball to eyeball with Mark Schwarzer. It wasn't looking at all good for Australia. Miraculously, from the edge of the penalty area, Recoba shot wide. It was a seminal point in the match. Many people think so.

And then there was Richard "El Chengue" Morales, who had two great chances to score for Uruguay. His best was a free header in the second half, from six metres out. He missed the target, totally, but as John Aloisi says, "Chengue Morales doesn't miss from there. I have watched him at training [they were team-mates at Osasuna] and those headers, he doesn't miss, they are his bread and butter." Not only did Aloisi have a close-up of Morales at Osasuna, he also had a close-up of "that" header, as he was warming up behind the goal at the time. His heart must have been in his mouth.

Arnold was always confident in the penalty shoot-out too. "If you look at the size of Schwarzer compared with Carini [Uruguay's keeper], I thought we'd have a good chance there also. But there was a problem with Bresciano being taken off late in extra

---

"I had a feeling right through the whole game that it was ours, even up to the penalty shoot-out. I had it before and during the game. I don't know why but I had this feeling that it's ours—it's time."

time. He was to be our third penalty taker and now there was a vacancy. We'd planned for Harry [Kewell] first, then Lucas [Neill], Dukes [Mark Viduka] at number four and Johnny Aloisi at five—he wanted to be 'the hero or the villain'. But who was going to be number three? I approached Jason Culina who didn't fancy it because he'd never taken a penalty before. Fair enough. I asked Skokes [Josip Skoko] who'd only just taken the field and 'hadn't touched the ball yet', and Vince Grella said he'd take one after Schwarzer, so he was really confident. And then Tony Vidmar said, 'I'll take one', and I'd never seen Tony take a penalty before so he was my real worry. I couldn't watch Tony.

"We told our blokes, and everyone listened except Dukes, 'hit it hard', at least you give yourself a chance. But I'd have been worried if it'd gone past five penalties.

"I said to my wife before I went to Holland and then to Uruguay for the qualifiers, next time I come back in this house, it's going to be different because we are going to be winners. And I'd pictured what I was going to do at the final whistle. I thought, well, I'll either get hold of Hiddink because he'll get all the photos or run to Harry [same philosophy] or run to the boys. But over the 120 minutes, I had drunk ten bottles of water and I was busting for a piss, so when Aloisi scored the last penalty, I had to shoot up the tunnel and go to the urinal. I ended up missing the first couple of minutes of the celebration or I would have pissed my pants."

Like everyone, Arnold is cock-a-hoop with what has gone on, but the situation as it developed with the end of Frank Farina's time with the national team presented Arnold with a very "tough personal situation". On 29 June 2005, only three months before the final round of Oceania qualifiers and four and a half months before the matches against Uruguay, Farina left the position of

Socceroos coach, an agreed "mutual separation" with Football Federation Australia. Farina had been in charge of the national team since 1999. Like most coaches, his tenure was marked by some fantastic results (the 2001 Confederations Cup, where his team beat Brazil to finish third, and the historic 3-1 win over England, in London, in 2003, to name two) and some dire ones (defeat at the hands of New Zealand in the 2002 Oceania Nations Cup and the 2005 Confederations Cup, to name two). The 2005 Confederations Cup, consecutive losses to Germany, Argentina and then, fatally, Tunisia, signalled the end of Farina's term. It was a bold move by FFA. It generated a lot of debate, particularly about the timing, as the qualifiers were but months away. Frank Farina was, and is, one of Australian football's favourite sons. This was not a decision that was going to pass easily. But the decision was made.

"When Frankie rang me and said there was something going on, I was on my way to a meeting at FFA. He told me to go and wait at a cafe around the corner. I sat there for four hours. He said that'd be finishing up and I said, 'That's it for me, I'm done as well'. But he talked me into staying. He was great the way he handled everything—he showed a lot of dignity. The more I spoke with him, the more it was obvious that this was all about the players and not about my position. Whoever was to come in and take over—and I didn't know that until about ten days later, when I had to meet with some of the candidates in Europe—it appeared as though it was going to be a part-time appointment. For the good of the players and with the minimum time available, that person was going to rely heavily on me to provide the information about our players etc.

"When I first sat down with Hiddink, he was worried about Frank's situation. He's a very sensitive person, we clicked straightaway. He gave me a lot of authority and a lot of say.

He was happy to rely on me. If you think about it and look at it, Hiddink was only involved twenty-five days and that's pretty remarkable. I said it to him after the game, that I think it's his biggest achievement ever, because with South Korea he had eighteen months to control things and do what he wanted. That is also a credit to our players because they were adaptable and changed as necessary for the new coach. It was very difficult with Frankie because he was, and is, such a good friend of mine. He is genuinely happy for the players and everyone involved."

Graham Arnold was renowned as being a player's player and now his reputation is as a player's coach. From purple and white to green and gold, and all the club colours of the rainbow in between, there has been a pot of gold waiting at the end.

Arnold believes that he is now ready to embark upon his own coaching career. One wonders if, for the next chapter of his life, he has a plan to which he will work or if things will just sort of happen.

Graham Arnold

Acknowledgements

I wish to acknowledge the impact and contribution of the late Johnny Warren on my life experience. It was profound then, and it continues today. Thank you and I wish you were here.

To Rebecca, continued thanks for the space you give me to inhale football. I know it gets tedious for you, but it greases my wheels.

Helen Bateman at Limelight Press for her tenacity and sense of purpose. Terrier-like, Helen pushed on when there seemed to be only darkness ahead. She had neither torch nor headlamp, only desire. With application like this, she could have had her own professional football career in Europe. Limelight, like football, is a team game, and whilst my contact has mainly been Helen, it would be an oversight not to send a cheerio to Jayne Denshire; behind every good woman is, well, another good woman.

Thanks to Football Federation Australia for their assistance with pulling this project together. Isolating individuals is fraught with danger, leaving someone off "the list" is to be avoided at all cost. So, this blanket thank you is offered as the alternative, but you know who you are, all of you.

To the Professional Footballers' Association, for its assistance and support. And Jeanne Ryckmans too, you are a great encouragement.

I will take this opportunity to acknowledge the investors who rolled out their readies to allow the A-League to happen. May the passing of time continue to vindicate your faith and passion.

I would like to thank the haste and blind panic that caused me to take the wrong passport to Sydney airport when I left for Europe to do the background for this book. When sent to the principal's office by the very obliging immigration officials, I was joined by Anthony LaPaglia who had been similarly impounded. We were both now running late for our planes, but after an embrace and a very brief exchange on Sydney FC matters, Anthony graciously accepted the invitation to write the Foreword. I thank him for that, and also for the "sliding doors" theory of life that brings these situations into play.

Finally, to my good friend Michael Cockerill, who'd sing the theme music to "Mission Impossible" down the phone to me, at every opportunity, when this project was commissioned. Such "motivational speaking" is usually reserved for the after-dinner circuit but it is received here with thanks, and returned with gusto. Cheers Beaker.

Special note

I would like to thank the players who have contributed to this book, for their willingness to assist with this project.

It should be noted, also, that given the lead time required to write and publish this book, it was impossible to wait until the World Cup squad was selected before writing could commence. In that case, the decision on whom to include in this collection of biographies was an educated guess, based largely on the Uruguay qualifying series. The exception to this was Craig Moore, whose absence from the qualifiers, it was presumed, was purely because of injury.

At no stage was any information about player selection provided by any FFA personnel (coaching or administration) on the "likely" final make-up of the team. Thanks are offered, however, to FFA for providing access to the players who were in attendance at the February training camp at Eindhoven.

It is accepted that between the time of the book's publishing and the final selection of the squad, players not included in the book will make the squad. Equally, it is accepted that there is the possibility, for reasons of injury or other, that players who have been included here, will not be included in the final World Cup squad.

At this point, one would like to wish all players the very best in their quest for World Cup selection and, beyond, to the World Cup itself, that they have the time of their life.